MISADVENTURES WITH COCO-OSCAR

A CONSCRIPT'S ROLE IN THE MALAYAN EMERGENCY

R A (BRAM) BRAMLEY

(WITH DAVID W CHESHIRE)

FOR CHESH

WHO NO LONGER REMEMBERS BEING THERE

AUTHOR'S NOTE

This is a work of non-fiction. The names of some individuals have been changed and identifying features have been modified in order to preserve their anonymity.

The goal in all cases was to protect people's privacy without detracting from the integrity of the story.

ISBN: 978-1-7640864-7-9 (Paperback)
ISBN: 978-1-7640864-6-2 (eBook)

Published by Richard Bramley
Copyright © Richard Bramley 2025

Cover design by Andrea James Bramley
Cover photography courtesy of The National Army Museum (www.nam.ac.uk)

CONTENTS

PREFACE

Between 1947 and 1960 the British government required all able-bodied eighteen year-old males not in reserved occupations to undergo National Service; initially eighteen months and, latterly, two years' service in the military. This memoir recounts the experiences of a reluctant conscript serving in a dysfunctional army unit in an undeclared, and now largely forgotten war known as the 'Malayan Emergency'.

Due for call-up in early 1958 I could have deferred my service by accepting a place at London University and, with National Service expected to end in 1960, possibly escaped it all together. Instead, my rugby ambitions and the prospect of playing in a Varsity Match at Twickenham led me to accept the offer of a place at St John's College, Cambridge. The downside of this decision was, along with all freshmen other than those awarded scholarships, I was required to complete my National Service before matriculating. Consequently, the Army became my 'university of life'.

The military path down which my ultimately unfulfilled Rugby ambitions took me could scarcely be called an adventure: it was more of an ordeal to be endured rather than enjoyed. Consequently, after being demobbed all I wanted to do was to forget about the Army and get on with my life. Never would I fall into the old nostalgia trap of saying, 'Ah, yes, National Service — best days of my life!', although eventually (albeit grudgingly) I did concede I did not regret having undergone the experience. The Army taught me a lot, but it was a far from agreeable learning experience. So why would I embark on a military memoir after having had nothing whatsoever to do with anything military for more than half a century?

Strangely, it was the introduction of the Goods and Services Tax in Australia, where I now live, which was the trigger. When the tax was introduced in 2000, I was living on a graduate research scholarship which was not adjusted for the impact of the new tax. Through a chance conversation I learnt that, having served alongside Australian troops in the Malayan Emergency, I may be eligible for Veterans' Health Benefits which would substantially reduce my medical expenses — so I applied.

This was no small undertaking; made somewhat easier because I had retained my Service Record and Army Medical History and still possessed all the letters I had written home during my time in Malaya. Together with my 1959 'demob diary' these letters provided a record of what occurred during my period of service. As it turned out, my application was to no avail. The period of the 'Emergency' during which I served was indeed a 'period of hostilities' and was deemed to be 'qualifying service' for Australian servicemen but, for some arcane bureaucratic reason, not for Australian citizens who had served with other Commonwealth forces. This was despite Australian troops and those from other countries being engaged in the same combat areas in pursuit of the same terrorists. This esoteric distinction rendered redundant the further need to prove I had actually 'incurred danger from hostile forces of the enemy'.

On re-reading my letters, it became clear my memories of the deficiencies of the battalion in which I had served were far too kind. The letters revealed the ineptitude of those in command was far worse than I had remembered and it was this re-acquaintance with the minutia of military buffoonery so many years ago which first sowed the seeds of literary ambition – but first I had a PhD to finish!

With the PhD completed (no mean achievement for a man who was described on his Certificate of Discharge as only 'fairly intelligent but not very industrious'), the next trigger was the death of the last of the original Anzacs. Until then I had considered the Anzac Day Parade to be no concern of mine; it was specifically an Australian and New Zealand commemoration, but by then I was an Australian. So, amid gloomy predictions at the time of the demise of the Anzac Day Parade, I thought I should participate.

In 2006 I marched for the first time, with the British ex-Servicemen's contingent. By the following year I had discovered the National Malaya and Borneo Veterans' Association, and not only marched with them but, after persuading myself I was not morphing into an Antipodean Colonel Blimp, joined the local sub-branch. My fellow veterans have proved to be agreeable company and our past service in Malaya is seldom discussed.

However, one significant service-related event was the Association's annual pilgrimage to Ipoh, where I had once been based. Here participants commemorated the murder of the three planters in June 1948 which triggered the Emergency and those servicemen who had lost their lives during the campaign that followed. In 2010, the year marking the 50th anniversary of the Cessation of Hostilities, I bribed my wife with a side trip to Laos and joined the pilgrimage.

Remembrance services took place at the Ipoh Cenotaph; at the Kamunting Road Christian Cemetery in Taiping (which contains the graves of several soldiers whose deaths I recalled), at Batu Gajah (God's Little Acre Cemetery), and at Syed Putra Camp (the former Gurkha Barracks where I had once been stationed). This visit stirred up a flood of memories, bringing to life the incidents described in my letters and was the final spur to embarking on this literary excursion – even though it is scarcely one of heroic military deeds.

Instead, it is the story of a poorly led and inadequately trained infantry battalion which, during its brief period on active operations, found itself in the wrong places at the wrong times to demonstrate any combat capabilities. The only casualties the battalion suffered were self-inflicted, the only hostile bodies it captured were sexually transmitted and the only fighting it engaged in took place in bars and dancehalls. The battalion's only taste of success in Malaya contributed nothing to ending the 'Emergency': it took place on the football field where the battalion won the Far East Army Football Cup. This was the pinnacle of the battalion's achievements during its tour of duty in Malaya.

CHAPTER 1
How I joined the Circus

It was high noon on a hot, humid Sunday in the jungles of South Johore. In a clearing a tall, lean, distinguished-looking man clad in olive greens glared down at the bare-headed, shirtless man standing rigidly to attention before him wearing only shorts, rolled-down socks and ammo boots. With his beer belly protruding over his low-slung regimental belt, the shirtless man gave the appearance of listing forward. The tall man carried a revolver in a holster on his hip. The short man had a large sheath knife stuck down the front of his regimental belt in the manner of an Arab *jambiya*[1].

'Give me the knife,' ordered the tall man in his pukka English public-school accent.

'No, sir!' replied the short man in equally pukka tones, 'it gives me confidence.'

'Give . . . me . . . the . . . knife!' repeated the tall man, his hand resting on the holster of the service revolver on his hip. The short man remained silent and motionless.

His defiance seemed to infuriate the tall man who unexpectedly lunged for the knife. Despite his inebriated state

[1] An Arabian knife having a curved, double-edged blade.

1

the short man leapt backwards with alacrity evading the tall man's grasp. After this brief flurry of action the two men remained in a face-off, the tall man gripping his revolver and the short man clutching the handle of his knife. At this point the Provost Sergeant, who had recently arrived on the supply launch, intervened; grabbing the short man from behind he placed him under arrest.

The tall man was Coco-Oscar, my Commanding Officer, the short man was Acker, his wireless operator. Their encounter was the first skirmish of the battalion's engagement in the Malayan Emergency and it was Her Majesty Queen Elizabeth II who enabled me to bear witness to this piece of military theatre of the absurd. Exercising her powers under the National Service Act, 1947, she conscripted me, along with all other able-bodied 18-year-old males not in reserved occupations, to donate two years of our lives to protecting her dominions around the world.

With a place awaiting me at Cambridge University, I was obliged to request an early call-up, or risk not being released in time to commence my studies in October 1959. The dreaded brown OHMS envelope arrived in mid-August 1957, instructing me to report for duty on the 12th of September.

So, on a dewy autumn morning, I walked to Attenborough railway station accompanied by my father who had served in World War II. He was the youngest of seven brothers and five sisters, who had been spared from the worst of the Great Depression by their father's voice. A big man with a big personality and big tenor voice, my

2

grandfather, Percy, started his working life as a cottage stocking frame operator. He earned extra money for his ever-growing family by singing in pubs, occasionally performing with the touring Carl Rosa Opera Company and singing at gentlemen's dinners, which brought him to the attention of a local brewery owner. Subsequently, in 1923, he was offered the tenancy of *The Rose of England*, a large city pub in Nottingham, where my father grew up.

During my early school-age years my family bred cocker spaniels which, in hindsight, I can only surmise must have provided a supplementary source of income because my mother had contracted tuberculosis (TB) and spent extended periods in sanatoriums leaving my father a sole parent during her absences. To ensure my brother and I shouldered our share of responsibility for feeding, grooming and exercising the dogs, especially during my mother's absences, my father was not averse to resorting to dog leads as instruments of discipline. Consequently, he and I were not close and, rather than addressing him using paternal nouns such as 'Father', 'Dad' or 'Daddy', I had settled for 'Squire'. Thus, on the day of my call-up, we stood on the long, deserted platform engaging in awkward small talk. Having served in an infantry regiment during World War II my father knew what awaited me but chose not to tell, and I, not knowing, chose not to ask. In true English fashion we shook hands and I boarded the train wondering what awaited me: an adventure or an ordeal?

Alighting at the grandiose Victorian-era station serving the grimy railway town where my assigned regiment was head-quartered I was greeted by a Provost Sergeant who was prowling the platform. Together with two Regimental Policemen (RPs) he was rounding up recruits arriving on different trains and herding them into the back of three-ton lorries for the drive to the Regimental Depot. Slamming up the tailgate of our lorry one of the RPs pointed along Railway Terrace and welcomed us with the following words:

'Take a look out there, that's Civvy Street. You won't be seeing that again for two years.'

That was the moment when the reality of what lay ahead hit home. The lorry jerked into life and set off for the Regimental Depot, a looming late 19th-century 'Fortress Gothic' revival-style military complex and, since 1881, the home of the Notts & Jocks[2]. After passing through the wrought iron gates our personal details were re-checked before we were assigned to one of two platoons. There were 50 of us in total, two of whom I knew from school. We were the Notts & Jocks' National Service Intake 5717. All but one of us, Jock McCrossan from Greenock, were from the Midland counties (perhaps he was the Notts and Jocks' token Jock?).

Formalities completed, we were hustled onto the parade square, and left standing in the cold, damp autumn air

---

[2] The 'Notts and Jocks' sobriquet came about during World War I when the 1st Battalion, of the Regiment was serving alongside the 1/5th Black Watch and this combined unit was temporarily called 'the Notts and Jocks'.

awaiting the arrival of the Regimental Sergeant Major (RSM). This was our introduction to the Army's customary *modus operandum* – '**hurry up and wait**!' Finally, the RSM marched onto the parade ground, pace-stick tucked under his arm. After a cursory inspection of his latest recruits, he told us how honoured we should be to serve in the Regiment before outlining the scope of our training programme. Following this the Lance-Corporals in charge of each platoon directed us to our barrack rooms and allocated us each a bedspace.

After a sandwich lunch it was full on as I joined the scramble heading to the QM's (Quartermaster) stores. It was like a coconut shy at Nottingham Goose Fair except we were the coconuts as all kinds of garments were thrown at us; socks, battle-dress, itchy shirts, ghastly khaki underwear, and berets. Then it was boots; reminiscent of a women's shoe shop during the Boxing Day sales blokes were scrambling around on the floor trying on boots amid a background of manic exchanges,

'Size?'

'Nine.'

'Try these.'

'They're too loose.'

'How about these?'

'They're too tight.'

'Make up your fucking mind! They'll stretch. Here's your other pair. Now fuck off.'

'Next!' and so it went.

Eventually, laden down with clothing and two pairs of boots draped around my neck by the laces I headed for the barrack room and sat there in a daze surrounded by my new military wardrobe.

'You!' yelled the Platoon Corporal, 'Don't just sit there like a fart in a colander can't get out for holes, get your arse down the webbing store!'

At the webbing store I was kitted out with backpack, small pack, ammo pouches, webbing belts and straps, helmet, mess tins, a water bottle, eating irons and a mug before struggling back to the barrack room under this new load. Then it was time to join the queue to collect bedding and lugging that back to the room as well.

Next it was dog tags:

'Religion?' asked the old sweat with the hammer and dies, and the blank tags.

'Agnostic,' I replied.

'Sarge, man here doesn't like our God.'

'C of E,' came the reply from the back of the store.

I persisted, spelling out 'agnostic', but this was beyond the old sweat's vocabulary, and thereafter I became an 'agnotic'.

Back in our barrack room our Lance-Corporal showed us how to make a 'bed block' and how to stow our kit in the bedside lockers. Next came our introduction to Army cooking. Our first meal was a glutinous stew dumped over mashed potatoes and tinned peas followed by steamed pudding, covered with what purported to be custard, washed down with large mugs of tea (laced with bromide to dampen our libido according to rumour).

Returning to the barrack room, we all sat around like cheese at fourpence taking in our surroundings. The room was one of two on the first floor, separated by a central stairwell and accommodated half of our intake with the room opposite accommodating the other half. The room was high-ceilinged, with 15 bedspaces on each side, a green metal locker between each, and a rifle rack along the end wall by the stairwell. The walls were dark green up to dado level, cream above with a white ceiling and a well-buffed timber floor.

As we took in our surrounds the Platoon Corporal suddenly bellowed out:

'Stand by your beds!'

We scrambled to our feet as an intimidating figure entered the room. He was a little over six feet tall, mid-20's, with a featureless slab of a face which looked as if it had been weathered from soapstone. He wore an immaculately pressed battle-dress, complete with a red sash encasing his muscular frame. His tight-fitting beret, furled precisely around his cap badge, looked as if it had been moulded to his head – not at all like the floppy things just issued to us. His trousers, complete with razor-sharp creases, fell evenly around the top of his gaiters which, in turn, encased the top of his gleaming boots. He was the exemplar of what we should aspire to look like. He strode through the barrack room, gently slapping his swagger stick into the palm of his hand as he cast his eyes over his latest batch of recruits.

'My name is Espinosa,' he proclaimed before swivelling on his heel at the end of the room, 'and I am English!'

Pausing to let this sink in he continued, 'I'm your Platoon Sergeant, and it's my job to turn you into soldiers.'

We all stood there thunderstruck as he continued to outline our training schedule.

'Now, any questions?' he asked in conclusion.

There were none; who would question this bloke? (who, we learnt later, had been the BAOR heavyweight boxing champion when stationed in Germany). After instructing our Platoon Corporal to have us washed, shaved, dressed in fatigues and standing by our beds at the ungodly hour of six o'clock in the morning, he left — just as abruptly as he had arrived.

Thereafter, we were subjected to eight weeks of torment only the Army knows how to inflict. There were three main places of torture. First, the parade square, where we were subjected to endless hours of square-bashing, accompanied by expletive-laden castigation for missteps or missed commands. Second, was the gym where, for me at least, climbing ropes and doing pull-ups on horizontal beams was the worst form of torture. Despite having played schoolboy rugby, I still found it difficult to achieve the requisite 10 pull-ups on the beam to satisfy the PULHEEMS[3] requirements. However, the thought

---

[3]   PULHEEMS – standing for **P**hysique, **U**pper limbs, **L**ower limbs, **H**earing, **E**yesight right, **E**yesight   Left, **M**ental Function, **S**tability (emotional), a system of grading

of being 'back-squadded' if I failed the test, being sent on a physical training course and starting basic training all over again was a fate too dire to contemplate. A surge of adrenaline during the final test was sufficient to enable me to make the grade. The third place of torture was the rifle range, learning how to fire a rifle and a Bren gun, and how to handle and throw hand grenades. At the time the standard infantry weapon was the Lee Enfield .303, a bolt-action, magazine-fed rifle first used by the British Army in 1895.

As a left-hander, this posed difficulties for me since it entailed the clumsy action of reaching over the top of the rifle to operate the bolt. After watching me struggling clumsily with the bolt, Corporal Doherty (also a left-hander **and** a marksman) suggested,

'You might want to try switching to right-handed.'

I gave it a try and became a sufficiently proficient right-handed shot to achieve a 1st Class range classification. The flaw in this conversion only became apparent six years later when spotlighting hares from the back of a farm pick-up truck: I could not hit a stationary hare sitting in the spotlight. My farming friends were in hysterics.

'Can't even hit a hare in a spotlight,' chortled one, 'I thought you'd been in the Army.'

'You still on the Reserve?' queried another, 'wouldn't want to rely on you to defend the country.'

---

physical and mental fitness used to determine the suitability of soldiers for posting into military zones

Eventually, the penny dropped — I was instinctively closing the wrong eye and so missing the target. Wouldn't have been great in a combat situation requiring rapid, accurate fire!

Evenings provided no respite. Our time was filled by the overarching Army fetish — **bull**! Apart from maintaining ourselves, our uniforms, webbing and weapons in an immaculate state, we had to maintain our barrack room to the same high standard. Beds and lockers were lined up symmetrically, not a speck of dust anywhere, rifles cleaned and oiled and locked in the rifle rack, and the timber floor polished to a high sheen with a 'bumper'.[4]

Along with the rest of the lads I struggled to smooth the pimples out of the toe-caps of my boots and work them up to a glossy sheen. Mixing Blanco[5] to the right consistency and applying it evenly to webbing without lumps or drips was another challenge, as was keeping brasses in a gleaming state. What infuriated me was the necessary boot polish and Brasso required to accomplish these tasks had to be purchased out of our miserable 28 shillings a week — a rate of pay not increased since National Service was introduced in 1947.

---

[4] Bumping the floor was a ritual in every Army barrack room. The wooden or linoleum-covered floor was 'bumped' with the heavy metal head of a broom covered with cloth to polish the surface. Sometimes a man stood on the bumper and was pulled along by several others to increase the cleaning pressure.

[5] Blanco, belying its name, was green, the colour most British Army units used for web belts and anklets.

The one cleaning task we did not begrudge doing was cleaning our rifles after range days. Unlike gleaming toe-caps or shiny brasses, a clean well-oiled rifle could be the difference between life and death. Consequently, we diligently hauled pieces of four-by-two flannelette through the barrel with the pull-through stowed in the stock and kept the exterior parts clean and lightly oiled.

Other skills we had to learn were ironing and sewing, which ate up yet more of our free time. Our battledress had to be pressed to Chinese-laundry standard with a ra-zor-sharp crease in the trousers and blouse but the most irksome task was sewing buttons on greatcoats. Handed in by soldiers returning from Germany for release, the greatcoats issued to us had 'General Service' (GS) but-tons. As we were home-based, these GS buttons had to be removed and replaced with regimental buttons bear-ing the regimental badge, and, if you didn't know how to sew, you quickly learnt. On completion of basic train-ing, in anticipation of us being posted to Germany to join the Battalion, we were ordered to replace the Regimental buttons on our greatcoats with the GS buttons we had removed two months earlier. As it turned out we did not go to Germany, but our intake formed the Advance Party at the transit camp in Worcester where the Battalion was to return before being posted to Malaya. Once again we were ordered to remove the GS buttons and replace them with Regimental buttons so it was out with the needle and thread again.

Early in the piece I naively thought it would be nice to have a batman to do all this bull for me, so I applied to become an officer. The first step was to appear before a

USB (Unit Selection Board); a screening process designed, essentially, to confirm whether you had the right attitude, came from the right sort of family and had gone to the right sort of school. My USB did not go well. After the standard 'Why do you want to be an officer?' questions, I was asked if my school had a CCF (Combined Cadet Force).

'Yes sir,' I replied.

'And did you join the CCF?'

'Yes sir.'

'And which branch of the CCF did you join?'

'The Army, sir.'

'And what rank did you achieve?'

'Private, sir.'

'And why were you not promoted?'

'I quit after one year, sir.'

My officer aspirations ended there, not even making it to WOSB. (War Office Selection Board). My family and school background might have passed muster but my attitude was found wanting — I was dismissed as a 'NAAFI' soldier *(No Ambition And Fuck-all Interest)*. Only two of our Intake made the grade, one of whom, Don Jackson, fresh from Oxford University had been three years ahead of me at school. Obviously, I should have obtained a degree before sitting my USB.

After the first month of 'at-the-double' training, we were scheduled for an inspection by the Brigadier and were subjected to even more extreme bull. We paraded before the Brigadier without mishap after which he inspected our barrack rooms. With lockers open and kit laid out as per regulation, we stood to attention by our beds. When the Brigadier reached us, we had been instructed to call out our Army number, rank, name, and whether we were National Serviceman or Regular soldiers. The occasion proved too much for Dave Satchell in the bed adjacent to me. With the Brigadier standing before him, he blurted out:

'Two, Three, Four, One, double Eight, Five, Six, Private Service, National Satchell-man, sir'! How the room did not explode into laughter was a miracle.

Soon after this inspection there was an outbreak of 'Alsatian Flu' in the Depot, and our scheduled inoculations were postponed — which, later, was to have unfortunate repercussions for some. Shortly after the flu outbreak, we went on a night exercise in the Dukeries Training Area. Here, 'B' Platoon had to defend a wrecked tank on a hilltop, representing a fortified emplacement. My platoon, 'A' Platoon, was given the task of penetrating the defensive line to place a 'bomb', in the form of a metal canister, under the tank. Divided into three sections of eight, each section was given a 'bomb' and set about the task. Our 1 and 2 Sections either set off trip flares or were soon intercepted by the defenders. My section, Section 3, contained all the smart-arses. Using six men as decoys, John Bilson and I set off with our 'bomb.'

'Don't see why we can't go up through the woods,' said John, 'if they're supposed to be out of bounds there'll be no defenders there.'

So that's what we did: flanking around to our right through the woods we approached the hill from the other side which turned out to be undefended. We crawled up to the top on our bellies, placed the 'bomb' under the tank, and crawled back unobserved to find all our Section's decoys had been captured. A whistle denoted the end of the exercise, and we re-joined the rest of the platoon.

'Where's your bomb?' inquired Sergeant Espinosa.

'Under the tank, Sarge, we found a back way up.' John replied.

'Well done , that should piss Sergeant Lovell off no end.'

When both platoons reassembled Sergeant Lovell, in charge of the defenders, stood gloatingly over the two 'bombs' captured from our other two Sections. Standing beside him was Sergeant Espinosa with the glimmer of a smile etched on his face as Lovell demanded:

'Three Section, where's your fucking bomb?'

'Up the hill under the tank, Sarge,' I said.

'How the fuck did it get there?'

'We went through the woods and up the back way.'

'You were told the fucking woods were mined and out of bounds.'

'We just took a chance, Sarge.' said John.

'Well, you'd better take a chance now; get your arses up that fucking hill and get your bomb back here quick-smart before we fuck off without you,' was his acerbic response. No trace of the melodic sing-song cadence of his drill commands.

John and I hurriedly retrieved our 'bomb' and re-joined the others. This was my first shot at flouting the strait-jacket of Army regimentation — in a combat situation we would at least have earned a 'Mention in Dispatches', even if posthumously.

After the exercise, we were driven to some freezing wooden huts, where we spent the rest of the night, nour-ished by nothing more than a mug of hot tea and some hardtack. In the morning, after a camp-cooked breakfast, it was back to the Depot and the continuation of the end-less grind of basic training.

This went on for a total of eight weeks until, finally, in mid-November it was time for our Passing Out Parade, to be presided over by the Commander of the Midland Division. On the morning of the parade, we were awak-ened early. Dressed in our immaculately bulled kit, we drew weapons and fell in on the square. It was barely light and foggy. Out of the gloom, an unseen band began to play, and we were marched around the square to the beat of the music. Having never marched to a band be-fore, only to the pace of the drill sergeants, it was not easy at first to fit in with the tempo of the music but eventually it all clicked.

After a hasty breakfast, we returned to the barrack room to draw our rifles once more and returned to the parade square for the big occasion. The RSM gave us a final once-over and we stood at ease awaiting the General — standard 'hurry up and wait'. Finally, the General ar-rived and we snapped to attention, presented arms, ordered arms and stood to attention while he moved along the ranks, speaking to the occasional soldier. Again, if spoken to by the General, you were to state your number, rank and name, and whether you were a National Serviceman or a Regular soldier. Stopping in front of me he inquired why I was not a Regular soldier. On informing him I had a place at Cambridge University waiting for me he replied enthusiastically:

'Good show, which College?'

'St John's, sir.'

'Jolly good, I was next door at Trinity,' he said and moved on.

After his inspection, the General took his position on the saluting platform. We did a smart left turn and, to the music of the now visible Regimental Band of the Royal Leicestershire Regiment, marched off led by our platoon commander, Lieutenant Nickelhead[6], bearing his ceremonial sword. After a circuit of the parade square, a sharp 'Eyes right!' as we reached the saluting platform and our basic training was over. Supposedly, we were now fully trained soldiers and entitled to a week's leave.

Not so: having missed our inoculations earlier due to the flu outbreak, our jabs had to come first. Thus, on the Friday before we were due to go on leave, we lined up outside the clinic for the MO (Medical Officer) to give us our jabs. Several lads had severe reactions to the smallpox jab and became feverish. One of the most comical

---

[6] So called because he had a metal plate in his skull following a fall from a horse.

sights of the night was 'Curly' Laming staggering around the barrack room in his greatcoat, with his swollen inoculated arm hooked into a clothes hanger, which in turn was hooked into the lapel buttonhole of his greatcoat. On Saturday morning Curly and several others were still feverish and unfit to travel and lost a day's leave. I later discovered dispensing inoculations on a Friday afternoon was standard Army practice so soldiers who suffered an adverse reaction did so on their own time over the weekend.

During the eight weeks of basic training my only respite had come courtesy of the Sheriff of Nottingham. Not only was he the Sheriff, but he was also Colonel of the Regiment's Nottingham TA (Territorial Army) Battalion and a Vice-President of Notts RFC. With the Club 1st XV seriously depleted due to representative commitments and the Alsatian Flu, he wielded sufficient clout to secure me a 36-hour leave pass on 'compassionate grounds' to make my 1st XV debut. A surprise win[7] over Northern RFC in Newcastle, more than a few beers with my rugger pals on the journey home, a night in my own bed, a late lie-in and a slap-up breakfast cooked by my mother, was a blissful escape mid-way through my training.

---

[7] Fortunately, the local Saturday evening paper did not carry the match report that appeared in the Nottingham Evening News, in which my name featured in the headline, so the real reason for my 'compassionate leave' was never revealed.

During my post-training leave conversation at home was filled with speculation about what awaited me in Malaya. My mother, by this time at home again and seemingly free of TB, was naturally anxious about the dangers I may face. As for me, the extent of my knowledge had been derived from reading *The Jungle is Neutral*[8] as a 15-year-old in which Freddy Spencer Chapman described his time in the jungle with the Malayan People's Anti-Japanese Army (MPAJA), a 'behind-the-lines' resistance force, during World War II.

On our return from leave, with our posting to Germany cancelled, we did general duties around the Depot including regular guard duties. Patrolling the Depot overnight in near freezing temperatures armed only with pickaxe handles with which to repel any attacks by the IRA was a far from enjoyable introduction to Army routine. On the plus side this interregnum enabled the 5717 Intake to spend a last Christmas at home before our embarkation.

During this period, I met the girl who was later to relieve me of my virginity. Liz was around four years older than me, with short wavy blonde hair, blue eyes, a wide Terry Thomas-like gap between her front teeth and a substantial bust. Whether it was my uniform or my youth which appealed to her I don't know but, as an occupational therapist, she evidently thought I was in need of some sex therapy.

---

[8] Spencer Chapman, F. (1949). *The Jungle is Neutral,* London. Chatto & Windus

Our affair got off to a calamitous start. Remaining late at the rugby club on the first Saturday of the New Year to watch the descent of the Russian *Sputnik* back into the atmosphere Liz missed her last bus so, for the first time, I brought her home. No way was my father having her stay overnight. Consequently, after checking how much I'd had to drink, he reluctantly let me borrow his sleek silver-grey MG Magnette to drive Liz home.

'Make sure you drive carefully, and come straight home after you've dropped her off, no lingering for a coffee or anything,' he said meaningfully. Perhaps he was mindful of history repeating itself given he and my mother, who was three years older, were married in Gretna Green five and a half months before I was born.

Liz and I took a while to say our goodnights and I arrived home well after 2.00 am.

'What time do you call this?' thundered my father, 'your mother was worried sick.' My excuse about the fog through Harlow Wood didn't wash.

'That's the last time you'll be borrowing my car,' were his parting words as he stormed back up the stairs to bed — and it was! By the time I returned from Malaya he had upgraded to a Jaguar 2.4 and no way was he letting me drive that car unaccompanied, even though I drove lorries for a soft drinks company in university vacations.

The following week we moved to Norton Barracks in Worcester to form the Advance Party for the returning Battalion, thus sparing me any further paternal ire. Norton was another late 19th-century 'fortress Gothic' style complex, with an imposing keep and barrack buildings

19

but, rather than occupying these substantial buildings we were accommodated in 'temporary' wooden huts built in the 1940's to house recruits called up during World War II. The huts were bare and cold, with a pot-bellied stove in the centre which, with a ration of two scuttles of coke per day, were only lit at night. To endure the coldest winter since 1947, we supplemented our coke ration by scavenging whatever additional fuel we could find, even resorting to ripping planking off the lower sections of vacant huts. This practice ultimately came at a high cost in the form of punitive barrack damages when we vacated Norton.

February saw the return of the Battalion from Germany and the Advance Party personnel were allocated to different companies to replace those National Servicemen with insufficient time to serve to be posted to Malaya — finally, I'd joined the circus that was the 1st Battalion!

Fortunately for me, one of the returning Orderly Room clerks was 'Buggy' Brown who had been a couple of years ahead of me at school. Buggy had a word with Doug Darby, the Corporal responsible for allocating the 5717 Intake to positions being vacated and Doug assigned me to a post as an intelligence clerk.

My posting to the Intelligence Section was triply fortuitous: first, because I escaped from being assigned to a rifle company and a life of endless square-bashing, weapons training, mind-numbing bull and, ultimately, the hardship of jungle patrols; second, it placed me at the centre of operational activities in Malaya and; third, being part of BHQ (Battalion Headquarters), I had direct access to the Orderly Room and all the battalion news and gossip.

The Intelligence Section (Int Section) comprised Captain Pavior, the Battalion Intelligence Officer (IO), Sergeant Kaz, a former Free Polish soldier, Lance-Corporal Osbert, another Regular soldier, plus myself and Trev, who had been in my training intake. Later, we were to be joined by Dan and Sammy, both National Servicemen, who were posted to the Battalion after completing their basic training.

Being part of the Int Section led to my first encounter with Coco-Oscar, the ringmaster of the circus that was the 1st Battalion. His sobriquet reflected both his double-barrelled surname and his sense of self-importance. It had come about by doubling his official designation of 'CO' (Charlie Oscar for Commanding Officer) to 'COCO', and combining it with 'Oscar' to form 'COCO- OSCAR'. In his early 40's, public school educated with an accent to match, he had been commissioned into the Notts & Jocks after officer training at Sandhurst. He had served with distinction in World War II when his youthful bravery had outshone his inherent ineptitude and he had been rewarded with medals both for his escape from a prisoner-of-war camp and his part in the D-Day Landings.

Coco-Oscar was tall, lean and distinguished-looking, especially in his dress uniform (which he loved to wear). However, by the time he rose to the rank of Lieutenant-Colonel and took command of the battalion, he was no longer young and no longer brave and scarcely up to the challenges of higher order leadership, although he was not without a streak of base cunning. On taking command of the battalion in Germany, his first act to demonstrate his toughness was to lead a 20-mile route march carrying a No. 38 radio set as well as his personal weapon and full ammo pouches. What was unknown to all but his batman was the radio contained no batteries reducing the weight of the set by half.

To aid the Int Section in interrogating captured terrorists Coco-Oscar's first bright idea was to have us learn Malay — in our own time, of course — from a recently returned Malay-speaking RASC (Royal Army Service Corps) Sergeant, stationed on the barracks.

'Doesn't the prat know all the Charlie Tangoes[9] are Chinese and mostly speak Fukien, Hakka, or Hokkien?' expostulated our mentor when we showed up for our first lesson. Nevertheless, with the incentive of an extra allowance for teaching us the Sergeant taught us the rudiments of the Malay language, as well as imparting some background on the origins of the Emergency, and some insights into the current situation.

According to him, following the defeat of the Japanese, the Malayan Communist Party (MCP) led by Chin Peng took advantage of the post-war power vacuum and tried to take control of the country through terrorist activities culminating in the murder of three rubber planters in Perak in June 1948. This caused the High Commissioner, Sir Edward Gent, to declare a 'State of Emergency' and the mobilisation of British and Commonwealth forces to defeat the communist insurgents. At the time the

---

[9] Charlie Tango – Communist terrorist

Sergeant had returned to Britain, over half of Malaya had been declared free of terrorists with pockets still operating in the southern state of Johore but were much more active in the northern state of Perak and along the Thai border. War had never been officially declared due to the impact it would have had on the availability and cost of insurance cover for the tin and rubber industries which underpinned Malaya's economy, as well as being crucial commodities during the 'Cold War'.

At Norton, preparation for our posting to FARELF (Far East Land Forces) continued apace. For the 5717 Intake this entailed replacing our newly sewn-on regimental buttons with GS buttons yet again — we were taking greatcoats to tropical Malaya? Newly enlisted men posted to the Signals Platoon underwent training as wireless operators; those posted to the MT (Motor Transport) Platoon were sent to Oswestry on a driving cadre; and those posted to the Medium Machine-Gun (MMG) and Mortar Platoons underwent training on these weapons. According to my friend David Cheshire (aka 'Chesh'), who I'd known prior to our call-up, rifle company training for jungle warfare comprised endless square-bashing and fatigues to keep the camp looking immaculate. They received no instruction whatsoever on the newly introduced Belgian FN SLR (Self-Loading Rifle) with which they were to be armed for jungle combat in Malaya — in fact the first time they clapped eyes on these weapons was on arrival in Singapore.

Surprisingly, after the stodge we had endured at the Depot, the food at Norton Barracks was exceptionally good: both plentiful and well cooked. We even had a choice of main course at the evening meal. What we didn't know while enjoying this excellent fare was the ACC (Army Catering Corps) Staff Sergeant in charge had been drawing rations for everyone for seven days a week, even though many of us were away most weekends — hence the plentiful food. Like the barrack damages for scavenging timber off vacant huts, there was a price to pay for our lavish dining: our ration allowance for the days we were on leave was deducted from our pay.

One blessing during that freezing winter was frequent weekend escapes. Whenever possible, Chesh and I would take the train to Nottingham, alighting at Beeston, home of our rugby club, hoping to pick up a game if weather permitted and, in my case, to catch up with Liz, my love interest. These snatched Saturday assignations culminated in a clandestine weekend in London shortly before I was due to embark. Rendezvousing at a small private hotel in Bloomsbury we enjoyed as good a meal as my meagre Army pay would buy followed by a few drinks in a nearby pub before returning to the hotel. Times being what they were we had separate rooms but, come midnight, after a furtive look both ways along the corridor, I made my way to Liz's room.

'At least,' I reflected as I padded my way back to my room in the early hours, 'I won't die a virgin soldier.'

One week later it was Embarkation Eve with 476 days to push!

CHAPTER 2
HI HO SILVER CITY

'Hands off cocks, feet in socks!'

It was 5:00 am on 22 May 1958 and this bellowed command brought our last fitful night's sleep on home soil to an abrupt end. We scrambled out of bed into the washroom before handing in our bedding, all before an early breakfast after which we assembled on the parade square ready to board the buses that would take us to the railway station. Remarkably, our train left Worcester at 9:25 am, the exact time stated on the movement order. After an idyllic journey through rural England nourished by a British Railways packed lunch we arrived at Southampton early in the afternoon. Here, a squad of Military Policemen herded us into a quayside shed where we downed a quick mug of tea and, in no time at all, it was boarding time – no 'hurry up and wait' with a ship to board.

After a 29-day voyage onboard the TT *Dilwara*, (a spartan 12,555-ton Glasgow-built troopship) we arrived in Singapore on 19 June 1958, berthing at the Victoria Dock to the stirring sound of the pipes and drums of the Argyll and Sutherland Highlanders, resplendent in their kilts and glengarries. After disembarking we climbed aboard a fleet of lorries which transported us to the transit camp at Nee Soon Barracks. It was on this journey

that my nostrils were first assailed by the olfactory over-
load that is Singapore – the unforgettable pungent stench
of monsoon drains clogged with all manner of unsanitary
detritus, *wok*-fried garlic, dried fish and tobacco smoke,
all blended together with the sickly fragrance of tropical
blossoms.

The voyage itself had been one of mixed experiences. I
clearly recall my last glimpse of England slipping away
into the darkness with the Land's End Lighthouse blink-
ing into the night as I spent a solitary moment reflecting
on what lay ahead. I was setting off to fight in a war, an
undeclared war but a shooting war nonetheless, facing
possible life or death situations. Could I kill someone?
Boiled down to kill or be killed in a contact situation
clearly the answer was 'Yes'. But what about killing in
cold blood, a 'shoot to kill' order, say in an ambush? In
that situation, could I pull the trigger and kill an unsus-
pecting person? The thought that, if I didn't, I might be
the next target was sufficient to convince me that I could.

The first ordeal of the voyage was the Bay of Biscay
where most passengers were sea-sick. Fortunately, I discovered I was a reasonably good sailor and only experienced one queasy moment when the ship rolled in the
night: in the darkness I grabbed the rail on the lower sea
deck only to find it coated in vomit from above.

On reaching Gibraltar, our first port of call, Trev and I
disobeyed the ironclad law of Army life — **never volunteer**! We responded to a call for volunteers to teach
the children of the officers and senior NCOs who were
travelling with their families. It was a good decision: not
only did we avoid all muster parades (except Emergency

Drills) and deck fatigues, but, during the especially hot period of the voyage, we got to enjoy at least some time in the air conditioning of the 1st and 2nd Class decks and chilled drinks while teaching. Best of all we got paid for it — both of us ending up £5.12.3d better off at the end of the voyage.

Denied shore leave at Gibraltar because it was the Whitsunday Bank Holiday, and also at Colombo because of political unrest in Ceylon, the only place we got ashore was Aden at the arse end of the Red Sea. Squeezed into the narrow coastal plain between the mountains and the sea, the town was a squalid, stinking hellhole, most of which was deemed out of bounds to us. The one upside of our brief time in port was riding hired bicycles up to the hilltop Lido operated by the NAAFI (Navy, Army & Air Force Institute) where we enjoyed our first cold beers since leaving Southampton.

By far the most interesting part of the voyage was passing through the Suez Canal. Protruding above the water as we entered Port Said we saw the superstructure of ships that Colonel Nasser had sunk during the Suez Canal crisis in 1956. This brought back sharp memories of my final year at school. At that time, it seemed my imminent National Service might see me engaged in a war with the Soviet Union following the Hungarian uprising in October 1956. Those fears were abated after the uprising was suppressed by Soviet tanks rolling into Budapest on 4th November. Changing trains in Peterborough the following day, *en route* to Cambridge for college interviews, the newspaper placards on the station jumped out at me – *British and French troops parachuted into*

Egypt. This Anglo-French attempt to take back control of the Suez Canal Zone following its recent nationalisation by Egyptian president Gamal Abdel Nasser, followed hard on the heels of the Israeli invasion of Sinai in late October. I spent the rest of my train journey to Cambridge contemplating the prospect of spending my National Service fighting in the Middle East against the UAR (United Arab Republic) rather than against the Soviet Union over Hungary. Instead, here I was aboard a troopship passing through the scene of Britain and France's last failed imperialistic hurrah[10] *en route* to another post-colonial conflict in the Far East.

The highlight of our brief stay in Port Said was the bumboats. As we entered the port, we were besieged by around 50 of them. Crewed by two men these small tubs were crammed full of wicker baskets containing all manner of merchandise. However, due to recent fractious incidents with bum-boatmen, all passengers had all been forbidden to even converse with the boatmen let alone take up a line and risk further trouble. After 20 minutes or so of MP-enforced silence on our part, the bum-boatmen realised no business was to be had. That's when they started to curse and swear at us in English, threatening to throw knives and other missiles. This entertainment was capped when one wag yelled to them,

'Can you piss?'

'Yes, plenty good,' replied one of the bum-boatmen.

---

[10] At least, in Britain's case, until Margaret Thatcher repossessed the Falkland Islands following the Argentinian invasion in April 1982.

'Well then, piss off!'

Enraged by this blunt dismissal several boatmen lifted their *jalabayas* [11] and proceeded to demonstrate their pissing prowess in front of all, including horrified wives and children.

The other source of amusement was the Egyptian police who swarmed aboard before we commenced our journey through the northern half of the Canal to ensure we did not take photographs of 'secret military installations'. The police wore white uniforms and were armed with a variety of pistols. The brass buttons on their uniforms were incongruous insofar as they displayed a crescent enclosing two stars, surmounted by a crown. By that time Egypt had become part of the United Arab Republic and no longer had a monarch; King Farouk having been de-throned by Colonel Nasser.

It was during our voyage through the Red Sea that the limitations of the ship's ventilation system became starkly evident, especially at night when the heat was truly oppressive. By this time temperatures were topping 120°F in the day and, in the two troop decks, remained around 90°F overnight. To make life more bearable for everyone, those in the bottom bunks were allowed to sleep on deck. Being in a top bunk I was condemned to remain below trying to sleep in the fetid atmosphere of farts, snores, and furtive wanking.

---

[11] *Jalabaya* – a traditional Egyptian garment native to the Nile Valley.

In Aden we had picked up our first mail delivery since setting sail. Among my letters, was the first copy of *Soviet Weekly*, a Communist magazine to which I had subscribed before we left England as a test of whether the Army might have concerns about my loyalty. Despite ostentatiously displaying the title when reading it, my communist magazine attracted no attention: the *Soviet Weekly* contained no photographs of scantily dressed girls, so was of no interest to anyone.

After arriving in Singapore, we spent four days in Nee Soon acclimatising. The first hours after arrival were spent handing in weapons, drawing bedding and exchanging the clothing and webbing we had brought with us from England for 44 Pattern lightweight jungle kit. According to the QM staff our greatcoats were considered to be 'gash'[12] and burnt (buttons as well?).

Our first taste of Army food Singapore-style was *tiffin* (lunch, in English parlance) — essentially standard English fare served buffet-style with a few oriental touches such as curry (somewhat noisy on the tongue for we 'nigs'[13] fresh from England). After lunch we were free to explore the barracks. It was a huge complex but it didn't take us long to find the NAAFI where I sampled my first pint of Tiger beer – icy cold and refreshing, and the start of a lifelong love affair with the brew[14].

---

[12] Gash - surplus or waste material/equipment

[13] Nig - a raw recruit, newcomer or novice.

[14] Since that time, I never transit through Changi Airport without sinking a Tiger – despite the extortionate airport prices.

We were accommodated in *bashas*, palm-thatched huts with concrete floors, atap walls to chest height above which they were open-sided and covered with wire netting. Basic, but remarkably cool and, on that first night, bed beckoned early. I crawled under my mosquito net and slept soundly until being awakened by a *char-wallah*[15] by my bed bearing a mug of tea — such luxury! After breakfast, we were introduced to the morning ritual of Paludrine Parade when anti-malarial tablets were dispensed. With little to do for the rest of the day we took advantage of the on-site swimming pool. Later, after tea[16], Filly, the Post Corporal, Trev and I ventured into Nee Soon village. The main street, leading right to the camp gates, was lined with gift shops, tailors (bespoke suits in 24 hours for as little as $16), tattooists, barbers, restaurants and bars. The street itself was crawling with prostitutes asking between $4 and $10 for a 'short time' *jig-jig*[17]. Most of these ladies of the night gave the appearance of painted dolls whose face-paint had seen too many re-coats. Nevertheless, despite their tarty appearance they didn't lack for trade from the newly arrived nigs.

At noon the following day we were subjected to a pep talk by Major Rocky, our short, stout, moustachioed Company Commander. His lecture covered arms

---

[15] *Char-wallah* – a camp trader who supplies tea and snacks.

[16] During my service the main evening meal was referred to as 'tea', rather than the more customary 'dinner' and lunch was known as '*tiffin*'.

[17] *Jig-jig,* vulgarism for sexual intercourse.

31

security, personal safety, health and hygiene matters, and especially sexual health.

'Stay well clear of the street prostitutes you see outside the gates,' he cautioned us, 'they are riddled with VD (venereal disease), and the same goes for the 'young virgins' that *trishaw wallahs* will offer to take you to.'

Strict abstinence was the message — a little late for some of the lads we had observed the previous night. Subsequent events were to prove that Rocky's admonition regarding sexual health had been totally inadequate. The far more comprehensive joint disquisition delivered by the MO and the Padre only came after the battalion had topped the VD infection rate for all units in FARELF (Far East Land Forces).

Having handed in our standard issue Lee-Enfield No 4 rifles on arrival we were issued with the short-barrelled, lighter No 5[18] version developed specifically for use in the jungle. These were smeared in grease, presenting us with a challenging cleaning task. At the same time, the rifle companies were issued with the newly introduced Belgian FN SLR rifles[19], the Notts & Jocks being among the first British units to use these weapons on active

---

[18] The Lee-Enfield No. 5, a lighter and shorter version of the Lee-Enfield No 4. It had such a hard recoil that the designers included a rubber butt pad.

[19] Other than being self-loading, the newly introduced FN rifle had the advantage of using .762mm calibre rounds which were slightly larger than the .303inch calibre Lee-Enfield rifles used by the CTs, most of which had been supplied by the British during World War II.

service. As Chesh was to tell me later, they too came smeared in grease.

On Sunday, the day prior to our departure for Kota Tinggi, we enjoyed the luxury of a lie-in — such bliss after four weeks of 6:00 am Reveilles seven days a week onboard ship. Over a pint in the Nee Soon NAAFI that evening, we read the Sunday papers proclaiming the arrival of the 'Fighting 45th' who, the paper declared, were going to rid South-East Johore of its remaining 73 Communist Terrorists (CTs) by 31st August – the first anniversary of Merdeka (Malayan Independence Day). If they read the papers, the CTs should have been surrendering *en masse*.

The following morning, after a 5:00 am Reveille and an early breakfast, the Battalion Advance Party, including the Int Section, set off for Kota Tinggi in pouring rain. After crossing the Causeway into Malaya, we arrived at FTC (FARELF Training Centre) mid-morning — finally, we were in the Fed[20]. By this time the rain had ceased, the sky had cleared, but the humidity had not. Dressed in our new olive green (OG) tropical uniforms adorned with 17th Gurkha Division shoulder flashes we were dumped on the roadside and left in limbo while the QM completed his formal take-over of the camp — yet more 'hurry up and wait!'

We found what shelter we could in the sweltering heat and cast our gaze over the camp that was to be our new home. Sprawling across the hilly terrain were rows of distinctive corrugated iron godolphins that gave the

---

[20] Federation of Malay States.

camp its sobriquet — 'Silver City'. The valley sides were terraced, subdivided horizontally by monsoon drains and water pipes and vertically by steep flights of concrete steps. No-one knew where we were to sleep, or where the armoury was to hand in our rifles, or where the bedding store was or, more importantly, where the cookhouse was.

Sitting there in my sweat-soaked OGs, I reflected on what lay ahead and wondering when I would receive more mail and, in particular, more copies of *Soviet Weekly* that I could leave around the NAAFI to kindle disaffection. As these subversive thoughts were passing through my mind, we were finally mobilised to begin the takeover. By this time, it was mid-afternoon and the rain had re-commenced. We were rushed around like blue-arsed flies, first handing in weapons before drawing bedding, which we had to manhandle down numerous steps to our allocated *bashas* in the pouring rain. Finally, we were enlightened as to the whereabouts of the cookhouse. Of course, it was on the hilltop across the valley so, to obtain our first meal since the early breakfast in Nee Soon, it was a downhill-uphill hike in the still pelting rain.

The next day was spent taking over the camp; carrying bedsteads, mattresses, pillows, bedlinen and mosquito nets from the unused cookhouse on our side of the valley to the respective rifle company stores. Once cleared, what was to become our cookhouse was ready for occupation by our regimental cooks, who were due to arrive with the Battalion on the coming Friday. Meanwhile, we had to eat in the distant cookhouse while we slaved away

34

on fatigues, distributing every sort of gear to each of the company stores.

On Wednesday the Int Section stores finally arrived from Singapore and we unloaded the four large wooden crates into a room adjoining the intended Ops Room — big mistake! By next day plans had changed and the Ops Room was relocated to another building 300 yards away. This meant manhandling all our stores across the hillside to our new offices. Here, with typical Notts & Jocks efficiency, the Int Section had been allocated two rooms, one at each end of the 20-yard long *basha,* with the other Tac HQ (Tactical Headquarters) offices in between. Thursday, however, did bring some compensation — we were paid! This spared us another drenching hike to the distant cookhouse: instead, I indulged in two suppers plus three pints of Anchor beer in the more adjacent NAAFI.

Finally, on Friday the rest of the Battalion arrived and our cooks took over the cookhouse on our side of the valley. Friday was also the day the Drum Major, who had been in charge of allocating accommodation, exacted his revenge on the Int Section for our persistent skiving through the week. Late that afternoon, with the NAAFI and a cold beer beckoning, he strode into our *basha.*

'You lot are supposed to be the intelligent ones,' he declared 'well use your fucking intelligence and find your way to that tent down the hill. This block's been re-allocated.'

'Arsehole!' muttered Trev as he left,

'Accommodation officer,' I chimed in, 'prat couldn't accommodate his arse in an armchair.'

Despite the inconvenience of the move, once installed, we liked our tent equally well. It was cramped, but weatherproof and serviceable, and came with ready-made clothes lines all around.

The arrival of the Battalion also heralded the arrival of the Int Section leaders, Captain Pavior and Sergeant Kaz. Our full complement of seven was now in place; a captain, a sergeant, a lance-corporal and four privates and we were soon put to work getting 'fully operational'. In charge of the Section was Captain Pavior who had attended High Pavement, the same Nottingham city grammar school as my father. He was prone to sunburn, with sparse red-tinged sandy hair, quite serious in demeanour, though ready to have a laugh at some of the bizarre occurrences that befell us.

Kaz, the Intelligence Sergeant, had escaped to Britain with the Free Polish Forces during World War II and had somehow wangled a transfer to the British Army after the war. He had a wide Slavic face and the breath of a chain smoker, which he tried to mask with chewing gum. No doubt due to his wartime experiences, Kaz was an inveterate scrounger and hoarder. When packing for the Far East, he stashed a gash greatcoat he had acquired in Germany into one of the Int Section packing cases. On arrival in Kota Tinggi, it was so mouldy he had to dump it.

Osbert, our Lance-Corporal, had enlisted as a boy soldier and was a perplexing, bespectacled oddball with a cowlick of dark hair, who was to cause us untold trouble over the year ahead. Apart from the pursuit of women, his interests included an eclectic mix of hobbies including fishing, shooting, photography and entomology.

The remaining four Intelligence clerks were all National Servicemen. Apart from me, bespectacled and 'built for comfort not for speed' as my Headmaster had once described me, the other ORs were Trev, Dan and Sammy. Trev, who had done his basic training with me, was a Lincolnshire lad and, like me, had a university place awaiting him after National Service. He had a pudgy oval-shaped face with a small mouth and almost rabbit-like front teeth all contained under a shock of dark hair. These rather bland features concealed a short fuse that was prone to land him in strife. Dan was sturdily built with a mop of curly brown hair who, prior to call-up, had been an apprentice footballer. He came with a ready grin and a mischievous nature especially with a few beers inside him. The fourth, and most junior member of the Int Section was Sammy. The smallest of the four of us, he had slightly protruding teeth and, being particularly gullible, became the butt of our often-unkind jokes.

This was the Intelligence team that was going to outsmart Chin Peng and his Communist guerrillas. Chin Peng, we were to learn, had joined the Communist Party of Malaya (MCP) as a teenager prior to World War II. When the Japanese invaded, he played a major role in establishing the Malay People's Anti-Japanese Army (MPAJA) which supported the British during the Japanese occupation. After the Japanese surrender, he led the MCP's attempt to seize control of the country before British control was restored. Subsequently, he was

37

instrumental in establishing the MNLA (Malayan National Liberation Army), the military wing of the MCP. Comprised mostly of former MPAJA fighters the MNLA, under Chin Peng's leadership, soon resorted to guerrilla tactics leading to the murder of three British rubber planters in June 1948. This caused the High Commissioner, Sir Edward Gent, to declare a 'State of Emergency'. It was this undeclared war in which we were now engaged.

Captain Pavior wasted no time in making his office the Ops Room, displaying maps of our intended operational area along with current SITREPs (Situation Reports). The Int Section's other office became the drawing office and map storage room occupied by we four clerks. Contrary to earlier rumours that our first deployment would be to Segamat, an inland district in the north of Johore State, the maps were of the area around Telok Sengat on the east bank of the Johore River.

Captain Pavior had high expectations of us but, having allotted a task, left us to it and did not interfere. All told, he was easy to work for; he treated us civilly, stood by us, and would scrounge anything we needed to get our office established. I felt fortunate to be answerable to him compared with some of the other officers I had already had dealings with.

Friday night saw a reunion with the BHQ lads in the NAAFI. This was when Henry Ford, our 'Mr Fixit'[21]

---

[21] Henry was in charge of duty rosters and was therefore a man not to get on the wrong side of.

Orderly Room Clerk, found out, to his cost, the strength of Malaya's national brew, Anchor beer.

'Bet you can't down a pint of Anchor as fast as a pint of bitter', challenged Sputnik, one of the Orderly Room clerks.

Not one to back down, Henry skolled his first in seven seconds, just to prove he could, before downing four more in quick succession. The effect was startling. At closing time, he raced back to his quarters stumbling into a monsoon drain on the way before storming into the room he shared with 'The Monk', a soon-to-be divinity student.

'I'm coming for you, Monk,' he yelled as he dived onto the Monk's bed, dragging down the mosquito net. Following this he was violently sick and had to be put to bed.

Our first Saturday at Silver City saw my introduction to '*ulu-*[22] bashing'. Little did I realise when reading Spencer Chapman's *The Jungle is Neutral* as a 15-year-old that four years later I would find myself in the same Malayan jungles[23], although not in nearly such dire circumstances.

---

[22] *Ulu* – jungle.

[23] Neither did I realise that 18 months later I would follow Spencer Chapman to the same Cambridge college, or that he had enlisted in the Seaforth Highlanders, the Scottish Regiment into which my father had been commissioned during World War II.

As our introduction to the jungle, the Int Section set off in Land Rovers as escorts for Coco-Oscar, the Battalion 2 i/c and the IO. Our esteemed leader, Coco-Oscar, of whom we had seen nothing during the voyage, wanted to reconnoitre a route for the whole Battalion to experience some *ulu*-bashing the next day. We were dropped off at a rubber plantation some three miles from the camp, making our way back on foot; first through the plantation, then on through a mile-and-a-half of jungle, followed by another half-mile of rubber.

The land was hilly and, while the rubber was easy going, progress through the jungle proved much tougher and involved wading through streams up to our waists. The tree canopy was closed overhead cutting off any direct sunlight. Combined with the dense foliage we found ourselves encircled in a surprisingly silent gloom, making it easy to lose sight of the man in front if you did not stay alert. Strangely, the ants and various other bugs and beetles did not bother me as much as I had expected — perhaps because I had become accustomed sharing my quarters with ants, cockroaches, big flying rhinoceros beetles, moths and small lizards. Thankfully, we did not encounter any leeches or biting ants otherwise it might have been a different story.

Addressing the Int Section during this scouting mission, Coco-Oscar announced his plans.

'Listen chaps, I want you to do as much jungle training as you can possibly fit in with your intelligence training,' his reasoning being, as I wrote in a letter at the time, that when we briefed rifle company platoons prior to ops:

' . . . *they will respect our judgement, knowing that we have experience of what conditions are like, and it will be a first-class experience for us in Tac HQ, as well as being good for the spirit of the men in the battalion if they have confidence in the Int Section.*' (Jolly good show!)

As it turned out, the Int Section's experience of jungle conditions was confined to a few more training sorties and not one member of the Int Section ever spent a night in the jungle. So much for our credibility in the eyes of the lads who did the real *ulu*-bashing. Like learning to speak Malay in Worcester, this was yet another of Coco-Oscar's misconceived and un-realised 'nice ideas.'

The next day, the full Battalion 'route march' bore no resemblance to the trek we had undertaken. The rifle companies went nowhere near any jungle. After hiking through a mile or so of rubber plantation, they were assembled in a clearing for a pre-jungle training pep talk by Coco-Oscar. This was my introduction to his bumbling oratory, exhorting us to uphold the proud reputation of the Regiment and become the absolute best battalion in service in Malaya. (Hear! Hear!)

With that exhortation to inspire us, Monday saw training begin in earnest with various lectures and demonstrations, and learning about jungle lore through patrols in the *ulu*. Later the same week, the whole of the Int Section, even including we lowly ORs, participated in a briefing of the Battalion's senior officers by Lieutenant-Colonel Lee, the CO of the Special Military Intelligence Branch. He prefaced his briefing with a succinct explanation of the origins of the 'Emergency', followed by an outline of the current 'state of play'. Following Merdeka Day on 31 August 1957, a further four months amnesty had been declared which had flushed out many more CTs, who were finding it increasingly difficult to gain access to food and other supplies due largely to the success of the New Villages[24] re-settlement programme. The only remaining areas where the terrorists were still active were in central and northern Perak, where they could more easily flee across the Thai border, and in south-east Johore where the Notts & Jocks were to be deployed. Other than that, security operations were confined to 'mopping up' in Negri Sembilan, southern Pahang, Selangor and in southern Perak.

One matter that Colonel Lee did not disclose was the reason for the change in the Notts & Jocks' initial deployment to Telok Sengat instead of Segamat. This became known later when it was revealed that Hor Lung, the MNLA's southern commander, had surrendered earlier in the year. His surrender was a closely guarded secret enabling him to visit individual CT camps around Segamat and northern Johore State encouraging others to surrender, for which he was well rewarded[25].

Colonel Lee's briefing was followed by a demonstration of air support for Army operations; radio-guided

---

[24] 'New Villages' were fortified communities into which squatters were re-settled to deny the terrorists access to food and other supplies, usually under duress.

[25] When his surrender was finally made public, he had orchestrated the surrender of over 100 other hard-core guerrillas thus decimating the MNLA's southern command.

Canberra bombers bombing a pre-identified jungle target, an Auster dropping a flare to guide four Venom fighter-bombers onto another target, which they attacked with rockets and machine-guns, a Dakota DC 3 'Voice Plane' demonstrating how propaganda leaflets were dropped, and messages broadcast over terrorist-occupied jungle, and a demonstration of a supply drop by a Valetta concluding with an Auster pilot showing off his prowess by dropping a full bottle of Tiger beer in the drop zone without breaking it. The final demonstration was by the helicopters, showing how they inserted and extracted patrols from the jungle and evacuated casualties (Casevacs[26]). All told, the RAF/RAAF (Royal Australian Air Force) helicopter demonstration was the most impressive, as was their assurance that they were on call anytime, anywhere, to support the lads in the *ulu.*

As the demonstration progressed, I was surprised to see my friend Chesh taking part in the helicopter demo. Last seen he had been suffering from a bad skin rash, boils and styes, which had led to talk of him being Medivaced back to the UK. This did not eventuate and he copped his full share of *ulu* bashing and was afflicted by skin ailments for the rest of his life, especially when exposed to the sun.

After two weeks at Kota Tinggi, we were granted a 48-hour weekend leave in Singapore. On Friday afternoon a convoy of four lorries set off on what proved to be a hair-raising drive to Johore Bahru led by Brummie George, one of our crazier drivers. To no one's surprise,

---

[26] Casualty evacuation.

43

after crossing the Causeway into Singapore, George soon became lost and had to flag down a taxi to guide the convoy to our destination, the Sandes Soldiers Home[27]. This was a lavish rest and recuperation (R&R) hostel on the edge of the city run by a Christian charity. The hostel was 'dry', but superbly equipped with games rooms, writing and reading rooms, chapel, a putting green, tennis court and swimming pool. It had civilised hours, with a cup of tea in bed at 6.30 am, and flexible meal times throughout the day with the freedom to come and go as you pleased, all for $10.00 for the weekend.

After a leisurely day around the pool, Saturday night saw us heading into the heart of the city. Here we first set eyes on the fusion of grand colonial-style buildings like the GPO and Raffles Hotel and high-end European style shops juxtaposed with streets of cluttered, open-fronted Chinese shophouses and open-air food stalls. As interesting as it was to see a city so different from urban environments with which I was familiar, I found Singapore something of an anti-climax: it did not seem to quite live up to its exotic image. Perhaps this had something to do with the prevailing stench of the open monsoon drains. However, one aspect of the city that did not disappoint us was the appearance of the Singaporean girls,

---

[27] Founded in 1869 by Elise Sandes in Tralee, where British soldiers were shunned by the Irish townsfolk, Sandes is a Christian charity working to support those who serve in the Armed Services, and their families.

especially those wearing *cheongsams*[28] with their provocative side slits reaching half-way up their thighs.

As in Nee Soon, there were scores of kids of all ages, running and crawling around until all hours of the night while adults lay around gonking[29] on pallets on the streets. At one point we lit upon a Chinese funeral, where relatives and friends had gathered in the house, wearing beautiful, vividly-coloured clothes, chanting and singing around the coffin and banging everything within reach with sticks and canes. There were realistic models of a car, a ship and furniture, made out of brightly-coloured materials — paper, cane, cardboard and tinsel — all near life-size except for the ship. These we were told were burnt when the body was buried and were supposed to go with the deceased person to the afterlife. The whole spectacle was enriched by loud and, to Western ears, discordant music: Elias and his Zig-Zag Jive Flutes had nothing on this funereal cacophony.

On Sunday afternoon, having found out from the Warden at Sandes that Pasir Panjang Road was close by, I set out to look up 'Pop' Homan, a neighbour from back home, who had recently arrived in Singapore as a civilian contractor for the Singapore Armed Forces. Somewhat confounded by the eccentric street numbering system, I eventually found Pop's guesthouse: a grand looking establishment on the seafront.   After making me

---

[28] *Cheongsam* – a straight dress, usually of silk or cotton, with a stand-up collar and a thigh-high slit down one side.
[29] 'Gonking' – sleeping.

welcome, we exchanged impressions of the Far East over a meal accompanied by a few gins and tonic.

Returning to Sandes, I joined the convoy for the journey back to Kota Tinggi. After sleeping on a proper sprung mattress, without the need for a mosquito net in a room with a ceiling fan, the prospect of going back to a tent was not in the least appealing. If anything, the return journey was worse than the outbound journey. After missing the well-signed road to the Causeway, our lorry came to a stuttering stop, apparently out of petrol. The rest of the convoy backtracked to locate us and found our driver standing alongside the main fuel tank looking mystified.

'Thought about switching over to your reserve tank?' enquired one of the other drivers. The penny dropped, problem solved, the journey resumed.

After a series of close shaves driving in pitch-black darkness, we arrived at Kota Tinggi after midnight, to learn that earlier in the evening the Notts & Jocks had taken the NAAFI apart. There had been an almighty brawl and the Guard had been called out. Chairs had been broken, tables rendered legless and lampshades damaged and the fibreboard wall separating the games room had holes in it where it had been penetrated by flying snooker balls. The damage was extensive: £250 worth at the final count. The following morning, we saw lads with cuts and bruises, a couple with bandaged heads, and counted ourselves lucky we had been in Singapore.

Naturally, an inquiry was held and renowned 'hard man', Big Ned, was accused of having started the fight. Still sporting his Yul Brynner hairstyle[30] from the ship, Ned vehemently proclaimed his innocence, swearing that he had left when the fighting started and had himself called out the Guard. He had the Adjutant bluffed until witnesses from the RASC pointed out that it was Big Ned himself (who was later to achieve even greater notoriety) who had thrown the first bottle. The outcome was that the Notts & Jocks were denied beer service in the NAAFI until further notice.

The other bad news was that we were due for a visit from the GOC (General Officer Commanding) on the coming Wednesday. This led to another outbreak of Notts & Jocks' bull fever; a particularly aggravating aspect being the introduction of elaborate new bed layouts. To that point, I had arranged my kit so that I could find anything within seconds; particularly useful in view of the typically late notice we were given for our jungle training sessions with 'C' Company.

Another negative aspect of Kota Tinggi was the deterioration in the standard of the meals after our own cooks had taken over the kitchen. This was especially noticeable after our weekend in Singapore, where we'd enjoyed excellent food at Sandes. The meals that came out of our battalion kitchen were a constant cause of complaint throughout my time in Malaya. In Kota Tinggi, bread and jam was our substitute for the barely edible, congealed offerings dumped on our plates. The attitude of

---

[30] Due to the heat when we passed through the Red Sea, Ned, along with about two dozen others had had their heads shaved.

47

the cooks was as bad as the food. Arriving late for tea one evening having been delayed at a lecture, the duty-cook flatly refused to serve us until ordered to do so by Cook Staff Sergeant.

That said, on the day of the GOC's visit, for which everything and everybody had to be bulled to the nines, the *tiffin* served was exceptionally appetising — funny that!

With Captain Pavior and Sergeant Kaz having escaped to Kuala Lumpur that day, Lance-Corporal Osbert had been delegated to escort the GOC around Tac HQ. Suitably impressed with our snappy saluting, marked-up maps, CT command displays and neatly filed SITREPS, the General's visit to the Int Section passed without incident.

The next day I found I was rostered on for guard duty the following night. Now that the Battalion had settled in, guard-mountings had become full-on regimental parades and, unfortunately, while I'd been in Singapore, it had rained on my best boots. This meant having to paying the star *boot-wallah* to shine them. Combined with my *dhobi wallah*-starched and ironed OGs, my immaculate appearance on Guard-mounting found me selected as the CO's 'Stick Orderly'. My reward was escaping that night's guard duty but, instead, I was delegated to be the CO's 'Runner' the next day. Apart from the 'honour' of being mentioned on Part 1 Orders, Friday saw me trotting around camp at Coco-Oscar's bidding wearing my white belt and carrying my baton of office: a first and last in my case, but at least I didn't lose a night's sleep. Meanwhile, the rest of the Int Section were out learning jungle navigation, returning soaked and exhausted.

Jungle training continued the following week, when 'A' Company was the first company to spend a night out in the *ulu* with Chesh being among the overnight guinea pigs. After surviving that experience, 'A' Company were also first to go out on an extended four-day training patrol. As Chesh recounted later:

After completing our jungle training, we spent three nights in the bush before our first real operation. We were kitted up with packs of rations, each one to last us 24 hours, which we packed into our Bergen rucksacks along with our clothing, ponchos[31] and bedding. We were introduced to our 'scout', a heavily tattooed little (even to me!) fellow who could read the jungle like we might recognise certain shops in a town. He was a Ranger Scout from North Borneo, and these chaps were called 'Ibans'. We were taken by truck to the rubber plantation on the jungle edge and set off in single file following a compass bearing, under the 'control' of our platoon commander, Second-Lieutenant Davies.

Unfortunately, South Johore is fairly flat and the maps didn't necessarily agree with the actual terrain. So where, from the map, we were expecting to find a river, there wasn't one! Water was a vital commodity, as the heat and humidity meant we perspired a lot and needed the water to replenish the liquid in our bodies.

Enter Jonny Iban. 'Water over there, about one hour away,' he announced. 'How do you know that?' he was asked. 'Smell,' he replied so we set off in the direction indicated, and eventually, after an hour or so, we came

---

[31] Poncho – groundsheet

across water of sorts, fairly brown and not flowing like a river. This was not totally unexpected. In anticipation of such an event we had each been issued with water filter bags and sterilisation tablets, which were put to use, resulting in just-about drinkable water after an hour or so.

Dusk on our first day arrived, and although we had been issued with hammocks, strangely there were few trees to attach them to so, without further ado, we made two-man bivouacs by clipping together two ponchos, which gave us a groundsheet and sloping roof. We had each been issued with a blanket and proceeded to wrap a blanket around ourselves and lay in pairs on our groundsheets on the jungle floor and attempted to sleep. Not exactly the Ritz, but it served its purpose. We were so tired we fell asleep almost immediately.

At this stage our officer hadn't got us lost. This happened later but, even so, the stress was too much for one individual who, quite literally, went a bit bonkers. We were in daily radio contact with HQ, and it was decided to Casevac him out. As I mentioned earlier, there was a lack of trees, just scrub undergrowth, but this was to the poor chap's advantage. It was decided to employ a helicopter to lift him out of the bush, so all we had to do was clear what trees there were over a reasonably large area in order for a helicopter to land. A suitable site was found and several of us were instructed to fell the few trees that there were.

We had all been issued with a 'golok',[32] intended to be used to cut through dense jungle and to fell trees to make frames for our hammocks. On this occasion, with the credo, 'many hands make light work,' those involved set to work willingly. When only a couple or so trees remained to be felled, I was attacking one when a colleague decided to help by putting this saying into practice. He commenced chopping the tree I was working on from the opposite side. A reasonable rhythm was going, he on one side and me on the other. Sounds reasonable enough, except he got a bit further round his side of the tree and, as my chopping stroke went down, his went in an upward direction and the end of his golok blade hit the tree and the middle finger of my right hand. Ow! Result, very nearly a severed finger, saved by the finger bone!

One member of our platoon had been given rudimentary training in First Aid, so he was the platoon medic. After a few stitches and a tight plaster, I was fine. I still bear the scar, but at least I have all my fingers – only one candidate for evacuation this time. Despite the wound, I was better off than the chap who was Casevac-ed out and we never saw him again. Apparently, he was taken to the psychiatric ward of BMH (British Military Hospital) Singapore and that was the end of his active service.

But back to patrol mode. As mentioned earlier, the maps were not like a one-inch to the mile OS Map used by ramblers and the like in the UK, but were created from aerial photographs taken prior to the 1939-1945 World

---

[32] Golok – machete.

*War. On one of our patrols, I think our Platoon Com-
mander, knew where we were supposed to be going but
getting there was not as easy as an afternoon hike in the
UK. By early afternoon we were hopelessly lost. This
fact was reported to HQ during the daily radio report.
We were ordered to find a not too tree-covered area and
lay out our Identity Panels provided for this purpose, in
a certain pattern. A helicopter would then overfly the
area and let us know the map reference of where we actually were. Amazingly, with this knowledge, we were
able to reach our rendezvous by the appointed time.*

While Chesh was busy *ulu*-bashing, the Int Section was
engaged in routine intelligence work, marking up maps
of our area of operation in preparation for Tac HQ's task
of coordinating the battalion's participation in Operation
Badak. The purpose of the operation was to eliminate the
MNLA's 9th Independent Platoon and any other CTs
found in the 63 Brigade area of South-East Johore. Finally, our 'Rogue's Gallery' identifying the command
structure of the terrorist units in Johore State, was being
put to use. The chart was based largely on Spencer Chapman's remarkable memory. After being posted to 101
Special Training School in Singapore in September 1941
to teach guerrilla warfare, he trained recruits to form eth-
nically mixed stay-behind parties in case Japan invaded
Malaya. By December 1941 the invasion was a reality,
and, by January 1942, as the Japanese invaded the Peninsula, Spencer Chapman had established only a few *ad
hoc* stay-behind parties. After what he termed 'The Mad
Fortnight', during which his own party blew up several
bridges, derailed trains and ambushed convoys, he and

his men ran out of supplies and made a disastrous break for the coast in which he lost most of his group.

Thereafter, Spencer Chapman spent the rest of the war in the jungle with the MPAJA trying to re-establish contact with SOE (Special Operations Executive) to set up re-supply lines and to sabotage Japanese operations. During this period, he trained the guerrillas in the use of their assorted weapons and in basic military techniques. The irony of all this was that the guerrilla tactics he had taught them, and the weapons supplied by SOE after contact was re-established in 1945, were now being used by the MNLA against Commonwealth forces.

After being exfiltrated from Malaya in 1945, Spencer-Chapman documented the organisational structure, military tactics, and support and supply operations of the MJAPA which, after the war, became the nucleus of MNLA. This background information became a critical source of intelligence during the immediate post-war insurgency leading to the declaration of the Emergency in June, 1948[33] and was a major source of intelligence from which my 'Rogues Gallery' was derived.

Until the conclusion of Operation *Badak*, estimated to take a month to six weeks, Tac HQ was to be based at Telok Sengat, a *kampong* on the east side of the Johore River. Here we had six weeks of bull-free isolation to look forward to, visited only by the ration launch and the occasional helicopter. The reasoning behind this

---

[33] Kenneison, R (2014). *Freddy Spencer Chapman: from John's to the jungle*. 'The Eagle', St John's College, Cambridge, Vol 96 35- 42

deployment appeared to be that, with 116 CTs having surrendered in the previous ten months, largely as a result of Hor Lung's surrender and his activities in soliciting further surrenders, a big propaganda campaign had been directed at the remaining CTs in the area. We were to operate in conjunction with the 1/7th Gurkhas and 2/10th Gurkhas, who were patrolling to the north and south of our operational area and were putting extreme pressure on the remaining CTs, having killed another terrorist the previous week.

We looked forward to the move, as we were heartily sick of Kota Tinggi. With our drawing office adjacent to the HQ Company office, we were privy to the officers' incessant bickering next door. It became even worse when HQ Company was ordered to move to another part of the camp. Major Rocky, the Company Commander, blew his top on hearing this news, erupting like the 1883 explosion of the nearby Krakatoa volcano. His top-blowing on the telephone usually climaxed with him raving 'Christ man!', at whatever poor sod was on the other end of the line before slamming down the phone. Face-to-face top-blowing climaxed with him slamming down his inkstand in sync with his 'Christ man!' exclamation.

Before our departure for Telok Sengat we managed to squeeze in one more weekend at Sandes Home in Singapore and, on Saturday night, headed for the Britannia Club. Here I encountered three lads from my 5717 training intake who had remained behind at the Depot.

'What the hell are you lads doing here?' I inquired, having not seen them around camp at Kota Tinggi.

'We flew in two days ago with a new draft and have been in Nee Soon ever since because the Battalion didn't know we were coming.' — Typical!

They went on to tell me they had flown out of Baghdad the day before the execution of King Faisal II in the midst of rising political tensions in the Middle East following the 14 July Revolution in Iraq.

'Lucky, we sailed when we did,' declared Trev, 'if we'd sailed from England a month later, we might have found ourselves diverted to Jordan or Lebanon.'

Not a pleasant prospect with half a million Russian troops reported to be massing on the Turkish and Persian borders and rumours that Krushchev[34] had already supplied guided missiles to Egypt and was talking of sending 'volunteers' to help the UAR. The situation was so serious that the Lincolnshire Regiment, due to return home in August, were already on notice that they may be ordered to depart early to act as a standby battalion in the Mediterranean.

On Sunday, Dan and Trev and I took our minds off these matters with a visit to the Tiger Balm Gardens, where we saw statues and models depicting aspects of Taoist life, including torture chambers representing Taoist purgatory; all strikingly realistic and painted in vivid colours. As the Gardens were close to Pop Homan's guesthouse, I used the opportunity to take up his open invitation to drop by, and was taken to the Officers' Club at Buenavista Gap for drinks — here I was, a lowly private

---

[34] President of the USSR

hobnobbing with the officer class masquerading as Pop's visiting nephew. After dinner at his guesthouse, he drove me back to Sandes in his newly acquired Morris Minor 1000 for the rather less comfortable ride back to Kota Tinggi.

With more regular mail deliveries since arriving at Kota Tinggi, the stream of *Soviet Weeklys* resumed so, given the rumours about the Russians, I continued to leave these lying around conspicuously in the NAAFI but they aroused no concern that there might be a Russian fifth column within the Battalion.

It was now six weeks since our arrival in Malaya and I felt I had fully acclimatised to equatorial conditions. I enjoyed being able to walk around all day in only a pair of shorts, boots and rolled-down socks, and only having to wear long trousers and a long-sleeved shirt in the evening as protection from mosquitos. Apart from the ever-present flies that infested our cookhouse despite daily spraying, mosquitos were the only really troublesome creatures we faced: how troublesome I was to discover later. Another benefit of serving in an equatorial climate was that it greatly reduced the amount of bull. Lightweight 44-pattern webbing did not require blancoing and, unlike gaiters, neither did puttees, OGs did not require constant pressing and, if razor-sharp creases were required for Guard-mounting or parades, we could always call on the dhobi-wallah.

The weekend before our departure for Telok Sengat, we were told that, in addition to our jungle order, Tac HQ clerks were only permitted to take one kitbag between two. To circumvent this limitation, we decided to pack some of our personal kit it in spare space in the Int Section packing cases. Typically, Lance-Corporal Osbert decided to pack all of his kit into one of these boxes, only to discover that this left insufficient space for all the Int Section supplies. Eventually, he managed to persuade Captain Pavior to allow us to take an extra kitbag between us. This done, he refused point blank to remove his own kit from the packing case and use the extra kitbag for himself.

'You blokes can have the extra kitbag,' was his generous offer, leaving four of us to remove our excess kit from the packing case and cram it into the one extra kitbag.

As departure day approached, tensions rose. In the adjacent office two officers from BHQ were squabbling over who was responsible for storing kit that Tac HQ personnel were unable to take to Telok Sengat, and who was responsible for ordering and arranging delivery of our NAAFI indent.

'That's a QM responsibility' argued Nickelhead, the Orderly Room admin officer.

'No, it has to go through the Orderly Room,' replied the QM.

'Not according to the Company Commander, sir.'

'It's not our job' replied the QM, 'you'd better check with Rocky again.' — and on it went.

Tac HQ was the unit directing the battalion's combat operations yet no BHQ Company officer wanted the chore of looking after the needs of its lowly squaddies. All this palaver over simple administrative matters. I shuddered at the thought of having to serve under these officers in combat conditions.

Loading Tac HQ supplies started the day before our departure. It was a shambles: Int Section supplies, wireless sets and batteries were loaded together on the same lorries as tents, cooking equipment, rations and camp latrines. Initially, only one lorry had shown up and, due to the late arrival of the others, we were late for tea, resulting in another confrontation with the duty cook.

'You're too fucking late,' he announced, 'tea service is over.'

'Like fuck!' responded an irate Trev to no avail, and it was only my threat of fetching the Orderly Officer, that brought about a resumption of service. Loading resumed after our late tea and, finally, the job was completed and we headed off to the NAAFI to enjoy the luxury of our last cold beers before setting out on our first operation early in the morning.

The eve of 'active service' with 407 days to push!

CHAPTER 3
DESTINATION TELOK SENGAT

After only five weeks' jungle training at FTC Kota Tinggi, the battalion was considered capable of undertaking its first operation. Tac HQ was launched into active service aboard a Royal Engineers' Z-craft on Wednesday, 30 July 1958. After a 4:00 am Reveille and a remarkably incident-free drive to Singapore, we boarded the Z-craft at RAF Seletar a little before 7:00 am. The vessel was crewed by five sappers[35] and an ACC (Army Catering Corps) cook, all of whom ambled around the craft in absolute shit-order. Instead of regulation berets, the crew wore blue peaked caps with RE (Royal Engineers) badges. The skipper, a corporal, looked more like buccaneer than an engineer. He wore patched-up shorts, crepe soled shoes instead of army boots and, beneath his peaked cap, sprouted a thatch of crinkly, tightly-curled blonde hair. Life aboard a Z-craft looked enticing — no bull, no loudmouthed Army-style discipline (and the skipper had the voice for it).

The three-hour voyage up the Johore River on an early morning incoming tide was my first opportunity to observe Coco-Oscar in command. Operation *Badak* was his first experience of commanding a battalion on active

---

[35] Sapper – archaic term commonly used for Royal Engineers.

service and, with thumbstick tucked tightly under his arm, he strode around the deck packed with vehicles trying to look authoritative. He seemed irked that a mere corporal was in charge of the vessel rather than himself. Desperate to take over as we approached the beach where we were to land, he called out to the skipper,

'We're not coming in straight.'

'Allowing for the tide,' was the gruff reply.

On landing, we unloaded all our stores and rations, along with Coco-Oscar's vehicles; a Land Rover and a Ferret armoured scout car. In addition, he was to have an RASC launch at his disposal and, close by, a helicopter at his beck and call. After everything was unloaded, we were driven to the top of a steep-sided hill nearby where we pitched camp in the now pouring rain — 11 large marquees, including one for the sole use of Coco-Oscar, one for the other three officers, and one for the Officers Mess — anyone would think they were on a camping holiday rather than active service.

The rain simply bucketed down the whole time we were erecting the tents — a true tropical downpour the like of which we had never experienced before. The floor of the tent in which we were to sleep was a lake. After a makeshift dinner cooked on the partially assembled camp kitchen, we returned to our tent and, using our basic carbide lamp for illumination, sought refuge in the only dry place we could find – in our beds under mozzie nets.

Thursday dawned to more rain. That morning the Int Section got to grips with establishing the Ops Room, while the wireless operators began setting up the Signals

Office. Map displays were erected as instructed by Captain Pavior and the SITREP system was established before we returned to digging: excavating deep, deep trenches around our waterlogged tent, deep enough to serve as defensible dugouts as well as monsoon drains. Camping on a hilltop one would have expected that water would drain away, but the soil had more clay content than a potter's wheel and water ponded everywhere. This was ameliorated by covering the tent floors with sand trucked from the beach. Even so, the floor of our tent remained a natural reservoir and walking on the sand felt like paddling around the waterline of an outgoing tide. That night, having spent most of the day digging trenches, we were again all pretty creased[36] so, after a surprisingly tasty supper prepared by Les Whitehand, our cook, on his now almost completed camp kitchen, we turned in early once again.

Throughout the settling-in process the officers surprised us by mucking in and working hard. Even Coco-Oscar lent a hand spreading sand, and Captain Pavior and Lieutenant Thistleton, the RSO, both worked like navvies loading and trucking sand from the beach in the Land Rover. The only person who contributed nothing helpful was Lieutenant Duff-Cannonier the commander of the Mortar Platoon, another hyphenated officer-class dolt who walked around bleating,

'Okay chaps, right, are we all happy with that? Okay, right-ho, jolly good!'

---

[36] Tired, exhausted.

Even the diminutive, bespectacled Doc Drew, the National Service MO, pitched in with the digging. At this stage distinction between officers and ORs was noticeable by its absence, as was the presence of the normally ubiquitous bull.

From the camp we had a panoramic view over the nearby *kampong* to the Johore River, which looked to be almost a mile wide at that point. The *kampong* was located on the edge of a rubber plantation with jungle beyond. Despite the discomforts, one aspect of camp life that did turn out to be amazingly good was the food. After our wretched culinary experiences at the Training Depot and at Kota Tinggi, this was a welcome surprise, all the more remarkable because our sole cook was producing quality meals out of a camp kitchen in appalling weather. No doubt this was because our meals were cooked together with the meals served in the Officers' and Sergeants' Messes.

Friday dawned fine. The rifle companies were in place and, finally, the Battalion was fully operational. The commencement of operations was marked by our first mail delivery including a 17 Gurkha Division tie addressed to the RSM — an essential accessory for anyone on active service!

Saturday night was the Int Section's turn for guard duty. It was the cushiest guard I had ever done. No formal guard-mounting and the first stag[37] did not go on duty until 8:00 pm, with two-hour stags through the night. The one aspect of guard duties here at Telok Sengat that

---

[37] Stag – the period spent on duty, in this case two hours.

I could not fathom was why, now we were operational in a 'black area'[38], was the guard not supplied with live rounds as we were back at FTC, in a secure 'white area'? What we were expected to do if confronted by armed CTs only Coco-Oscar knew. However, that night it was Coco-Oscar himself who provided the entertainment. Striding into the Ops tent like a prize peacock in his full regimental mess kit, complete with miniature medals he turned to the IO and inquired,

'Do you think I look like Mark Clark, Paul?'

Why he would want to resemble a World War II US Army general remained a mystery. Especially Clark, who had been heavily criticised for ignoring the orders of General Alexander, his British superior officer, by letting the German 10th Army off the hook in his drive to take Rome.

It was this apparition that brought home to us that, extraordinarily for an infantry unit on active service, among the stores that we had unloaded from the Z-craft had been some of the Regimental silver, to be used nightly for formal dining in the Officers Mess tent. Meanwhile, we mere privates had been allowed to bring only one kitbag between two. It also brought to light why, among the Tac HQ complement, there were four batmen and an Officers Mess waiter to serve four officers, making a complete mockery of Coco-Oscar's statement

---

[38] 'Black Area' - an insecure area requiring an armed escort to travel through.

before we left Kota Tinggi that 'there will be no passengers in Tac HQ'.

The following week life settled into a routine. Most of the intelligence work was done by Captain Pavior or Sergeant Kaz, and we lower ranks were left with little to do. In our free time we went swimming, played football on the *kampong* pitch or simply had an afternoon gonk. Nevertheless, the powers that be seemed to consider we were doing it hard, because every five days ten of us were taken back to FTC for R&R (Rest & Recuperation). I went on the first party, and clean sheets (sheets of any kind were non-existent at Telok Sengat), a good shower, a trip to the cinema and a cold drink were welcome luxuries.

It was during this period that Coco-Oscar's letters to impress the Colonel of the Regiment in England became another source of entertainment. Reading the drafts that he gave to Bryn, the Tac HQ typist, we were convinced that he was only semi-literate. He used 'farther' instead of 'further'; was unsure whether the 'a' came before the 'e' in Zealand and spelt the ordinal number 'fourth' without a 'u'. In hindsight, had the condition been known at the time, he probably would have been diagnosed as dyslexic. Bryn, a cadet journalist prior to call-up, tried surreptitiously to correct Coco's spelling when typing his letters, but was often reprimanded and ordered to re-type them with the wrong spelling. Doubtless the Colonel of the Regiment would attribute these spelling errors to Coco's ill-educated typist. Coco also liked to write the SITREPs himself but, as soon as he was out of the way, either the IO or the RSO re-wrote them.

While life at Tac HQ was pretty cushy, the rifle companies were doing it much harder. Although they had found a few tracks and several food dumps, they failed to find any CTs. This was probably because we had been deployed into the area too late to intercept CTs fleeing north to escape from the 2nd/10th Gurkhas who had them on the run at the southern end of the peninsula.

Returning to Tac HQ after my second R&R at Kota Tinggi, the improvements to our camp made me wonder why we needed R&R at all. Rather than doing it tough, the camp was beginning to look like a holiday camp; all we lacked was cold beer and a cinema. We were now able to keep the water out of our tents when it rained, life had been made comfortable by building wash-stands and tables, the Mortar Platoon had built a shower and laid out a badminton court.

Then, out of the blue, a single incident caused discipline to be tightened, formal guard-mounting parades to be introduced, and live rounds issued to those on guard duty. These changes were in no way due to CT activity, but were solely the result of the antics of Acker, Coco-Oscar's wireless operator and a most unlikely 'hard man'. Acker was in his late twenties, a nine-year Regular soldier with previous service in Malaya, and clearly good at his trade, having been selected as the CO's wireless operator. Around five feet four inches short, he was built like a barrel with matchstick legs, a pukka accent and a quick wit. Since arriving in Telok Sengat he had taken to wearing a large sheath knife stuffed down the front of his Regimental belt much like an Arab *jambiya*.

One Friday, as was his weekend custom, Acker headed for the bar in the nearby *kampong* for his weekend ration of cold Anchor. On his way back, he accosted a villager and had him detained for being unable to produce his identity card. This came to light in the morning when the local Royal Malaya Police lieutenant visited Tac HQ to report the incident. The hapless villager was freed and Acker was reprimanded by Coco-Oscar, and ordered to be back in camp no later than 8:00 pm in future. However, this was Saturday which, from lunchtime until lights-out on Sunday, Acker considered to be his time, not the Army's. So, undeterred, and in the company of 'Joe Belly'[39], another old sweat who was rostered for guard duty that night, Acker once more headed off to the *kampong*.

Come eight o'clock, when Joe had not reported for guard duty and Acker could not be found in camp, Sergeant Kaz the Guard Commander set off to find them. He accosted the pair in the village bar and ordered them back to camp. By this time, both men were well into their cups and Acker, one hand on his knife for emphasis, informed Kaz,

'We'll come when we're ready.'

Unable to persuade them otherwise, Kaz drove back to camp returning with two armed guards.

'Are you ready to come now?' said Kaz before escorting the pair back to camp where they were placed under

---

[39] So-called because he had the word 'Belly' crudely tattooed across his scrawny stomach.

open arrest. But that was not the end of it — in fact that
was only the start of it. Appearing unshaven on Muster
Parade on Sunday morning, Acker was gripped by Captain Pavior.

'Acker, get that fuzz off your face and report to me,
cleanshaven, at 11 o'clock.' As it was a Sunday, Acker
declined, citing the bible:

'Six days shalt thou labour and on the seventh shalt thou
rest,' he declared.

'Battalion Orders take precedence over God's word in
this camp. My tent, 11 o'clock, clean-shaven, understood? Now fall out.'

When Acker failed to appear at the appointed hour, a
search was mounted and, once again, he was found in
the *kampong*, this time sitting in the barber shop sipping
Anchor beer from a small glass while being shaved. Captain Pavior himself drove into the *kampong* to collect the
recalcitrant. Had he not been bareheaded and shirtless as
he sat alongside the Captain in the Land Rover, cheroot
in hand, Acker could almost have passed as a visiting
Brigadier as they drove into camp.

By this time Coco-Oscar had been made aware of events.
He confronted Acker, demanding that he hand over the
knife which, as usual, was tucked into his low-slung
Regimental belt. Still shirtless and standing rigidly to attention, Acker refused claiming that wearing the knife
was good for his confidence. Infuriated at Acker's defiance, Coco-Oscar unexpectedly lunged for the knife.
Despite his inebriated state Acker leapt backwards with
alacrity evading Coco-Oscar's grasp. After this brief

flurry of action, the two of them remained in a face-off Coco-Oscar gripping his revolver and Acker clutching the handle of his knife. The stalemate was broken by Sergeant Weller, the overbearing Provost Sergeant, recently arrived on the supply launch. Grabbing Acker from behind he placed him under arrest and escorted him to the launch. Still drunk, but now knifeless as well as shirtless, Acker was fuming at the indignity.

'Give me any trouble on the way over and you won't reach the other side,' he told Weller.

It came as no surprise when, after serving 21 days in detention at Batu Pahat, Coco-Oscar did not want him to return, nor did the RSO. Sadly, Tac HQ had lost it's one outstanding 'character', banished to a rifle company and the prospect of jungle patrols with not an Anchor beer to be had. With his cartoon-like shape, quick wit and penchant for quoting the Bible, Acker had been a constant source of entertainment. But the real price we paid for all this entertainment was a ban on evening visits to the *kampong* and the introduction of formal guard-mounting parades.

The following night I was rostered on guard duty under the new regime and, for the first time since arriving at Telok Sengat, the guard was issued with live ammunition. The reason for this change being known only to Coco-Oscar. One of the guard's duties was to give Les Whitehand, the camp cook, an early wake-up call. Gently prodding him in the ribs with my rifle butt I announced it was time to get up. Receiving no more than a mumbled response ending in '...off', I prodded Les more vigorously and coaxed him from beneath his mozzie net and left him sitting on the edge of his bed in the pre-dawn gloom. No sooner had I left his tent, than I was stopped in my tracks by a piercing yell from behind me. I swung around, rifle at the ready, but could see nothing untoward. Making my way back to Les's tent, I discovered that, in pulling on his jungle boot in the dark, his foot had encountered a snake nestling inside.

August, was punctuated by a succession of 'flaps.' First, a lad out in the *ulu* collapsed with intense stomach pain which ultimately was diagnosed as a blocked bowel. The MO recommended an immediate Casevac by helicopter but, after the ignominy of having a soldier evacuated from a training patrol, Coco-Oscar flatly refused to authorise it (bad for what he perceived to be the good reputation of the Regiment to have another Casevac on his first operation). Instead, he ordered that the man be carried out through 4,000 yards of dense jungle to a beach, so he could be evacuated by boat from there.

By the next morning the soldier's condition had deteriorated further. After liaising by radio with the Platoon Sergeant, who had first aid training, the MO was flown to the nearest helicopter LZ (Landing Zone) and had to walk into the *ulu* to treat the casualty who, by this time was delirious. Under sedation he was carried out to the beach from where he was flown by helicopter to BMH (British Military Hospital) Singapore, where a surgeon was on standby to operate.

On his return to Tac HQ, the MO told Coco-Oscar in no uncertain terms that, had the surgeon not been on standby, the soldier may well have become the battalion's first fatality. Clearly, the fault lay squarely with Coco-Oscar, who had refused the MO's initial request for a helicopter evacuation. At the time, the incident had certainly unnerved Coco-Oscar. Following the MO's departure to treat the soldier, he could scarcely sit still for a second and cut a gaunt, chain-smoking, figure pacing up and down the Ops Room tent running his hands through his silver-grey hair which, after three weeks in the *ulu* had taken on a greenish tinge at the tips as if affected by mildew.

Unbelievably, the day after the MO's return, another lad cut his leg to the bone with his *golok*; again Coco-Oscar refused to authorise a helicopter Casevac.

'This man has lost a lot of blood and could possibly lose a leg,' asserted the MO.

Coco was having none of it.

'The man can easily be stretchered back to his Company base camp and evacuated by road from there,' he responded.

This time, Captain Drew, the National Service doctor, asserted his medical authority, demanding that Coco-Oscar authorise a helicopter Casevac. Finally relenting, Coco authorised the evacuation. Only after these two incidents did Coco-Oscar begin to show a little more concern for the lives of his men than he did for what he considered to be 'the reputation of the Regiment', and two more helicopter Casevacs were authorised before Operation *Badak* concluded.

By this time, to add some interest to life in Telok Sengat, and to open a new avenue for testing the limits of army regulations, I ceased shaving above my top lip.

'Why try and cultivate hair on your lip when it grows wild on your arse?' asked Dan, but I was not alone with Trev, Bryn and, eventually Dan himself, also ceasing to shave above their top lip. It was a new challenge — Army moustaches are bound by strict regulations: they may not extend beyond the width of the top lip, nor allowed to grow beneath the level of the mouth, so moustache cultivation became a constant test of how far you could extend the area of growth before being gripped.

Soon after the outbreak of moustache growing the Int Section acquired a dog. Osbert, our oddball Lance-Corporal, asked Coco-Oscar for permission to keep a dog. Astonishingly, the request was granted. As my family had bred dogs when I was a boy, I went to the *kampong* with Osbert to examine a month-old Alsatian pup before he bought it. The pup's mother was a retired War Dog, and the sire an Alsatian from the War Dog Training Wing in Kota Tinggi. The pup was extremely timid and, at first, seldom emerged from beneath Osbert's bed. With a dark coat and muzzle, she was like a young foal, all legs and nothing else. After a couple of puppy pukes we wanted to call her 'Pukey' but, it being Osbert's dog, he christened her 'Joy', a total misnomer given the life that lay ahead of her.

It was around this time the ban on evening visits to the *kampong* was lifted, and Dan, Trev and I decided to explore. Standing outside the local bar comparing beer prices with NAAFI prices, a Eurasian-looking fellow called out to us from inside in exceptionally good English,

'Come in and have a beer with me,' he said, so we did. We soon learnt that he had been in the Royal Engineers in World War II and had been a prisoner of the Japanese on the Burma Railway for three-and-a-half years, alongside many British POWs. This experience had given him a huge respect for the British which he demonstrated by continuing to get the beers in, refusing to let us buy a round. His name was Edward, and he was the tractor supervisor on the local rubber estate. After several beers, he sent his driver away with $20. The driver returned a short time later with a bottle of 'Black & White' whisky, sourced from who knows where? Edward insisted we finish the bottle and, not wishing to offend our host, we duly obliged. That was singing liquor and Edward soon launched into *Three German officers crossed the Rhine*, and we continued with everything from *Cats on the Rooftop* to *The Ball of Kirriemuir*. It wasn't long before we had half the village clustered around the bar seemingly enjoying the show. When we ran out of songs our host insisted on buying a couple of large bottles of Guinness as a nightcap. Having downed these, we lurched back into camp around midnight, waking up most of the lads before falling into our scratchers[40].

A few days later we visited the *kampong* again and came across a Malay wedding taking place at a big house. The groom's brother invited us to join the proceedings, sat us at a table and fed us savoury pies, cakes and scented tea, making us most welcome. We were a great hit with the kids, who revelled in wearing our jungle hats as we practiced our Malay and taught the kids a bit of English. As

---

[40] Scratcher – bed.

we understood it a Malay marriage is a contract between the groom and the girl's father and, if the prospective groom offers the right price, he can marry the girl. We watched as sisters, cousins and aunts of the bride-to-be came forward and scattered flower petals before the weeping girl who clearly did not want to marry the man in question. Meanwhile, across the road in an open *ba-sha*, the heads of the families were negotiating the legal and financial details of the betrothal.

Next day brought big news: eavesdropping on a conversation between Coco-Oscar and the other officers, I learnt that, after concluding our current operation, we were being sent north for two months to relieve the Loyals[41] in Ipoh, while they went to Hong Kong on R&R. Ipoh was reputed to be one of the best postings in Malaya, where the infantry battalions operated out of permanent barracks. Rather than having to build our own Tac HQ, as here in Telok Sengat, we would simply take over the Loyals' Operations Room — at least that was the theory but events were to prove otherwise. The move sounded good to me: I'd see more of the country and a change of scenery would help speed up the passage of time.

The day before pulling out of Telok Sengat was spent dismantling and packing up the camp ,the major dilemma facing the officers that night was whether to dress for dinner. In the morning, after another early Sabbath Reveille, it was discovered that the battalion flag, which had always flown proudly over Tac HQ, had disappeared

---

[41] Loyals – The Loyal North Lancashire Regiment.

overnight. On muster parade Coco-Oscar was ropeable (so to speak).

'This is not a joke,' he thundered, stating that, 'provided the flag is returned before we break camp, that would be the end of it.' Nobody from Tac HQ owned up but, by the time we drove to the beach, the flag had mysteriously re-appeared, neatly folded, on the seat of Coco's Land Rover.

At the appointed departure time of 7:15am, all our vehicles were lined up on the beach ready to board, but no sign of the Z-craft. 'Hurry up and wait', again! An hour passed before it was finally sighted. Crewed by the same motley band of sappers who had ferried us here a month ago, it ran aground something like two cricket pitches short of the beach. Observing the expanse of shallow water, the skipper bellowed to Coco-Oscar in his Cockney foghorn of a voice,

'Ain't enough water.'

'Yes, the tide is going out,' confirmed Coco-Oscar.

'Yer wot?' bellowed the skipper, cupping his hands around his ears.

'The tide is going out,' repeated Coco-Oscar.

'Yeah, have to wait for tonight's tide now,' replied the skipper before lighting a smoke and ambling back to the bridge.

On the beach we were in stitches at this scruffy corporal, again in his patched-up shorts, crepe soled shoes and blue peaked cap addressing Coco-Oscar in that manner. The prospects for the rest of the day, however, were less amusing. Here we were, marooned on an open beach with only our vehicles for cover, and only the rounds in the magazines on our rifles to defend ourselves. All the other ammunition was stowed away somewhere on who knows which lorry? Absolute sitting ducks if any of the MNLA's 9th Independent Platoon, who we had failed to even sight, let alone capture or kill, ventured this way. With this in mind sentries were rotated throughout the course of the day which was spent swimming and sunbathing, with little concern over the prospect of a surprise attack.

For *tiffin* we were taken to 'B' Company's base camp in a three-tonner driven by 'Ton-up Trev'. It was a hair-raising drive as Trev barrelled over decrepit log bridges running cycling rubber tappers off the road and clipping a stray chicken, which he collected to supplement that night's tea. On the return journey he ran a tractor and trailer off the road — 'Ton-up Trev' was in a class of his own.

While at 'B' Company we learnt how the battalion flag had gone missing. During the Tac HQ guard mounting the previous night Freddie Miner, the 'B' Company CSM, had arrived in a canopied Land Rover. While one of his corporals had kept the Orderly Officer talking, two other 'B' Company lads crept out of the back of the Land Rover, cut through the halyard with a *golok*, hauled the flag down and driven off with it.

Back at the beach, chatting with one of the crew I discovered that Z-craft's delayed departure from Seletar was due to a big demob party in their NAAFI the night before — have to get your priorities right, partying

75

comes before early morning sailings. Meanwhile, the Z-craft's late arrival was causing considerable anxiety among the harassed Gurkha engineers who were onboard with a bulldozer and large supply vehicle to off-load. Onshore, Coco-Oscar was equally anxious about getting all our vehicles, plus a huge Aveling Barford grader, boarded before the tide ebbed again.

The tide finally peaked a little before sunset and the crew tried once again to nose the ramp into the sand but, even on the high tide, there was still water between the ramp and the shore. Consequently, we had to use battens stored onboard to extend the ramp. With these in place, the Gurkha driver gunned his dozer up onto the ramp before crashing down with the blade digging into the sand under the battens, lifting and snapping them as the driver kept going at full throttle to avoid getting bogged in the sand. Coco-Oscar who, true to form, was trying to direct operations from the beach was sent scuttling for safety much to the amusement of all.

The makeshift ramp extension was reinstated to allow the other heavy wagon to be driven off, snapping yet another batten in the process. Off-loading completed, it was our turn: as each of our vehicles was driven aboard the tide kept washing the remaining battens away and we had to keep replacing them in position before another vehicle could drive onto the ramp, again at a furious pace, to avoid becoming bogged in the sand. The last vehicle to be loaded was the grader by which time the tide was beginning to ebb. With a roar and a plume of exhaust smoke the grader rumbled up the ramp onto the deck miraculously pulling up inches short of the already-loaded vehicles. With all aboard it was time to depart and the ramp was raised at seven o'clock.

'Be a bastard if we can't get off now,' observed the skipper to Coco-Oscar. Failing to get a reply, he repeated his observation, again without response. Coco was clearly having difficulty dealing with an NCO who seemed to be unaware of the word 'Sir' and had evidently not been introduced to the practice of saluting. After further gravel-voiced orders to the crew, the anchor was raised and the Z-craft went hard astern. We were midstream before anyone noticed that the tender had come adrift and was drifting away on the tide. The skipper manoeuvred the Z-craft closer to the tender before ordering a deckhand to dive overboard to reclaim it. With the tender secured we headed downstream for Singapore — only 12 hours and one high tide behind schedule.

Arriving at Selctar a few hours later, all vehicles were driven off the Z-craft without mishap and we arrived back at FTC at midnight where the usual 'chooks without heads' routine resumed. First, we were sent to 'D' Company arms store at the top of the central hill to hand in our weapons, then on to 'C' Company cookhouse at the far end of the camp for a meal where we were fed a surprisingly appetising late-night supper. After finishing our supper, we were hustled along to the nearby QM's store to draw bedding where the unloved Acting Sergeant Brannock was rewarded with a rousing chorus of *Why was he born so beautiful?* as he grappled with the task of handing out mattresses, mozzie nets and bedlinen. To conclude our 20-hour day we then had to hump our bedding all the way back to our *bashas* in 'D' Company lines, before collapsing into our newly made beds. But there was no respite. After not getting to bed until well after one, we were roused at sparrow-fart[42] to unload the vehicles and store all the Int Section gear while the signallers and Mortar Platoon did likewise.

That evening in the NAAFI we chewed the fat with the Orderly Room lads and the Pay Corps clerks, who were over from Batu Pahat to sort out the paperwork for our move to Ipoh. It wasn't long before we were joined by a few blokes from the assault pioneers and rifle companies who had already returned to FTC. This was when the unofficial post-mortem on the Notts and Jocks' first operation commenced.

As the night wore on the reasons for the Battalion's lack of success became evident. 'Westie' a 'D' Company NS Lance-Corporal kicked off,

'Our prick of a platoon commander was a total 'Nancy', couldn't, or wouldn't, do anything for himself. Even had one of the squaddies erect his *basha* and cook his meals for him and the medical orderly constantly inspecting him for tinea, footrot, leeches and bites of any kind.'

Sputnik from the Orderly Room chipped in,

'Yeah, not surprising, his father's a Foreign Office diplomat.'

---

[42] Sparrow-fart – colourful British Army term for very early in the morning.

'Nancy's' pedigree and cut-glass public school accent probably explained how he passed his WOSB but the wonder was that he had completed officer training.

'He had no fucking idea how to organise patrols,' continued Westie, 'and he was scared of crossing swamps for fear of footrot.' An accomplished pianist he might have been, as he had demonstrated at the ship's concert on the way over, but a soldier he was not – lucky Daddy was an ambassador.

On CO's Orders the following morning, three of 'Nancy's' Lance-Corporals were stripped of their rank for incompetence or insubordination. In giving evidence, the platoon sergeant did not hide his contempt for his platoon commander and, apparently, came perilously close to being charged himself by reporting the platoon did not do half as many patrols as recorded in its SITREPS. His account of false SITREPS was corroborated next day when six Lance-Corporals from other companies appeared on CO's Orders and were stripped of their 'tapes' when evidence of similar falsified SITREPS came to light. Several other men lost up to 28 days' pay for sleeping on guard in the jungle, accidentally discharging weapons or refusing to obey orders. In reality, Company SITREPs were made up mostly of half-truths at best, making the battalion's impressive sounding performance little more than a load of hogwash. If other battalions operated like ours, it truly was a wonder that the campaign was going as well as reported.

All told, the Notts and Jocks contribution to Operation *Badak* amounted to three-quarters of five eighth of bugger all. Rather than eliminating the remaining 73 terrorists believed to be at large in the Pengerang Peninsula by Merdeka Day, as foretold in the *Straits Times*, the Battalion had returned to FTC a week early having not clapped eyes on a single terrorist. This record did not bode well for our move up north to Perak State where the terrorists were much more active.

First operation survived, 379 more days to push.

CHAPTER 4
ADVENTURES IN IPOH

On a steamy Saturday night, after a five-day turnaround at FTC Kota Tinggi, we boarded the night train for Kuala Lumpur (KL) at Johore Bahru Station where we were crammed into squalid third-class carriages with hard wooden seats and dirty worn linoleum floors. The insides of the carriages were painted dark green from floor to sill level and light green above. The inside of the once-white, now nicotine-stained, curved roof was reminiscent of the trolley buses that took me to school, missing only the clear vertical white streaks where condensation had bled through the nicotine stains. The elegant looking chocolate and cream railway carriages that we had seen leaving Singapore Station on our initial drive from the docks to Nee Soon had flattered only to deceive.

We travelled overnight, sleeping where we could — on and under seats, or in corridors. I gonked on the floor with my head under a seat out of the way of stray boots and managed several hours sleep until near dawn when blokes started walking over me as their bladders demanded release. Apart from guard duties, it was the worst night's sleep I'd had in the Army. Dirty, sweaty and tired, we pulled into Kuala Lumpur Station in the early hours — a great way to greet the first anniversary of Merdeka Day.

After breakfast at the nearby NAAFI, we had time for a quick look around, admiring the clean white and cream facades of the more grandiose city buildings, all bedecked in bunting and Merdeka banners. The railway station[43] itself, completed in 1910, was a distinctive example of the unique architectural style of the region. After this glimpse of the capital, we continued northwards, stopping only at Tapah Road around midday for a packed lunch and a mug of tea. The last lap of the journey saw us arriving at Ipoh Station around two o'clock, only half an hour late — impressive over 400 miles on a largely single-track system.

Ipoh itself was situated in a fairly level valley floor surrounded by steep-sided limestone mountains (*gunungs*) rising to 7,000 feet. Although pleasing to look at with the sun glinting on them and clouds kissing their summits, I didn't envy the rifle companies who would have to patrol them. First impressions of the town itself, as we were driven through in Loyals' lorries *en route* to Colombo Barracks, were favourable with lots of greenery and some impressive, mostly white or yellow rendered buildings.

On arrival at our new home we were shown to our living quarters; a long, well-constructed *basha* sleeping 18 men and beds with Dunlopillo mattresses — utter luxury! After settling in we unpacked and stowed all the Int Section

---

[43] A building I was to become much more familiar with 17 years later, when overseeing an Australian Aid project to assess the feasibility of relocating the Railway Goods Yard, then part of the station complex.

equipment, which had arrived separately by road, in our new operations centre. This was a long building with the Int Clerks' office at one end, the Signals Office at the other end separated by the CO's office, my new northern CT Rogue's Gallery, the aerial photo room, and the Ops Room — all smartly furnished with the Ops maps mounted on the pastel blue and white painted walls.

Our sleeping quarters were central for everything except the Loyals' cookhouse where we were to be fed, but it was worth the walk. The meals cooked by the Loyals' cooks before they departed for Hong Kong were the best we'd eaten since Nee Soon. There was also an excellent NAAFI and cinema located within the barracks which, to us, was luxury indeed. Despite all these comforts, the Loyals Orderly Room lads we talked to griped about the conditions. They had clearly been there too long.

It soon became clear that Operation *Ginger*, in which we were now about to participate, was a major operation. We were temporarily replacing 1st Loyals in 28th Commonwealth Brigade, which comprised 3RAR (Royal Australian Regiment), 1NZR (New Zealand Regiment) and 2nd/6th Gurkhas, with armoured support from a squadron of KDGs (King's Dragoon Guards), plus an SAS (Special Air Service) Troop on stand-by. These units had been putting the heat on the CTs, with the Loyals and 1NZR chalking up seven kills and three surrenders in the fortnight before we arrived. This had caused a senior Communist guerrilla commander, accompanied by several other CTs, to surrender because they could not obtain food.

This news inspired Coco-Oscar. In his pep talk prior to commencing operations, he declared 'we must kill someone' — a terrorist, I wondered, or just 'someone'? It was clear from the Loyals Ops set-up that we would be fully occupied. Captain Pavior summarised the current situation before allocating each of us specific jobs — something he should have done much earlier. None of the intelligence work had been delegated to the lower ranks during our time at Telok Sengat with Captain Pavior and Sergeant Kaz doing it all. Addressing Trev and Sammy, he announced,

'You two will be in charge of the filing and the typing', before designating Dan as our draughtsman. Pointing at me, he said, 'I know you like to play the comedian, but can you manage the maps and CT ORBAT (Order of Battle) as well?' Demonstrating my agreement, I immediately set about my new task of becoming familiar with my northern 'Rogues' Gallery'.

Of course, our takeover of the Loyals Ops Room could not have been achieved without a drama or two. First, it was our precious regimental signs which, on our return from Telok Sengat, had been repainted by two Pioneer Platoon tradesmen specially dispatched from Batu Pahat for the task. After they had been re-erected outside the Ipoh Tac HQ Coco-Oscar noticed that all the signs, bearing the regimental badge, had been badly scratched during the journey. Sergeant Kaz bore the brunt of Coco's ire over the damaged signs,

'Sergeant, what's happened to these signs? Look at the state they're in.'

'Mortar Platoon pack them and bring here, sir,' Kaz pointed out in in his Polish-accented English.

'It doesn't matter who brought them here, Sergeant, get them re-painted immediately,' said Coco leaving Kaz in a major panic over how to get this done. When we returned late from lunch shortly after this incident, we bore the brunt of his anger and frustration over the signs.

'Why for you late back?' he yelled.

'Because Loyals' mealtimes are later than ours, Sarge', replied Trev.

'You should get there earlier.'

'Kitchen wouldn't be open, Sarge,' I chimed in — that did it!

'I report you to Captain Pavior for being late.'

Fortunately, Pavior acknowledged that, while the Loyals were still operating the kitchen, it was unrealistic to expect us to return by two o'clock when *tiffin* was not served until 1:30 pm on the other side of the camp, and he sanctioned our late return, within reasonable limits.

We were becoming accustomed to Kaz's temperament getting the better of him whenever Coco-Oscar gripped him, or when anything unforeseen happened. Every minor hiccup became a major drama. The way that he and the rest of the Regular NCOs flapped around at a word from Coco-Oscar was truly nauseating. It would have been understandable if Coco-Oscar was a commander who warranted respect but, as I wrote at the time:

... he is the original cream of closets with his bleating, um-ing and ah-ing voice and the way he must have minute things looking 'nice', such as the angle that the regimental signs faced and having the sand floor of the Ops tent at Telok Sengat swept smooth, when his main concern ought to be commanding his battalion efficiently. This morning when he was raving about his beautiful signs being scratched, he complained of our 'couldn't care less' attitude. I think that it is about time somebody told him it is the prevalent attitude in the battalion and the reason is because it is commanded in such a sloppy manner – 'Shall we dress for dinner tonight?' being the main concern of the officers. Promotion, at the expense of the private soldier, who they bugger around to bring attention to their 'efficiency', being the main concern of the sergeants and some corporals; whereas the buckshee privates merely think of demob, the next pay day if he has no money, and where to go tonight if he does, and to hell with CTs.

This was borne out chatting to some of the Loyals lads. Mainly National Servicemen like us, we had a lot in common with them but, overall, they seemed more motivated and appeared to run things much more efficiently than we did. Whether this was due to superior leadership (not difficult) or the success they were having on operations, with four CTs killed in the last fortnight, was open to conjecture.

One feature of our battalion that astounded the Loyals lads was our collection of animals. The menagerie included Osbert's timid pup, Pukey; a honey bear belonging to Lieutenant Duff-Cannonier, the Mortar Platoon commander; and the RSO's Alsatian, plus numerous pet monkeys. The Padre's monkey was perhaps the star of the circus, occasionally pissing on the epaulettes of his bush jacket when being carried around perched on his shoulder.

For Trev and I, the dawning of September 12th was a 'red letter day'. It was the half-way point of our National Service. One benefit of reaching this milestone was that we became eligible for star classification and Captain Pavior recommended both of us for two stars, which brought with them a modest pay increase. Celebrations in the NAAFI, the only source of reasonably priced beer, were postponed until pay day when our stay in the NAAFI was short-lived: it was packed with Loyals celebrating their imminent departure for Hong Kong so we headed into Ipoh. After a red hot, spicy chicken curry in the Ipoh Bar, we moved on to Darkie's Bar, which we found over-run by KDGs in full song celebrating their own imminent return to the UK. The whole town seemed to be in celebratory mood, so Trev and I joined in — over the hump, days to do are getting few!

Operationally, our rifle companies were gradually taking over the areas previously patrolled by the Loyals but were failing to make any contacts with CTs. In, fact, it was the Mortar Platoon that got as close to a terrorist as the Notts & Jocks ever would, escorting a surrendered CT to recover a Bren gun and ammo from a jungle arms dump.

Back at Tac HQ, Coco-Oscar was still grappling with his spelling. In the absence of Bryn, the cadet journalist who had been posted to BHQ in Batu Pahat, Trev and I had taken over going through and correcting (with a red pencil) the handwritten letters Coco gave Sammy to type. Unfortunately for Sammy, Coco disagreed with some of our corrections and asked Sammy to bring him the original handwritten draft. Sammy had no choice but to oblige. Seeing all the red pencil corrections such as taking the 'a' out of 'knowleadge' and the 'u' out of 'fourty', Coco-Oscar saw red himself. He was particularly livid with my correction of 'accur', where I had written a large letter 'O' over the 'a' with the comment – 'No! 'O' for Oscar.' Poor Sammy copped a full-on Coco rant.

'How dare you change my letters? Do you think you know better than me?' he raved, 'You need to show more respect for your senior officers and don't go changing what they have written. Do you understand?'

To his credit Sammy wore the blame and did not bubble[44] the real culprits, Trev and I. Coco-Oscar took the matter no further: perhaps charging Sammy for correcting his own spelling mistakes would have been too embarrassing? Thereafter, Trev and I ceased our voluntary proof-reading. It was this incident that brought to light why, when we were in Telok Sengat, the IO and RSO were both so keen to get their hands on any SITREPs written by Coco-Oscar before they were sent out.

As the demands on the Int Section increased with all four rifle companies out on ops, the Polack was getting more and more frazzled, biting everyone's head off over the most minor bungles. Fortunately, that weekend he went off on two weeks leave having rented an apartment in

---

[44] To bubble - to report someone for a misdemeanour.

Ipoh and was bringing his family up from Singapore in a huge Studebaker Champion he had purchased. Maybe this was to celebrate his signing on for another 10 years; news that resulted in little notes appearing around the Ops Room, saying, 'If you're thick, sign on quick'. However, given his limited career choices in civvy street, it was probably Kaz's only option, especially as he was near the top of the list for promotion to Colour Sergeant.

Meanwhile, the Ops Room routine continued with an average of one cock-up per day. The Monday after Kaz had departed on leave it was an extra big one — a secret document had gone astray in dispatch and the IO and RSO were flapping around trying to trace it. As it turned out the dispatch had gone out but not been recorded and had arrived late at its destination — hence the panic!

This was followed by an alarming cock-up over collecting the MO from a routine visit to 'C' and 'D' Companies. Johnny, his regular driver, had not driven him out that day because his Land Rover was being serviced, but had been ordered to collect him from the 'C' and 'D' Company base camp. The RSO signed his work ticket and I was detailed as an escort. The last three miles into their base camp were along a 'Black' road through jungle. On reaching the RV(Rendezvous) point at the end of the plantation road there was no sign of the armoured Ferret that was to escort us the rest of the way.

'Wouldn't you know it,' said Johnny, 'the bastards are never late when I've got the Doc on board.'

'Déjà vu — Telok Sengat beach all over again!' I thought, but this time there were only two of us armed only with a .303 rifle and a Sterling Machine Gun (SMG), each with a single magazine — no match for any CTs in the vicinity who may have heard our approach. Johnny turned off the engine and we listened for any sound of an approaching Ferret. The silence was broken only by the tick-tick-tick of our cooling engine.

'Fuck this for a game of soldiers,' said Johnny as he re-started the Land Rover, turned it around and pulled in behind some fringing undergrowth facing the plantation road.

And there we sat, back-to-back, Johnny in the driver's seat, Sterling on his lap, ready to hotfoot it at the sound or sight of anything untoward, and me crouched in the rear with my .303, each with a 180° arc of fire; the pair of us shitting ourselves at every unfamiliar sound. Yet more '**hurry up and wait**', and wait we did for almost an hour by which time I'd had enough.

'These bastards aren't going to show,' I said, 'not even 'C' Company could be this late, so the Doc will have to spend a night in the *ulu.*'

'Agreed,' replied Johnny, happy to get out of our exposed position, 'I'll stop at Chemor Police Station on the way back and phone Tac HQ from there to see what's happened.'

At Chemor I stayed with the vehicle while Johnny went into the police station.

'Typical', he fumed as he walked back down the steps, 'The Doc's at 'A' Company, been there all fucking day; wants to know where we've got to.'

We arrived at 'A' Company base camp right on tea time to find the MO had decided to stay and dine with the officers. The upside for Johnny and I was that we were given a hot meal in the Officers' Mess kitchen, eating off regimental crockery and using regimental cutlery no less. This was another eye-opener. I knew from Telok Sengat that Tac HQ officers dined formally off regimental silver but rifle company officers dining formally in the field on operations? Unbelievable! Hope the Doc had the fore-sight to bring his dress uniform with him.

Before leaving 'A' Company, I caught up with Chesh, who was smeared in Castellani's paint for his latest tinea outbreak. Although called up several months after me, he was boasting he would be back in Blighty before me.

'How come? I asked.

'Well,' he declared confidently, 'once I've passed my USB (which had been postponed because of operational duties) they'll fly me back to England for a WOSB'

'Bet you a quid they don't,' I said. 'Even if you pass your USB, the Army won't fly you back unless you sign up for three years.'

I knew my money was safe: Chesh would never sign on for an extra year.

Finally, back on the road with the MO aboard, we ar-rived at Colombo Barracks well after 10:00 pm. On turn-ing in his vehicle, Johnny was greeted by the news that he was on CO's Orders next morning for speeding that afternoon while trying to reach the wrong RV point on time. It was not the local speed limit he had exceeded but the lower WD (War Department) limit imposed on all military vehicles — he was steaming!

It was around this time, with Sergeant Kaz on leave, meaning more work for the rest of us, that we first lost patience with Osbert and his antics. Other than Sergeant Kaz and Captain Pavior, he was the only Regular soldier in our section. On first meeting him in Worcester, I had concluded he was something of a nutcase as he used to volunteer for all manner of jobs in the office, none of which he had ever completed satisfactorily.

Even at Telok Sengat, where we had been in an active operational area and our jobs carried some real respon-sibility, Osbert was always skiving off with his fishing rod or camera at every opportunity and otherwise doing as little as possible and not even doing that well. In ad-dition to his Int Section duties he had been appointed the Post and Dispatch Clerk for Tac HQ and the four rifle companies stationed in Ipoh. If his intelligence work clashed with his personal activities, he'd leave us to cover for him and left any unsorted mail lying around until he returned. Any official mail he was unsure about he dumped in a file tray until the shit hit the fan over non-delivery. He was an expert at blame-shifting: on one occasion accusing Trev of taking some missing official mail from his desk and filing it — how much mail was lost or went astray was anybody's guess? Without a sin-gle redeeming feature, he was so clueless that he once sent the Int Section mail to 'D' Company.

Our frustration with him peaked one Saturday night, af-ter Sammy had agreed to stand in for him as duty clerk until six o'clock, while Osbert spent the day in Ipoh with his new Chinese lady-friend. He did not return until after 10. In his absence his dog, thin as a rake after living on two corned beef banjos[45] a day, had been whining for food. On his return we gave it to him in spades. Dan's message was succinct:

'Osbert, feed your fucking dog, and don't ever mess your mates around again when they do you a favour.'

'Yeah, you're more interested in getting your end away than doing your fucking job,' I added.

By this time, it had become clear the only way we could deal with him would be to 'bubble' him as soon as he dropped his next clanger. Remonstrating with him made not the slightest bit of difference. As I described him at the time:

... he is childish, incompetent, selfish, untruthful, and just bloody useless yet, because he has been in the Army longer than any of the other intelligence clerks, he is a Lance Cpl and, because he is a regular soldier, he gets paid $69 a week while the rest of us National Servicemen, even though we have stacks more ability, only get $27 a week and no promotion. Osbert is a representative ex-ample of the type that is going to make up Britain's 'new' Regular Army.

Following this episode relations with Osbert remained icy, but at least he did start going to the cookhouse to get food for his dog, yet she remained pitifully thin and had no vitality. We even considered adopting her ourselves

---

[45] Banjo - a sandwich or bread roll usually containing a fried egg.

since Osbert seemed to have lost all interest in her but thought better of it, deciding Osbert needed to learn that dogs came with responsibilities.

It was on the same Sunday, that the Notts & Jocks cooks had arrived and taken over the cookhouse from the now departed Loyals. Without any notice they had changed the mealtimes so, when we arrived 'late', for our tea, the miserable Brummie cook with whom we had previously had run-ins, greeted us saying,

'You're too fucking late, kitchen's closed.'

'And since when did you have authority to change meal times without it being on Part 1 Orders?' I asked. This riled him a treat and he jumped over the counter and shirt-fronted me.

'The fucking kitchen's closed,' he rasped into my face.

Fisticuffs were averted when Johnny and Dan (six-footers both) intervened and pulled him away — stalemate! But with the menacing presence of Johnny and Dan, and an ever-lengthening queue behind us, Brummie-boy was persuaded to resume serving. With our own cooks back in charge there was an immediate dip in the quality of meals which fell away to the abysmal standard well remembered from Kota Tinggi. With the same ration allocation sourced from the same suppliers, it was scarcely credible that the meals our cooks turned out were so inferior to those cooked by the Loyals' cooks.

The following week saw more Notts & Jocks' incompetence. One of our well-trained riflemen on an 'A' Company patrol accidentally discharged his rifle and put a round through another lad's leg requiring yet another helicopter Casevac. Returning from a patrol later in the week, a Corporal from another platoon handed in his leading scout's shotgun to the armoury, allegedly having cleared it beforehand. Before servicing the weapon, the armourer pulled the trigger and blew off part of the armoury roof. Typically, the National Serviceman to whom the shotgun had been issued was docked 21 days' pay for not clearing his weapon before handing it over to the Corporal. The Corporal, who had confirmed the weapon had been cleared, and the armourer, who had pulled the trigger, both of whom were regular soldiers, got off Scot free.

To Coco-Oscar, however, poor arms handling practices were not nearly as important as ensuring our drivers did not exceed the WD speed limits. After numerous drivers had found themselves on CO's Orders for driving within the civilian speed limit but exceeding the WD limit, Coco-Oscar cracked down and began docking drivers 21 days' pay for exceeding the WD limit, in one case by a mere by three mph. The week also saw a major SITREP cock-up where one of 'A' Company's Sections had been given a wrong map reference and strayed into the 2/6 Gurkhas operational area. Brigade HQ raised hell setting Coco-Oscar off in pursuit of someone to blame.

It was during this period that anxiety levels were heightened further, not by the CTs, but by the 'Quemoy' crisis in the Taiwan Straits. As a test of American support for Taiwan the People's Republic of China (PRC) began shelling Kinmen Island and the Matsu Islands in a threat to the Republic of China (ROC). In Malaya this aggressive action by China failed to stir up any Communist support and Prime Minister Tunku Abdul Rahman restated that there would be no change in the Malayan Government's hardline policy towards the Malayan Communist Party.

My next turn on night duty brought a new drama. At around 8:30 pm in the evening, I received a phone call from the RAF squadron in Kuala Lumpur that airdropped supplies to our platoons in the jungle. They had received a late signal requesting additional supplies be added to an earlier airdrop request which they had not received. After searching our office, I found the missing airdrop request in the Signals Office, and spent over half-an-hour dictating the original request over an insecure telephone line to Kuala Lumpur.

Why or how the original signal had failed to make its way from the Signal Centre at one end of the Tac HQ building to us at the other end, no one knew. It had not been booked out in our dispatch book, so presumably we had not received it from the Signal Centre. Unfortunately, the blame could not be laid at Osbert's door, as he had been at the GPO (General Post Office) collecting mail at the critical time. Had there not been a supplementary airdrop request, the RAF in Kuala Lumpur would simply have assumed that the platoon in question had been withdrawn and no longer needed a re-supply drop. Later, I discovered that it was Chesh's platoon that would have missed out — another beer he owed me!

The next demonstration of the Notts & Jocks obsession with 'bull' came the following weekend. With the departure of the Loyals for Hong Kong, we had to share Regimental duties, such as Guard Duty and Fire Picquets, with other units in the camp. Lieutenant Duff-Cannonier, our Mortar Platoon commander, took it upon himself to out-bull other units by ordering that not only would our Guard wear best kit in future, but so too would the Fire Picquet. This only came to our notice when the Mortar Platoon Sergeant (also in charge of Tac HQ discipline), brought in the new Fire Picquet orders for Sammy to type. The bulled-up dress standards for Guard duty were of no concern to the Int Section because, having to do overnight duty clerk shifts, we were excused Guard duties. Fire Picquet dress standards, though, were a different matter.

We brought this to the attention of Captain Pavior, who promptly over-ruled the orders, leaving curt notes for Duff-Cannonier and his Sergeant, stating best kit was not required to put out fires and that Tac HQ Fire Picquet would continue to parade in second best kit. He also advised that picquet mountings should be brief to avoid people missing tea if they were late from picquet mounting, and that no more than one Int Section soldier was to be rostered on Fire Picquet on any day.

For the Battalion, the latest news was that, after the Loyals returned from Hong Kong, Malaya Command intended to base us permanently at the FTC in Kota Tinggi as a semi-operational unit, responsible for refresher training for non-combat units and training newly arrived draftees — some training they would get from us!

Naturally, Coco-Oscar was livid: he thought it was grossly unfair to put us into a secondary role after such a short period on operations, with not a single CT contact to our credit, let alone any surrenders, captures or kills.

Even more important, at least in Coco-Oscar's eyes, was that if we moved back to FTC, Notts & Jocks officers would have to share the Officers' Mess with the various service corps officers based there; a total anathema to Coco-Oscar. He couldn't bear the thought of having dog doctors from the War Dog Training Wing or, even worse, jumped-up motor mechanics from 221 BVD, lowering the tone of his mess.

However, with the political situation in Malaya becoming more unsettled, our movements remained uncertain. Tin prices had fallen after the USSR flooded the market, and this had created unrest among the miners. Three newspapers had been closed, one for 'obscenity' and the other two because they'd printed what the Government regarded as subversive propaganda. Unemployment was rising, which had led to demonstrations outside parliament in Kuala Lumpur and the Selangor Democratic People's Independence League had been declared illegal, both because of its contacts with the outlawed MCP and suspected subversive activity. Concurrently, in Singapore, under the Emergency Regulations, people were liable to be detained for up to three years without trial, in a move to stamp out the secret societies.

Back in Colombo Barracks, the next to go on leave after Sergeant Kaz returned was Osbert. In his absence, Dan was delegated as Post Clerk for the first week, and me the second. The weekend after Osbert's departure, I found myself free of duties and sought respite from Army life by going to the *padang* in Ipoh to watch a rugby match between Perak and Kedah in the Inter-State Cup. Here I bumped into Chesh who had finally sat his postponed USB that morning and had been offered the opportunity to return to the UK for a WOSB but, as I had foretold, only if he agreed to sign on for an extra year. Since he was expected to join the family business on completion of his National Service, he declined the offer. So, having won my bet about who would return to the UK first, and saved his re-supply drop, the beers were on Chesh.

Over the course of the evening, he recounted the tale of his personal terrorist contact which, in his words, happened as follows:

On one patrol we found a hoard of uncooked rice which had been left by the Min Yuen[46] for the terrorists. Our aim was to starve them out and keep them on the move so that eventually they would surrender. This hoard of rice would have been like manna from Heaven for the terrorists, so it was thought likely they would know of its whereabouts and collect it at some point in the not too distant future. It was decided therefore to lay an ambush by surrounding this hoard and, if and when the terrorists arrived, either get them to surrender or kill them.

After a couple of days, we were running short of food ourselves and a re-supply was some distance off. This re-supply would have consisted of seven days rations per man, plus any kit that was required, e.g. boots, which had a habit of falling apart, and any clothing which had passed its 'sell by date'.

---

[46] The civilian support network for the Malayan National Liberation Army.

We still wanted to prevent the terrorists getting this rice, so our platoon commander decided to leave a one-man guard to keep an eye on it. The Bren gun was an automatic weapon with pretty fierce fire power. As I was in charge of the Bren gun section, I was the chosen solitary guard. I settled myself behind the gun with the food cache in sight but not too far away.

After a couple of hours or so I thought I saw three or four terrorists approaching the cache, so I cocked the gun in readiness to fire. This was not the quietest of operations and the terrorists must have heard it, as they were off in a flash. For the next hour or so, until the platoon returned, I was very scared that the terrorists may return with reinforcements and that would have been my lot. Eventually our blokes returned and, when the platoon commander saw me, he asked me what was the matter. Apparently, I was whiter than the best Persil-washed sheet. We never found the terrorists nor another cache of food, but I'm sure our platoon commander would have left two or three lads to guard it had we done so. Personally, I've never been so scared in my life!

That same evening, Johnny, the MO's driver, told us the MO was becoming increasingly concerned about the number of VD cases since we had been in Ipoh, with new infections being reported almost daily. With the incidence of infections assuming alarming proportions, Coco-Oscar took decisive action. He sent a stern warning letter to all Company Commanders — as if that would make any difference, it wasn't them catching the clap. There was also a serious outbreak of scrub typhus in 'B' Company. Tinea was also rife, reportedly passed on when the clothes of affected men were laundered along with those of others who were uninfected. As a result, Trev, Dan and I clubbed together to send our *dhobi* to a civvy contractor on the camp.

Another consequence of Osbert's absence was that we were rostered for weekend duty clerk shifts every other weekend and it wasn't going to get any better when he returned, because Dan was going to Penang on two weeks leave. It was these extra shifts that deprived me of a trip to the Cameron Highlands the weekend following Osbert's departure. Coco-Oscar had generously granted the MO a long weekend break and, had I not copped a weekend duty clerk shift, Johnny could have wangled me along as an escort. However, I was not to be deprived — I would get my trip to the Cameron Highlands later, in altogether different circumstances.

My first week as postman brought a welcome change providing me with more work than I'd done for as long as I could remember. It was stimulating to be busy doing something useful that occupied the whole working day, and the week passed quickly. My first weekend as postman I set about sorting over 100 items of mail that I had found in Osbert's cupboard: dumped because he didn't know where the recipients were located and was too lazy to find out. With a little help from the IO and RSO, scrutiny of the nominal rolls, the Signals rolls, Battalion Orders and draft distribution orders, I identified the correct destinations for all but 17 letters in a single afternoon.

During this period circus life continued to follow its normal chaotic course: a patrol crossing a fast-flowing stream lost a shotgun and had to spend two days

101

searching for the missing weapon. No sooner had that been recovered, than the Mortar Platoon lost another shotgun in similar circumstances when a lad had been swept away in a torrent and almost drowned. A diver had to be called into retrieve the shotgun.

Politically, the situation continued to be unsettled. Picketing over unemployment was ongoing, and the People's Progressive Party — the Socialist-oriented opposition — appeared to be acting as a mouthpiece for banned organisations, vehemently protesting recent arrests and the detention of people for subversive activities. With the increasing suppression of terrorist activities, and the MCP's failed attempt to gain control of the Trade Unions some years earlier, the Communists were now trying to infiltrate Socialist youth organisations as a means of gaining power. Given the diminishing success of their terrorist activities, the Communists were also trying to infiltrate the widespread network of Chinese Secret Societies but, again, with little success.

It was during this unsettled period that camp life was enlivened by the arrival of an SAS troop on a four-day stay before being chopper-ed into the jungle near the Thai border for one of their extended operations. Notwithstanding their formidable reputation, never had I seen such an unkempt bunch of British soldiers. Haircuts seemed to be optional; moustaches were rampant (they made mine look like something out of a Noel Coward play), complemented by long sideburns that would give our RSM apoplexy. Their OGs were in tatters, looking as though they never took them off. Accompanying the

SAS troop was a mob of equally ragged looking Se-mang[47] porters.

No doubt justifiably, the SAS fancied themselves as the true 'hard men' of the British Army and while on camp were a law unto themselves. They drove around as if they owned the place, 'No Parking' signs were ignored and, during their stay, they must have come close to drinking the NAAFI dry. They began grogging-up at six and stayed until closing time every night. They turned up in all manner of scruffy outfits, some with shirts and some without, but no Canteen Corporal was game to say a word to them about dress standards. Their appearance brought to mind the words the Duke of Wellington who is reputed to have said on inspecting a new contingent of troops sent to Spain during the Napoleonic War: 'I don't know what effect they'll have upon the enemy, but, by God, they frighten me.'

The Saturday on which my postal clerk duties were due to end proved to be the start of an eventful weekend. First, I found myself on CO's Orders, thankfully not on a charge but as a witness in connection with a collision involving the driver of the one-tonner that did the mail run. Preparing to turn left into the narrow lane beside the GPO, and aware there was a car behind him, Jordy, the driver, had given a clear left-turn hand signal, checked his mirrors, and made the turn, never dreaming that the driver behind would attempt to overtake on the inside. Wrong! In my witness statement, I affirmed that I was

---

[47] Semang — indigenous ethnic-minority people who live in the mountains and forests.

aware Jordy was preparing to turn left and had noticed the car behind us continuing to move up on the inside of the lorry immediately prior to the collision, but there was nothing I could do.

'Why didn't you give a hand signal from the left-hand side of the cab to warn the following driver?' Coco asked me.

'Because I wasn't in the cab, sir. I was in the back of the lorry with the mail.'

Coco persisted, turning back to Jordy he told him,

'You should have looked through the rear window of the cab as well as using your side mirrors'

'The window in the back of the cab was covered by the canopy, sir,' replied Jordy. At this Coco relented, declaring both drivers were equally at fault and Jordy was admonished.

With Osbert still on leave, I found myself doing another weekend duty clerk shift on top of my last scheduled day of postal duties. But it wasn't all bad. The duty signaller that night was one of the Battalion's numerous Smiths, all known as 'Smudge'[48] or 'Smudger' In this case it was 'Signals Smudge' who had acquired half a mug of rum from the Sergeants Mess. Together with Coco's un-

---

[48] Despite the number of Smudges in the battalion, it was usually clear in conversation which Smudge was being referred to, by adding a prefix, e.g. 'MT Smudge', or an 'r' on the sobriquet, or by the tone of the reference e.g. 'You'll never guess what Smudge has done now!', which usually meant 'REME Smudge'.

drunk thermos of coffee, which I had discovered in his office, we settled down for a nightcap of rum-enhanced coffee and a good night's sleep. Not to be. Shortly after midnight my phone rang with a message for Smudge: a signals corporal from 'D' Company advising his set was off-net and he needed a tuning and netting call in order to make a scheduled contact with his platoons at 2:00 am.

That same weekend, further news came to light on our subsequent deployments. With the Loyals returning from Hong Kong at the end of the month, Tac HQ would have to vacate the operations centre at Colombo Barracks. Initially, we were to be relocated to Sungei Kuang to operate out of 'C' and 'D' Companies' base camp before moving on to the Gurkha Barracks at Suvla Lines in mid-November to direct the concluding Notts & Jocks operational activities from there. At the beginning of December, we were to return south, spending Christmas at either FTC Kota Tinggi or the dreaded 'Bull Capital' at Batu Pahat where the Battalion HQ Company was based. Following a period of retraining after Christmas, we were scheduled to commence a new operation in the riverine area north of our previous base at Telok Sengat to finally eliminate the terrorists' 9th Independent Platoon.

The big operational news of the weekend, however, was the Notts & Jocks first 'capture'. A Home Guard patrol from a nearby *kampong* had discovered some unidentified tracks in a secured area and our mighty Tracker Team was put on the trail. The team followed the tracks of one man around the jungle edge before losing them among some cattle tracks. They soon picked up the tracks again and captured the man in question, taking him to Chemor Police Station for questioning. It turned out that he was a villager out checking his pig traps who had inadvertently strayed into a security cleared area — a brilliant first capture for the Notts & Jocks!

But this achievement was surpassed by Osbert on his return from two weeks leave. Officially, leave could only be spent staying with friends or relatives, or in authorised Army Leave Centres. Osbert, apparently with Sergeant Kaz's concurrence, had stated that he was staying with Kaz. In reality, he had been staying in a hotel in Ipoh with his Chinese lady-friend where he became ill. The pair did a flit from the hotel leaving a $240 unpaid bill, with Osbert moving in with his paramour. Returning to camp on Sunday looking like death warmed up he tried to borrow $90, allegedly for hospital fees, where he claimed he had spent the last three days. This sounded highly implausible because, had he gone to a civilian hospital, they would have contacted the Battalion. In all probability he was trying to raise a part payment on his hotel bill.

Having failed to borrow any money, he took off in a taxi, returning an hour later with the lady-friend in tow. By that time we had notified both Captain Pavior and the MO of his condition. After examining Osbert, the MO rushed him straight off to BMH Taiping with suspected malaria. Evidently, he had not been taking his Paludrine while away and, more than likely, had not been sleeping under a net. It seemed that we no longer needed to find a way to 'bubble' Osbert — he'd succeeded all on his own. By our count he would be facing multiple charges on his return from hospital; self-inflicted harm by not taking his Paludrine, not staying in approved accommodation, not reporting to a military medical centre when he became ill, incurring civilian debts, and returning from leave in an unfit state to perform his duties. Quite enough breaches of Queen's Regulations for the Adjutant to get his teeth into.

Captain Pavior was livid, Kaz more so for being let down so badly when doing Osbert a favour. But the icing on the cake was the arrival of a cable from Osbert's 'fiancée' in England reading; 'Regret unable to send money, Marge.' Next day, another lad, returning from BMH Taiping, brought a letter from Osbert for his lady-friend which he expected us to deliver for him. Incredibly, he had also forwarded an application to Captain Pavior for permission to buy a .22 rifle to go pig shooting. If he wanted to shoot things, why not transfer to a rifle company and go shooting Charlie Tangoes? And where would he would find the money to buy a rifle? From what we could work out, he owed approximately $400 including the hotel, the record shop where he had bought a gramophone, the civilian doctor he saw when he first became ill, and last, but by no means least, the camp *char-wallah.*

On Sunday lunch time, while I was in the cookhouse, Sammy took a call from Osbert's lady-friend, whose name he had discovered was Lucy, asking for Osbert's letter to be delivered to her home. In my absence, the ever-helpful Sammy suggested that she could meet me at the GPO in the morning to collect it. She dismissed this arrangement insisting I should deliver the letter to her home.

'No way, Lucy,' I told her when she called back, 'meet me at the GPO, I'll give you the letter there.' There followed what I took to be a barrage of Chinese obscenities but the letter remained undelivered.

Osbert's chutzpah knew no bounds, another lad returning from BMH Taiping brought a second letter from him, this one addressed to the Int Section wishing us the 'best of luck' in his absence and asking us to tell Captain Pavior how sorry he was for 'mucking him about' and, the sting in the tail — could Kaz send some money to Lucy?

The following Monday heralded the start of an even more action-packed week. First, the Adjutant was visiting from Batu Pahat so everything had to be immaculate. There was more flapping over a visit by the unloved Captain Toff, who strode around with his head tilted slightly back as if he had a permanent bad smell under his nose, than when we had visits from the 28 Commonwealth Brigade Commander. In the office, it was 'Sweep this,' 'Tidy that,' 'Bull your toenails,' 'Trim your pubic hair,' etc, etc. In addition, we were flat out preparing for a visit from the Secretary of State for War, who was in Malaya to study the conditions under which British and Commonwealth forces were serving.

Apparently, Battalion HQ in Batu Pahat had known of the Minister's visit since early September but had made no preparations. So, on the orders of the Adjutant, the Int Section spent the whole week, day and night, drawing up charts and signs for a 'demo' that 'C' and 'D' Companies were to carry out for the Minister — such utter bullshit!

In my opinion, instead of watching some contrived demonstration and dining in the Officers' Mess, the Honourable Secretary would have become much better informed about the conditions being experienced by those on active service if he had shared a meal or two with the squaddies in a rifle company operational base — but my opinion was not called for.

That same week, there was mounting evidence that, after six weeks of constant *ulu*-bashing resulting in numerous cases of tinea and footrot, the troops were getting frazzled. At 'B' Company a snap FFI (Freedom From Infection) inspection was called at Reveille on a Sunday morning. Corporal Jack, attached from the Signals Platoon, turned up on muster parade unshaven, and was sent off to shave by the CSM. While he was away his name was called for his medical inspection, whereupon the CSM charged him for being 'Absent from Parade.' Appearing on Orders before his Company Commander later that morning, an incensed Jack simply refused to answer to the charge. For his silence he was remanded under close arrest to appear on CO's Orders at 11:00 am. In response to Coco-Oscar's questioning over what had led to the charge, Jack let rip.

'Sir,' he said, 'it's a fucking stupid charge, how does the CSM expect me to be shaved minutes after Reveille? It was him what sent me off to get shaved so he knew where I was, so why the fuck did he charge me?

With my 'Rogues' Gallery' located adjacent to Coco-Oscar's office, I eavesdropped on the whole episode. Coco was stunned that a junior NCO should address him in this manner.

'Don't ever use that kind of language again when speaking to me, Corporal, is that clear?' I couldn't hear Jack's muffled reply, but Coco went on.

'The trouble with you junior NCOs is you're simply not pulling your weight and stupid behaviour like this is setting a bad example to the other ranks,' he blustered.

Equally gobsmacked, given the circumstances, Jack was momentarily silent before letting rip again:

'It's not the junior NCOs what's acting stupid, sir, it's the senior NCOs what's giving the stupid orders.'

Further incensed that a junior NCO should contradict him, Coco-Oscar launched into a long-winded tirade on the responsibilities of junior NCOs, concluding with the exhortation that:

'You junior NCOs must uphold the proud traditions of the Regiment by providing leadership, not undermining morale by refusing to obey orders!'

Coco-Oscar seemed totally unaware that his own leadership had never come close to capturing the hearts and minds of his men. The upshot was that Corporal Jack was docked a week's pay for insubordination — not even a reprimand. Being responsible for the 'B' Company communications network, he was too valuable a wireless operator in our current operational situation to be placed in detention like Acker at Telok Sengat, who served 21 days detention for a lesser act of insubordination — more Army double standards. In my opinion, which again was not sought, Jack should have been given a commendation for having the guts to spell out a few home truths to Coco-Oscar.

Later in the day, presumably as a result of Osbert contracting malaria while on leave, Coco-Oscar fired off another stern memo to all company commanders, this time stressing the importance of the men taking their Paludrine while on leave. It probably did as much good as his letter regarding VD infections.

The Osbert saga resumed the following weekend. While I was relieving Sammy during Saturday lunch time, the phone rang. It was Osbert. Trying to be pally, he told me he should have been discharged from hospital on Friday but that they couldn't find his records which sounded unlikely. Consequently, he'd discharged himself that morning and had caught the train to Ipoh and was now waiting at Ipoh Station for transport back to camp. I said I'd contact the MT Section to send the duty driver to collect him. He said he'd already phoned the MT Office and there was no answer, so he was taking a taxi.

So why call me? I thought.

On arrival he stopped the taxi outside the Officers' Mess, and asked for Captain Pavior. Dragged out from his Saturday lunch Pavior, on being asked to pay the taxi fare, refused point blank.

'If you are too dense to phone for transport, you can pay your own damned fare,' he said. In response Osbert trotted out the same line he'd given me, that, he'd phoned the MT Section and got no answer. By this time, Pavior's patience was wearing thin.

'If you are too impatient to wait for the duty driver to get back from *tiffin*, that's your problem.' Undeterred,

111

Osbert pushed his luck even further, asking if he could claim the fare through the PRI.[49]

'You're welcome to try, but don't expect any support from me!' snapped Pavior before disappearing back into the Mess.

After this rebuff Osbert returned to our *basha* and tried to borrow the taxi fare — it did not wash with anyone except Sammy, who lent him the fare. To further relieve Osbert's dire financial situation Sammy offered to buy his camera at a knockdown price — a real bargain for a quality camera; one that Osbert had bought off Kaz in Worcester, who, in turn, had smuggled it back from Germany. Maybe Sammy was not as green as he was cabbage looking.

That evening Dan, Johnny and I went to the *padang* to watch the Merdeka Cup Rugby final between 1NZR and 3RAR. It was a big occasion, drawing the biggest crowd I had yet seen at the *padang*. Both teams were immaculately turned out and were presented to the Mentri Besar (Chief Minister) of Perak before the match. Most of the New Zealand team were Maori, few of whom, if any, would have been officers, and, remarkably to British eyes, the captain of the Kiwi team was a Maori corporal,

---

[49] PRI – President of the Regimental Institute. The PRI is the Regimental shop, selling a range of Regimental items along with various items to make life on operations or exercise more comfortable. The PRI Fund is used for the benefit of all serving soldiers of the Regiment.

Rangitataura (Sam) Christie[50]. A stark contrast with British Army rugby teams which were mostly made up of, and captained by officers, with NCOs and ORs merely making up the numbers.

The match itself was a fast, hard fought, end-to-end contest, with the Aussies exerting early pressure before the Kiwis asserted control and ran out convincing winners 17-0. After the first New Zealand try, the 'Diggers' on the touchline began to get at their own team, the scrum-half in particular, an officer named Newman. He was having a poor game, not helped by the barracking of the Aussie spectators.

'What ya' doing out there, Newman, making up the numbers?'

'Yer wouldn't be on the team if you weren't an officer, Newman.'

'Newman ya' blonde bastard, don't ya' know the game's started?'

As the Kiwi lead increased, this only raised the ire of the Aussie spectators, especially against the unfortunate Captain Newman[51].

---

[50] Christie was a huge slab of a prop forward, bigger and, in all likelihood, fitter and stronger than Tam Elliot, the Gala and Scotland prop who was the biggest prop I had ever played against.

[51] I next encountered Captain Newman in 1978, standing on a sand dune near Ayers Rock, looking at a lagoon of raw sewage. He was there as Minister for the Environment, being shown the environmental damage to Ayers Rock (now

The Malayan Police were helpless to stop the touch line antics, and the RPs from 1NZR and 3RAR were either too drunk or too interested in the game to bother.

After the match, we decided to leave the town to the Anzacs and headed back to the NAAFI. On the way back across the *padang*, we spied Osbert and Lucy in the distance. It was the first time I had seen her and, from that distance, she did not look worth a $400 debt and a dose of malaria.

'Wouldn't knob her with yours,' was Johnny's cryptic observation.

Just to fill in the time during my duty clerk stint the following night, and exasperated by the disgusting late tea I had been served, I spent part of the evening composing a memo to the IO about the barely edible late meals we were being served when doing duty shifts and left it on Captain Pavior's desk. The following day, after my marathon stint of two nights as duty clerk and two as relieving clerk, I was given the day off. My hopes for a relaxing lie-in were ruined by Sergeant Kaz turning up to

---

Uluru-KataTjuta) National Park being caused by the inadequate infrastructure supporting the tourist facilities then located adjacent to the Rock. I was there as leader of the team planning the relocation of the facilities outside the National Park. Just to emphasise the inadequacy of the existing septic system, a Red Setter owned by one of the motel owners went for a dip in the sewage. On being called back, the dog came and stood by the Minister, shook himself and then wagged his tail against the Minister's trouser leg. The 'Diggers' on the touch line in Ipoh would have loved it.

inspect our *basha*. Seeing Dan still in bed and me lying on mine with a mug of tea, munching an egg banjo, he went into a typical rant, but, since I was off duty for the day and Dan's leave had started at Reveille that morning, his threats were empty.

The next visitor to our *basha* was Captain Pavior by which time Dan was out of his bed and in the shower and I was engrossed in an extract from Monty's memoirs in the *Sunday Times* in which he expressed his lack of confidence the competence of regular British Army personnel (I'd second that). To my surprise I learnt Captain Pavior had taken my complaint to the Loyals' Adjutant, who had already returned from Hong Kong with the Loyals' Advance Party. So too had their cooks who had replaced ours who had already left for Sungei Kuang. Captain Pavior told me the Loyals' Adjutant had promised to reprimand the Cook Corporal on duty the previous night (more than our Adjutant would ever deign to do). Astoundingly, he also offered to shout me a banjo at the *char-wallah's* in compensation (another indication of why the Loyals' morale appeared to be so much better than ours). After facetiously checking whether I needed to wear my best OGs to eat with an Adjutant, I accepted the offer — after all it was my day off!

Later that day I learned that Osbert had been placed on CO's Orders, and was facing numerous charges. He had been relieved of the Post NCO's job, which I was continuing to do, and was to take over permanently (no extra pay, of course). At least I now had something useful to do rather than routine chores and counting the days to demob. Osbert was to return to his Int Section duties, including typing up the SITREP every other night rather than pulling rank and always passing the job on to Sammy.

That day was also Johnny's birthday. Due to his late arrival back in camp after driving the MO on his rounds of the rifle companies we didn't get started on his birthday feast until he arrived at half past eight. We tucked into some hotdogs cooked on jungle-issue solid fuel stoves, together with bread and cheese I'd bought in town that day, all washed down with rum and coke — a worthy celebration for a good mate.

Friday that week was the day of the big move to Sungei Kuang and the night before the move I copped yet another night as duty clerk. Any thoughts of catching up on some shut-eye were dashed by Coco-Oscar who remained in the Ops Room, working until after 11:00 pm. Busy pretending to be busy until he left, I spent some of this time chatting with 'Bluey' the red-headed[52] Aussie signaller who had been on attachment with us. During the course of the evening, he corroborated my opinion of British Army food by revealing that Aussie troops were paid an extra 9/2d a week if they were posted to a British unit. Obviously, the Aussie Army thought their lads needed a subsistence allowance to live with the Brits.

So, it was 'So long, Colombo Barracks!' with 313 days to push!

---

[52] An idiosyncrasy of Australian slang is that red-haired people are known as 'Bluey' and bald people are known as 'Curly'.

CHAPTER 5
WELCOME TO SUNGEI CESSPIT

The last day of October, and we're making another month-end move. it was the usual shambles with Sergeant Kaz flapping over a missing mattress. Reassured by a recount, loading began and the Ops Room was handed back to the Loyals. The main party left at 11:00, but I remained behind with the Rear Party to help Tiss and Patto, the Tac HQ Signals corporals, take down our two aerials and officially close our command-net at Colombo Barracks. Not knowing what to expect at Sungei Kuang we hung around long enough to take advantage of a last Loyals-cooked *tiffin* before leaving. Our work at Colombo Barracks was done.

Arriving at what we discovered was known to its inmates as Sungei Cesspit, the Rear Party found all the work done. The Tac HQ advance party had spent three frenzied hours setting up the Ops Tent and organising our accommodation. My only task was to collect a bed and bedding from the stores tent. All Tac HQ personnel had been accommodated in muddy-floored, crowded tents but, thankfully, Trev and Osbert had prevailed on Captain Pavior to let the Int Section sleep in one end of the Ops Tent, which had a concrete floor. Convenient for work, more space than anyone else, and no muddy floor.

The downside was that the tent roof leaked in several places so beds had to be positioned to avoid the drips.

As at Colombo Barracks, we were handily located for all camp amenities except the cookhouse and the only problem with our new home was that it was swarming with mosquitoes due to the pools of water resulting from the daily afternoon storm. The first person I ran into on my first night in the NAAFI I was Acker, of Telok Sengat fame. After his expulsion from Tac HQ, he was now in charge of the base telephone exchange and apparently doing a good job, always provided he was relieved for his nightly ration of Anchor in the NAAFI.

My first day on duty at 'C' and 'D' Company base camp found me being harassed by the two company commanders over the slow delivery of mail. Not my fault I protested; now the post was on-forwarded from Sungei Siput[53], it meant that, if the airmail into Ipoh was late, it missed the night train to Sungei Siput and arrived a day late. Notwithstanding these delays, I set about getting on top of the mail sorting and deliveries and the timing of the SDS (Signals Delivery Service) runs. Another issue I faced was the non-arrival of letters containing cash rather than postal orders, sent by senior NCOs to their wives in Singapore — this too was my fault. Thankfully, my spirits rose that evening when the lads already *in situ* produced a rugger ball and, after tea, we spent an enjoyable half hour having a kickabout on the MT park.

---

[53] Sungei Kuang was about 10 miles north of Ipoh by road. and did not have a train station.

The first disciplinary matter after our arrival was Osbert's appearance on CO's Orders charged with not reporting to a military medical unit when he fell sick on leave, and for not taking his Paludrine whilst on leave. Other than being subjected to one of a Coco-Oscar's rambling rebukes, he got off surprisingly lightly with only a reprimand. And much good that did because the following day Lucy came to camp in a taxi to collect him. The pair also took Sammy along to meet one of Lucy's friends, no doubt as some recompense for bailing Osbert out financially and for feeding his dog while he was on leave and in hospital. Evidently the date fell short of Sammy's expectations because he returned that night on the shuttle truck from Ipoh, with Osbert only returning next morning in a taxi.

Once settled into the Sungei Cesspit routine it proved to be quite an easy-going camp with a notable absence of bull, plenty of opportunity for skiving and, remarkably, given the incessant rain and the basic camp kitchen facilities, the meals were a cut above what the same cooks had produced at Colombo Barracks — how can this be, I wondered, maybe because the officers' meals are coming out of the same kitchen?

Less to my liking was Coco-Oscar's nauseating attitude towards his men. In conversation with a visiting Army Public Relations Officer, he opined that:

'The private soldier has no personality . . . does he, Private?' he said, turning to Sammy for confirmation. Sammy dutifully jumped to his feet and agreed. Oh, that the arrogant bastard had addressed the question to me!

Coco's mood was not helped by being put upon by Brigade HQ demanding that he provide umpires for an internal security exercise in Singapore. To our Adjutant, visiting from Batu Pahat, he blustered,

'I'll bloody well bring Brigade to heel!'

Responding to the Brigadier on the phone later in the day, it was,

'Yes sir, no sir, three bags full sir!' Two-faced clown that he was!

But his absolute classic came the following day when he asked me,

'Where's Dick Turpin's tree in Notts?'

'I think you mean the 'Major Oak'[54], sir.'

'Yes, whatever it's called, where is it?

'It's near Edwinstowe, sir.'

'Where?'

'Edwinstowe sir, not far from Mansfield,' I added, thinking that, coming from East Anglia, he may not be familiar with the counties from which the regiment he commanded drew its recruits, but would at least have heard of my birthplace. My answer seemed to satisfy him and he returned to his office.

---

[54] A large mature oak tree in Sherwood Forest in which Robin Hood is reputed to have hidden from the Sheriff of Nottingham's soldiers.

Our tent continued to leak and, on returning from leave in Penang, Dan was far from impressed with his new quarters, having been living in fan-cooled luxury and did nothing but gripe about the conditions. Also, he'd returned with tinea which did nothing to improve his mood. Since I was suffering from prickly heat around my stomach that went on to develop into tinea, he had my sympathy, but we were not alone — there were dozens of cases in Sungei Cesspit with every other lad covered in scarlet Castellani's paint. However, with Sammy going on leave on Dan's return, we still had sufficient space to move the beds around and avoid the worst leaks.

Apart from Acker, evening entertainment in the NAAFI, was provided by the camp mascot, 'Half-Track', a podgy little sausage-dog pup belonging to one of the Signals Corporals. When he behaved himself, Half-Track was promoted to Corporal, and wore two brass chevrons on his collar but, if he misbehaved by cocking his leg or crapping in the Corporals' tent or in the NAAFI, he was busted back to private and lost his corporal's chevrons. He also lost his second water bowl in the NAAFI, the one that contained his 'malt ration' in the form of Anchor beer. For a dog of his size Half-Track had a surprisingly deep bark and growl and was really gutsy. He played boisterously with the RSO's Alsatian and with the 'War Dogs' on camp, and was more than a match for Osbert's Pukey.

Despite his recent reprimand Osbert's cock-happy antics continued. After a Friday night duty clerk shift, I was waiting on Saturday morning for him to relieve me. As usual, he had headed off to Ipoh on Friday night to visit

Lucy. With no sign of him, Trev relieved me while I went to breakfast. Returning from the cookhouse, I saw Osbert smooching with Lucy at the camp entrance. I saw red.

'What the fuck are you doing hanging around here necking? You should have relieved me two hours ago.'

'Just giving Lucy some money for her taxi back to Ipoh'

'Looks like you're giving her more than that — anyway Trev's still covering for you in the Ops Room, so you'd better get your arse over there.'

'OK, OK, keep your hair on.'

'And don't expect me to relieve you for meals today . . . or ever again for that matter, arsehole,' I muttered *sotto voce* as I stormed off.

On arrival at the Ops Room Osbert copped another fiery reception from Trev. As threatened, I did not relieve him for the rest of that day, leaving him to suck up to someone else if he wanted a meal break. With his little pal Sammy on leave, he was at the mercy of Trev and Dan.

That was the night Trev got utterly stocius in the NAAFI, more drunk than we had ever seen him. Mid-session, we had to take him outside for a puke before dragging him off to his bed. After 'Lights Out', such was our level of anger at Osbert, fuelled by copious quantities of Anchor, Dan and I went to the Ops Room, tipped him out of his bed, which we heaved outside.

Monday morning found Trev waking up in a soggy mess having, in the vernacular, 'pissed the mattress'. That day, with eyes like piss-holes in the snow and a sickly green pallor he couldn't remain in the hot, humid Ops Room for more than 10 minutes without having to go outside for a puke. That was the same morning it was confirmed that Tac HQ was to return to Ipoh, moving into the 2nd/6th Gurkhas Barracks at Suvla Lines before our relocation back to Johore. This move presented several problems. For Trev the most acute was his piss-stained mattress. The *dhobi-wallah* would be able to get the stains out of the mattress cover, but the mattress itself would remain stained. Since Tac HQ was moving out ahead of the rifle companies, this would inevitably be discovered when we handed in our bedding, with Trev having to pay damages. Fortuitously, a subsequent drama in the camp would present a solution to this dilemma.

The first problem we foresaw at Suvla Lines was the escalated level of bull that Coco-Oscar would impose to impress the Gurkha officers. We were not to be disappointed, the initial indication came when we had to parade for an inspection in our best kit. Several of us were told to exchange our shorts, bush jackets and even berets for new ones – we had to look our best on arrival at Suvla Lines. The second concern was meals: due to the different ration allocation for Gurkhas, and their cooks' unfamiliarity with cooking Western food, we were to be trucked three times a day to 3 Company RASC for our meals, meaning extremely early starts for breakfast.

These concerns were overtaken by the highlight of the week which was the Notts & Jocks' first ambush. For almost two weeks rotating platoons from 'C' Company had lain in ambush on a CT food dump located in a narrow crescent of land encased by a river on one side and a road on the other. Other platoons were keeping the river under surveillance for CTs crossing and the 13th/18th Hussars were patrolling the road in armoured cars. What could possibly go wrong?

As tracks would later reveal, what did go wrong was that two CTs walked right into and out of the ambush without tripping a flare or being seen or heard and made off with the food. When this was discovered, pandemonium broke out, Coco-Oscar was incandescent.

'How could you let this happen?' he ranted at the 'C' Company Commander who was equally mystified.

'Were men sleeping on watch? Coco demanded. Again, no one knew. The situation required a nicotine fix but with Sergeant Kaz, Coco's usual provider of cigarettes, not present Coco, who never carried his own in the belief that he didn't smoke, turned to Dan,

'I don't smoke, sir,' replied Dan. Turning to me he received the same answer and, in one sweeping condemnation, we were both dismissed as 'Useless'.

A cigarette having been found Coco dispatched our Tracker Team to the ambush site to track the elusive CTs who had made off with the food. They were never located, but later that morning, a 'D' Company patrol found an arms dump in a cave that also contained a trumpet, a trombone, a euphonium and a bugle — only the Notts & Jocks could have made a such a euphonious discovery.

Soon after the ambush incident I received a letter from home enclosing a cutting from the *Daily Express,* proclaiming, with typical Beaverbrook bombast, what a great job British troops were doing and, that following the recent surrender of Hor Lung[55], the MNLA's southern commander, the British had Chin Peng on the run and the 'fighting' would be all over by Christmas. In the article there was no mention of the Australians, New Zealanders and Gurkhas who, at the time, were having considerably more success than British units (especially the Notts & Jocks, who were having none). No mention either of the Royal Malaya Army, Police or Home Guard, who were playing equally valuable roles. In reality, the hard core of CTs that were left were jungle-savvy guerrillas, and no way could I envisage the 'fighting' (or, more correctly, patrolling) being over by Christmas the following year, let alone in six weeks.[56]

Following hot on the heels of the failed ambush, the next drama involved a Second-Lieutenant in 'C' Company. Fresh out of the jungle after being part of the unsuccessful ambush operation, he ordered a driver and two escorts to take him into Ipoh in a Land Rover for a night out. Returning to camp he insisted on taking the wheel and set off driving like a crazed charioteer. The

---

[55] Hor Lung had, in fact, surrendered some four months earlier and been held in secret while persuading others to surrender for which he was well rewarded. When his surrender was finally made public, he had orchestrated the surrender of over 100 other hard-core guerrillas thus decimating the MNLA's southern command, resulting in Johore State being declared a 'White' area.

[56] In fact, the 'Cessation of Hostilities' that ended the 'Emergency' was not declared until 31 July 1960.

authorised driver appealed to him to pull over but was ignored and the hair-raising drive continued until coming to grief on a sharp bend at speed. The Land Rover rolled and came to rest in a monsoon drain. The lucky subaltern escaped without a scratch, the two escorts suffered minor cuts and bruises, and the authorised driver, who was thrown out of the vehicle, sustained a deep gash to his back, but luckily no broken bones. Of course, Coco-Oscar tried to keep the incident quiet, concocting an accident report stating that it was an authorised journey (which it was not), and was caused by a stray animal (which it was not) on a wet road (which it was not).

'Bad for reputation of the Battalion if this came out,' was Coco-Oscar's summation.

The subaltern paid a heavy price for his escapade, having to contribute to the cost of replacing the vehicle and being confined to camp for three months, but no other disciplinary notation appeared on his service record. Meanwhile, regular MT Platoon drivers were having their pay stopped for minor speeding infringements. Had a private soldier written off an Army vehicle driving while drunk, his punishment would have been much more severe — one law for officers, another for ORs.

Coco-Oscar's dramas continued when he was the first army person to arrive on the scene of a head-on collision between an RASC three-ton truck and a 1st Loyals three-tonner on the Chemor Road, quite close to our camp. Both trucks were travelling at an estimated 35 mph, their fuel tanks ruptured on impact and the trucks burst into flames. Four soldiers were burnt to death and two others were thrown clear and survived[57]. Naturally, Coco-Os-car took charge of the situation and that night he kept Osbert busy typing his statement. This described how, on arrival, he had 'jumped up to look through the flames to see if anyone was still in the vehicle cabs', how he sent his driver to call the Fire Brigade, detailing what time they arrived and what time the water came on. He also detailed how he commandeered two civilian drivers to take the two injured soldiers to hospital and how he did not leave the scene until the SIB[58] and civilian police had arrived and taken charge. — November 13th was not a good day.

The day after the accident Coco-Oscar spent most of his time phoning almost everyone in FARELF, telling them how he had dealt with the situation but, sadly for him, that day's newspaper report omitted to mention the vital role he played. It later came to light that the driver of one truck had only five weeks to push, and had his bags packed ready to sail home the following week.

The following weekend brought another crisis. The Saturday afternoon peace was broken by a voice yelling,

---

[57] I experienced a stark reminder of this event 52 years later when attending the service commemorating the 50th anniversary of the 'Cessation of Hostilities' at the Kamunting Road Christian Cemetery, Taiping where, among the headstones, I saw those of the four soldiers who had died on that day.

[58] SIB – Special Investigation Branch of the Royal Military Police.

'Fire! Fire! Fire!'

This brought Coco-Oscar bursting out of the Ops Room tent, Captain Pavior and Sergeant Kaz hot on his heels. Fastening his shorts on the run (must have been a good mess lunch!), the sight that confronted him was the 'D' Company stores tent ablaze to the ridge line. Men with water buckets were running this way and that, pitching water at the fire and re-filling their buckets.

'Find more buckets!' yelled a corporal as men scrambled around: those with full buckets kept slipping in the mud or colliding with others rushing back to refill their empty buckets. It took fully five minutes for Coco-Oscar to organise a bucket chain to the nearest wash-house, and even longer for anyone to think of driving the water wagon and trailer to the scene of the fire. A fat lot of good all the fire drills had done! Rather than add to the chaos, Trev and I watched on from within our tent located almost directly across the road from the burning stores tent. Acrid-smelling smoke billowed out from the walls as flames penetrated the roof.

The fire was gradually brought under control and finally extinguished after around 25 minutes, but not before our brave Colonel had taken it upon himself to make an aerial inspection of the seat of the fire. He climbed up a guy rope and straddled the ridge of the tent where he was drenched by a bucket of water thrown over him by Sergeant 'Stonker' Storr, who claimed he had slipped as he released the water. It was at this point that the tent collapsed and Coco-Oscar disappeared into the smoking wreckage, only to re-appear from the charred remains, blackened but largely unburnt. By this stage, Trev and I were convulsed in laughter as we watched Coco-Oscar, the only casualty, making his way to the MI Room[59] to have burns on his knees and fingers bandaged by the MO (almost worth a Mention in Dispatches!)

With the fire extinguished and the entertainment over, Trev and I set off for tea, sheltering under his poncho as the rain set in. We almost jumped out of our skins when a thunderclap, the like of which I'd never heard before, crashed overhead, and simultaneously a bolt of lightning flashed all around us. With all remaining embers now totally extinguished by the storm, the local fire engine finally appeared to lend assistance, having become bogged along the road into camp. But for the storm the fire might have spread to the POL[60] store containing petrol and Avgas, which would have made the fire brigade's attendance worthwhile. After the rain eased the 'D' Company CQMS (Company Quartermaster Sergeant) set about supervising the erection of a temporary stores tent out of the serviceable remains of the burnt-out tent and any other available canvas.

The events of the day made for a lively session in the NAAFI that night. It was a small gathering as most of the lads had gone into Ipoh for the night and, with the rain again pelting down around us, much time was spent discussing the important business of the evening — how we could avoid all the excessive bull awaiting us at Suvla Lines. The word was that we would have to wear best boots, hose-tops and puttees, starched shorts and shirts

---

[59] Medical Inspection Room.

[60] POL – Petrol, oil and lubricants.

129

all day, with room inspections every morning. Kit, including mess tins, knives, forks, spoons, and mugs was to be laid out on our beds in the prescribed manner — all to impress Gurkhas who were unlikely to ever set foot in our *bashas*. The immediate problem though, for which we still hadn't found a solution, was Trev's piss-stained mattress which would be discovered when we handed in our bedding on Monday morning.

The solution presented itself on the way back to our *basha*. In the improvised 'D' Company stores tent we noticed a mattress bearing the name and number of Corporal Dyer, pressed against the netting enclosing the tent. Dyer, who was out on patrol, was one of the same unloved, fair-haired, short-arsed, short-tempered, bossy breed of NCOs as Corporal (sometimes Acting Sergeant) Brannock, only the Dyer version came with a toothbrush moustache. So, in the early hours of Sunday morning, after the rain had abated, Trev removed his mattress from its freshly *dhobi-ed* mattress-cover, while Dan and I did likewise with Dyer's mattress. A surreptitious swap was achieved and Trev had a pristine mattress again.

Sunday was spent packing the Int Section gear (yet again), after which we adjourned to the NAAFI for a final session with the 'Rear Link' crew — two cockney signallers from the Royal Signals and 'Bluey', the Aussie signaller, together with, who else, but Acker. It was a fitting finale to our sessions in the Sungei Cesspit NAAFI. Nothing more than a couple of leaking tents slung together but, with a good crew around the long table and Half-Track for entertainment, it had more atmosphere than any other on-site NAAFI in which we had imbibed.

On the move again, with 285 days to push.

CHAPTER 6
LIVING WITH THE GURKHAS

Monday morning, and we were awakened early to the sound of dogs howling over at the Tracker Wing, and the return of Osbert, who had been staying in Ipoh with Lucy since Saturday. After a hurried breakfast, we set about final packing and loading. At 8:30 am we were supposed to be on parade, resplendent in best boots, puttees, hose tops, best shorts and shirts, webbing belts and berets ready to leave. At the appointed hour Trev, Dan, Sammy, Osbert and myself were still finishing loading our gear, dressed only in PT shorts. Kaz went off the deep end:

'Why for you not dressed?'

'Balls, Sarge, how can you load wagons when you're all bulled up?'

'What about what it say on detail?'

'Detail's all balls, Sarge.'

Eventually, after changing into our best togs, we set off, passing the Rear Link boys, all casually dressed in PT shorts and flip-flops ready for their return to Taiping. We arrived at Suvla Lines around midday. After unloading, we were driven three miles to 3 Company RASC for *tiffin*, where we feasted on pork pie, corned beef, fresh tomatoes, cucumber, beetroot, crispy lettuce, potato salad, hard boiled eggs and fried spuds, followed by fresh fruit salad and whipped cream. It was a wondrous meal but, there again, if the Service Corps can't eat well who can?

As anticipated, our worst fears were realised on the first morning at Suvla Lines. We had to be awake at sparrow-fart to board the lorry to the RASC camp for breakfast. On our return, it was into our best boots, hose-tops, put-tees, starched shorts, shirts, belt and beret, standing by our beds at eight o'clock for the first of what were to become daily room inspections with kit laid out in pre-cise order on our beds. We couldn't be seen on a Gurkha barracks in our normal slovenly Sungei Cesspit state, es-pecially wearing 17 Gurkha Division flashes on our sleeves. This called for drastic action.

Immediately after the room inspection, Dan, Trev and I reported on Sick Parade. Poor Trev was diagnosed ail-ment-free but Dan was packed off to BMH Cameron Highlands with weeping tinea and I was excused boots with a touch of footrot that I had been cultivating at Sungei Cesspit — no more boots, hose-tops and puttees for me for at least a week, hopefully longer. I was also prescribed treatment for my prickly heat, little red spots that appear all over the affected area and feel like you are being constantly prickled.

When Trev and I returned to the Ops Room, me in flip-flops, and announced that Dan had been sent off to hos-pital, Kaz hit the roof yet again. He already had an ink-ling something was afoot when he had spotted us at the office collecting our medical records when we should have been on Muster Parade.

'What we do with man short?' he demanded.

'Shit, Sarge,' I shot back, 'you might have to do some work yourself.'

In the contrast to the early days in Telok Sengat when Captain Pavior and Sergeant Kaz did everything, and we clerks were entrusted with nothing, Kaz was now passing all jobs on to us while he sat around reading books or comics and smoking: always on call if Coco-Oscar needed to cadge a fag. In fact, he was so out of touch with operations that, if Coco asked him a question about an operational matter, he frequently had to come to us for the answers. The question neither he nor anyone else had the answer to was why the British taxpayer was paying him £25 a week for doing stuff all.

As the first day at Suvla Lines wore on, it became apparent that Coco-Oscar's insistence on such a high level of bull and dress standards was totally needless. Yes, the Gurkhas had elaborate bed layouts, and their soldiers on Regimental duties were immaculately turned out, but the Gurkha lads going about their normal duties wore boots, rolled-down socks, PT shorts, vests and either jungle hats or berets, like any other unit in Malaya.

Suvla Lines [61] itself was large and spread-out (you needed a bike to get around it) with an enormous parade

---

[61] Suvla Lines was later re-named Syed Putra Camp and became the home of the Royal Malaysian Rangers. When I visited in 2010 in the Australian delegation attending the 50th anniversary of the 'Cessation of Hostilities', I found it little changed, apart from the addition of several high-rise accommodation towers. These had clearly not weathered nearly as well as the original single storey blocks that I

square. The accommodation blocks were stone and concrete, with tiled roofs, surrounded by closely cut lawns with neatly trimmed borders and manicured shrubberies. Each Gurkha block had its own garden, which the Gurkhas turned out to trim and cultivate first thing every morning. They even dusted under the eaves of their barrack block verandas. Anything not living and trimmed to size was painted. Road edges and intersections were clearly marked with white and red paint, as were fence posts. Judging from the paint-work and polished brass studs in their wheel hubs, the Gurkha vehicles looked like they were just for show and never used.

A definite plus though was that there was a huge sports ground, and, within days of our arrival, a soccer match was arranged between the Gurkha Signals Platoon and Tac HQ. In order to make up the numbers I had to forget my footrot, don a pair of plimsolls and, swallowing my pride, participate in the round ball game, doing my impersonation of Tom Finney at outside left. It wasn't enough — we lost convincingly. The whole of the Gurkha Battalion who were not out on patrol turned out to watch wearing their off-duty attire of black shorts, light blue shirts, long dark blue socks and black shoes. Coupled with their youthful looks and short stature, this 'uniform', almost gave them the appearance of English public schoolboys. To me the highlight of the afternoon

---

remembered, which still looked in excellent condition. Fortunately, I did not need a bike to get around, as I was given a guided tour by two young Rangers officers in a Land Rover, who could not believe I had been stationed there 52 years earlier.

came after the match, when the Gurkha pipe band marched onto the field and played for 20 minutes. The sight and sounds of their stirring marches took me back to my childhood when my father was stationed at Fort George. Here I would sometimes sit outside the cook-house with a mug of tea, watching the pipe band of the Seaforth Highlanders rehearsing on the parade square.

The first night in our new quarters we ventured over to the Gurkha NAAFI, which had an impressive interior with photographs on the walls — more like a rugby club-house than an Army NAAFI. What immediately attracted our attention was a sergeant supervising the rum allocation. Six bottles of over-proof rum were poured into a bucket, topped up with a pint of water. Truly generous measures, probably around a gill (a quarter of a pint) of the only slightly diluted mix, were sold for 25 cents a tot. Top up two of those with Coke and you had a 50/50 pint of rum and Coke — lethal! The downside was that only Gurkhas were allowed to buy the rum but, as we got to know them better, we soon came to mutually beneficial arrangements whereby the Gurkha lads bought us rum and we bought them beer, which they found expensive on their pay.

By Tuesday, having had no mail delivery on Sunday, and having missed the mail collection on Monday due to the move, I was faced with five bags of mail to sort, no small task given the amount of misdirected mail. Sorting completed and mail despatched, I found 'Signals Smudge' in the NAAFI who informed me that the British REME (Royal Electrical & Mechanical Engineers) mechanics attached to the Gurkhas had their own accommodation block with a carpeted lounge and dormitory furnished with individual wardrobes. They had their own wash-room with hot and cold running water, showers, a bath and flush toilets plus a separate dining room with waiter service and were not subjected to bulled-up kit layouts — nice work for some!

On Wednesday, 'Signals Smudge' was again the bearer of good news: it had been decided that in future duty clerks and duty signallers would also get to enjoy this REME dining service. Arrangements had been made for those on duty to eat with the REME contingent. Being duty clerk that night I was the first to enjoy this luxury. Dining tables were laid with polished wooden table mats, cutlery all set out like a hotel restaurant, with a butter knife, water glasses, and butter, jam and a variety of sauces in individual bowls. All this with waiter service and excellent food. It was almost like eating in the Of-ficers Mess. Even the operational news was good. That night, as duty clerk, I took a phone call bearing the news that 3RAR had killed three CTs that day.

Reporting to the MI Room each morning for treatment on my footrot and prickly heat enabled me to escaped the full kit inspection following Paludrine parade. Given the slow progress of my footrot treatment, I figured I should be able to avoid wearing boots for the remainder of our time with the Gurkhas. My prickly heat though was responding much better to the prescribed lotion, but it wasn't being helped by Coco -Oscar's insistence that we wore shirts to work.

Repugnant though it was after the casual life at Sungei Cesspit, we soon fell into the routine of rising at 6:30 am, washing and shaving before boarding the wagon to take us to the RASC camp for breakfast, returning for Paludrine parade and kit inspection. During my morning visits to the MI Room, I soon became friendly with Pete Ranbahadur, the Gurkha medical orderly who treated me. Pete, spoke good English and was multi-skilled: in addition to his basic infantry training, he was a qualified driver as well as a medic. He also became my source of cheap rum in the Gurkha NAAFI.

During our first week with the Gurkhas, it was officially announced that we would be moving to Batu Pahat on 2nd December. The contemptible Osbert was to be sent to Batu Pahat immediately with the Advance Party. The logic behind this was threefold; first, for him to make a start on establishing the Int Office in Batu Pahat, second, to bolster the number of junior NCOs needed for Regimental duties there and, third, to get him away from his Chinese fancy woman in Ipoh. With Osbert gone to Batu Pahat and Dan in hospital enjoying the drier heat and cool nights in the Cameron Highlands, Sammy, Trev and I were hard at it with overnight duty clerk shifts again coming around every third night.

In the office, irrespective of what time the meal wagon returned from the RASC Mess, Kaz continued to be stroppy if we were even a minute late. Overall, it was worth wearing Kaz's wrath because the meals at 3 Coy RASC were well worth the three-mile drive, even though we don't get the waiter service we enjoyed when eating with the REME crew. Even so, the RASC food was always well presented, with dishes for jams, butter and condiments, rather than being served out of tins or packets as in the Notts & Jocks cookhouse. On his Mess rounds, the RASC Orderly Officer would not only ask about the food, but would also taste dishes for himself, and the Orderly Sergeant rebuked the cooks if the food wasn't up to scratch. In our cookhouse, no Orderly Officer would dare ask how the food was, but would sweep swiftly through the Mess saying, 'Everything alright, chaps?' and disappear.

By this time the Loyals, who'd now returned from Hong Kong, had resumed operational duties and our rifle platoons were gradually being withdrawn. Our brief role in Operation *Ginger* was at a close. We knew that what awaited us was worse — returning south to join Headquarters Company at Batu Pahat, the notorious 'Bull Capital'. Prior to this, however, we were to be farewelled by the Director of Operations in Perak state. In preparation for his visit, I was hunched over a drawing board drawing a large complex chart for the big occasion.

While concentrating on making sure no drops of sweat fell on the chart and smudging the wet ink, I heard a voice asking,

'Where's Captain Pavior?'

Unaware that I was the only person in the room, I continued stencilling and the next thing I knew was receiving a sharp jab in the ribs with what turned out to be Coco-Oscar's thumbstick. This caused me to push the stencil up the board, smudging the text I was printing — 'what the fuck?' was my immediate thought but I managed to reply civilly,

'He's gone to the Orderly Room, sir.'

'Stand up when you speak to me,' Coco snapped, looming over me. This I did, throwing him a smart salute for good measure.

'Now answer my question!' he said.

'Captain Pavior has gone to the Orderly Room, **sir**!'

'Why couldn't you have said that in the first place?' was Coco's brusque response as he turned to go in search of the IO. Fortunately, I bit my tongue because, if the arrogant sod had said one more word, I might well have lost it a said more than I should. Instead, I returned to the task of rectifying the smudged chart.

The condescending attitude of Coco-Oscar when speaking to ORs was getting me increasingly riled. At least the IO and RSO treated us like human beings. They would share a joke and allow us to speak our minds, as long as we remembered who was in charge. However, from overheard snippets of conversation, it was apparent that even they shared my irritation with Coco-Oscar, if not my intense dislike of the man. The RSO, despite being a Regular officer, often gave vent to his frustrations over Coco's clownish administration. This probably had a lot to do with the fact he was a reluctant soldier, being a National Service officer who had re-enlisted after failing to secure a satisfactory job on his return to Civvy Street. Unlike Coco-Oscar, he was held in high esteem by his men in the Signals Platoon, whose morale and operational performance outstripped other units within the battalion commanded by more fire-and-brimstone style officers. Unfortunately for the RSO, in the eyes of those officers in the battalion whose opinions counted, he was thought of as being too familiar with his men. No bad thing in the opinion of the Rear Link operators from the Royal Signals who had been attached to the battalion: they rated our communications set-up as the best of all units involved in Operation *Ginger*.

Later that day, Coco-Oscar had more on his mind than the whereabouts of the IO. Following hot on the heels of his heroics at the truck smash on the Chemor Road, news came of another road accident. This time it only involved only one fatality rather than four but had far more serious consequences for the Battalion. Five miles out of Batu Pahat an Ipoh-bound Notts & Jocks three-ton lorry knocked down and killed a young Chinese girl riding her bicycle. Unlike the recent Land Rover escapade, this one could not be covered up, especially as the lorry was being driven by an unauthorised and unlicensed driver. The official driver, an inoffensive National Serviceman, had been bullied by one of the escorts, would be 'hard man' Butch Marcello, into letting him to take the wheel. Marcello had never held either a civvy or Army driving licence in his life. His time in the MT Platoon had been short-lived after he backed a three-tonner into the 2 I/C's car during his first week and had failed to own up. It looked as if a court martial was looming, for both Martello and Bob Jones, the hapless driver.

With this on his mind, Coco Oscar also had to contend with a farewell visit by the Director of Operations for Perak. With nearly half of his men suffering from tinea, thus rendering them unfit, or barely fit for jungle service, Coco-Oscar had ordered that they should all be dressed in jungle boots, long trousers and bush jackets to hide their condition from the Director. All 'A' and 'B'

Company personnel who had already been withdrawn from the *ulu* were to be trucked to Sungei Kuang to join 'C' and 'D' Companies for the occasion, all looking 'nice' with their extensive coatings of Castellani's paint concealed beneath their jungle greens.

The first port of call for the Director of Operations was Tac HQ for a briefing. Aided by my smudged chart Coco-Oscar attempted to demonstrate what a great contribution the Notts & Jocks had made to Operation *Ginger* — which, of course, they hadn't. Apart from the seizure of a few musical instruments, the battalion's contribution had been imperceptible. After the Tac HQ briefing, the Director moved on to Sungei Kuang to thank the rifle companies for the important role they had played during their deployment to 28th Commonwealth Brigade and to farewell them before their return to Johore.

During our final week in Perak, with only one platoon remaining out in the *ulu* in an area of high CT activity, this was the Notts & Jocks' last chance to salvage some combat credibility. It was not to be. A 1NZR patrol, searching an area adjacent to 12 Platoon's operating area, had found the tracks of seven CTs no more than 12 hours old. Following the tracks, the Kiwis discovered they led into the Notts & Jocks operational area. The whole of 12 Platoon was withdrawn to Company base camp and clearance given for the Kiwis to continue following the tracks. Hot on the trail of the seven CTs, led by an Iban tracker, the Kiwis stalked into the vacated 12 Platoon bush camp[62].

'Tracks stop here,' announced the Iban, gravely. The tracks were those of a 12 Platoon patrol which had inadvertently strayed into the 1NZR area — and here were the Kiwis hot on their tracks looking for a big kill. A fitting finale and a fine demonstration of how much the Battalion had contributed to Operation *Ginger*.

At Suvla Lines our last week was notable in several respects, not least for me in in my role as Post Clerk. First, though was the return football match between Tac HQ and the Gurkha Signals Platoon. With a much-strengthened team, including several lads who had returned from leave or from hospital, we won 4 - 1. Needless to say, my participation was not needed.

The night of the match I made my first trip into Ipoh for three weeks due to the frequency of the duty clerk

---

[62] This could have had dire results, but the procedure when a patrol from one unit wishes to move into another unit's operational area is quite clear. A request is made at Battalion level from on Battalion HQ to the other and an agreed area is allocated to the incoming patrol. The host Battalion HQ then withdraws all its own troops from the agreed area. As a further precaution the incoming patrol keeps a radio set on the frequency of the withdrawing platoon, hence radio contact with the host Battalion is maintained. That the NZR patrol entered the 12 Platoon camp without being fired on indicates that the procedure had been followed and communication had been maintained. If these protocols are not observed it can lead to clashes between friendly forces.

schedule. Along with Trev, I set off for the Ipoh Bar where we compared notes with a few of the other lads we met there before heading for the Boston Bar where I found Chesh, recently released from hospital following a bout of dysentery. As he told it:

I was given medication, but to no avail and after a couple of weeks was carted off to BMH Taiping. Diet and different medication were the order of the day and after three weeks I was passed as OK to return to my unit. That was on a Saturday and I was deemed fit enough to go on an op the following Monday.

Monday came and off we went. I had lost a fair bit of weight and was certainly not really fit enough for jungle bashing, but orders are orders! After three or four hours I was more than beginning to flag so our Platoon Commander (the same Lieutenant Davies who got us lost in Johore), decided to leave me with two other lads whilst they pressed on to where they were meant to be. We cooked ourselves a meal, made a shelter and turned in, as by now it was nearly dusk. I think we must have stopped in a mosquito nest, as virtually the whole night was spent swatting mozzies. Despite face nets and insect repellent we were all bitten, not exactly to death but near to it. In the morning, we breakfasted and set off to catch up with the others. From this base camp I did go off on a couple of sorties, but as we were in a base camp, we didn't have to carry all our kit in a rucksack and I managed to continue with the op.

Back in Kota Tinggi during training, we had asked our training officer what was the likelihood of seeing a snake, to which his reply had been that snakes were more frightened of us than we were of them, and would usually not be visible. Best left alone if you should see one, was his advice. On this op we saw a big snake lying along a branch adjacent to the track we were on. As each person passed it, he would point it out to the next person in line. This is what I did but the lad behind me, perhaps to test the reaction of the snake, poked it with the end of his rifle barrel. I moved off very quickly but fortunately the snake slid off in the opposite direction and none of us, nor the snake was the worse for wear.

On the subject of wild creatures of the jungle, this incident reminded me of what had happened to me on a previous op. We had set up camp and prepared our 'nosh' and were at liberty to amuse ourselves, although there is not a lot in the bush that offers much amusement. Unfortunately, as darkness fell quickly, there was not a great deal to do to pass the time. However, despite being in the middle of nowhere, a guard had to be posted. At a spot near the middle of the camp, a solitary person, the guard, had to remain for an hour, after which he woke the next guard who, likewise, stood on duty for an hour and so on through the night. On one occasion I was the guard from 2.00-3.00 am. Pitch black with nothing to do or see. I amused myself for an hour singing rugby songs to myself. Suddenly, without any warning there was a rustling in the undergrowth very close to where I was sitting. The hairs on the back of my head 'froze' and then something hairy jumped into my lap and sped off into the bush. Truly frightening I can assure you. I checked with our platoon Iban, who gave a short laugh and said, 'Nothing to worry about, probably tree rat.' Possibly the Malayan equivalent of a grey squirrel.

After being regaled with Chesh's jungle yarns and his definition of a true friend as someone who will remove a leech from between the cheeks of your arse, we had a lively choral session before calling it a night. Fortunately for me and Trev, who was somewhat worse for wear, the driver taking the rifle company lads back to Sungei Kuang agreed to drop us off at Suvla Lines. Once inside the gate, as I was trying to steer Trev towards our *basha*, we were challenged.

'Halt! Who goes there.'

We looked around but could see no one. Where had the voice come from?

'Hands up!' was the next command.

We raised our arms and once in this position of surrender, a couple of Gurkha sentries, SLRs at the ready, emerged from a monsoon drain in which they had been concealed. We established our identities and, duty done, the Gurkhas sent us on our way with broad grins across their faces. After almost shitting ourselves, Trev and I resumed our meandering way in a much more sober state.

The unpleasant finale to my time at Suvla Lines came on the Friday morning before we were due to leave Ipoh and the timing could not have been worse. The previous day had been payday and I had sought out Gurkha Pete, my medical pal. We had become good friends over the course of my treatment and I had promised to buy him a beer or three before I left. Being paid only once a month and this being the end of the month, Pete was flat broke. I shouted him a couple of bottles of Anchor for starters but he flatly refused the money I offered him to buy me some Gurkha-issue rum. Instead, he borrowed money from one of his mates to buy for me and started getting them in, big time. It didn't take long, drinking 50/50 rum and coke, before I was pretty gibbered and bowed out early as gracefully as I could.

In the morning, with the killer of all hangovers, I headed to the dispatch office I shared with the SDS clerks when handling the mail. As I slumped into my chair in marched Captain Pavior accompanied by a Royal Military Police (RMP) Sergeant. Surveying the room, the Sergeant announced that mail containing money from some 'C' and 'D' Company senior NCOs to their wives in Singapore, had gone missing. Army logic had determined that, since I had been handling the mail for the last two months, I was the obvious suspect.

'Which one's the post clerk? demanded the Sergeant. Captain Pavior pointed me out and left.

Turning to the SDS clerks and drivers he told them to wait outside until he called them before plonking himself down in my chair leaving me standing there like cheese at fourpence.

'Did you know NCOs send cash through the mail to their wives? he asked.

Of course I knew, from the earlier complaints about missing mail when we first moved to Sungei Kuang but I wasn't going to admit it, so I answered,

'No, sarge . . .,'

'It's Sergeant!'

'Right, Sergeant,' I replied, 'but I am authorised to buy postal orders on their behalf at the GPO if they send me the cash with the SDS.'

'Have you ever opened any outgoing mail?

'No, Sergeant, all I do is deliver the outgoing mail to the GPO in Ipoh and the Malayan Postal Service handles it from there.'

'Have you ever looked to see if there are bank notes inside letters?'

'No, Sergeant, I only check to make sure they have the correct stamps.'

'Have you ever seen anybody else tampering with letters?'

'No, Sergeant.'

'Has any of the outgoing mail from 'C' and 'D' Companies been tampered with when you receive it?'

'Not that I've noticed. . ."

'Has it, or hasn't it?' (Alright, keep your hair on, arsehole)

'Like I said, not that I've noticed. I only check for correct postage so I don't look at the back of the envelopes to check if they have been tampered with.'

'Sure you're not lying?'

'Positive.'

'Be worse for you if you are'

'As you like, Sergeant, just go ahead and prove it.' (Shit! I'm answering back: is my head clearing under this interrogation, or am I still pissed?) The Redcap was not impressed,

'That's enough lip from you, soldier, go and put your statement in writing and send in the next suspect.' he snapped.

After putting the SDS clerks and drivers through the same interrogation, he escorted each of us in turn to our *bashas* and searched our kit, scattering it everywhere — all without finding anything incriminating.

This half-arsed investigation, confined to only the Army side of the mail-handling operation, left the SDS lads and myself seething with anger at having our honesty questioned: all as a result of the rank stupidity of senior NCOs (including a CSM) in sending bank notes through the mail. Theft and/or incompetence on the part of the Malayan Postal Service was the more likely explanation. After dealing with the Malayan Postal Service for a couple of months, I had little faith in their operations, having frequently had to redirect clearly addressed mail intended for other units, some of which were not even stationed in Perak.

Despite my hangover and the inquisition I had endured in my fragile state I later discovered that buying Gurkha Pete a few beers the previous night had been a far better option than taking my last chance to go into town. A couple of the Smudges, along with 'Curly' Laming, Patto, Tiss and Mick McC had hit the Boston Bar. After preventing Mick from getting into a fight with a gigantic

Maori, they had moved on to the Jubilee Cabaret, a dance hall.

Asian dance halls bear no resemblance to the likes of, say, the Arboretum Rooms in Nottingham where, after a few pints of Dutch courage in the pub, male teenagers would seek out a good-looking girl and, risking the embarrassment of rejection, ask her to dance. In Ipoh it was different. The girls were known as 'taxi dancers', and you needed a ticket (three for a dollar) to dance with them. This arrangement was not to Mick's liking and, without producing a ticket, dragged the girl he fancied onto the dancefloor. The Chinese bouncers pounced, making him produce a dollar to continue. Seemingly smitten, Mick used his remaining two tickets for further dances with the same girl. After the third dance, she refused to continue dancing with him without another ticket. Seething, Mick re-joined the lads at their table. A few rums and coke later he took umbrage when he saw 'his girl' dancing with a Chinese local, and cut in.

That was it. The Chinese bouncers dragged him off the dance floor *en route* to the exit at the head of the stairs. Mick resisted and started throwing punches, and the bouncers laid into him. Curly and the Smudges went to his aid, 'Signals' Smudge getting a chair smashed over his head for his trouble. Bottles and chairs flew, tables were overturned, the mirror behind the bar was shattered by a flying bottle. A couple of chairs went clattering over the balcony into the street, bouncing off cars below attracting the attention of Aussies and Kiwis in nearby bars, who came looking for the stouch. Somehow, aided by an RAMC (Royal Army Medical Corps) Corporal, Patto and Tiss managed to drag Mick out of the dance hall and down the stairs while the others held off the bouncers, but not before Mick had been glassed and stabbed.

With blood streaming from gashes on his head and several knife wounds to his arms and torso the medic took Mick and 'Signals' Smudge back to the Ipoh Medical Reception Centre (MRC) to get patched up. Mick was kept in overnight but Smudge was discharged after having a dozen or so stitches in his scalp.

Mick McC returned to camp the following morning, head swathed in bandages and with dressings on his arms and torso. When questioned over how he had sustained his injuries, he had a convenient bout of amnesia — couldn't remember a thing after getting to the Jubilee, or how he got to the MRC.

The fracas made headlines in the *Straits Times*, which reported that, apart from Mick, five Chinese men had also suffered knife wounds. The fallout was that the Jubilee Cabaret was placed 'out of bounds' to all Commonwealth service personnel. A great farewell triumph for the Notts & Jocks.

So, on departure from the hottest operational area in Malaya with no surrenders, no captures, and no kills, days to do were down to 282.

CHAPTER 7
BATU PAHAT AND ALL THAT BULL

After my horror hungover Friday, Saturday heralded my last overnight stint as duty clerk. Our last platoon came out of the jungle that day and the Battalion officially ceased operations at midnight. On Sunday we packed our personal kit, leaving Monday free to pack and load all the Int Section gear again for yet another early departure on Tuesday. With Dan still in hospital, Osbert already in Batu Pahat and Sergeant Kaz nowhere to be found with work to be done, the remaining three of us, as usual, had to pull our fingers out to get everything loaded. The *piece de resistance* during this operation was overhearing a telephone conversation between Coco-Oscar and the Adjutant in Batu Pahat.

'Ken, I want all the Battalion to be together over Christmas, with the minimum number of men on leave. I think we can make the men very happy.' — Christ, does the man have no idea?

After three months on operations, I doubted any of the lads would relish the idea of returning to the Batu Pahat 'Bull Capital' for a jolly regimental Christmas, let alone be subjected to Coco's 'nice ideas' for making us happy — what did he have in mind; tombola or charades perhaps? However, before he got around to writing to all Company Commanders advising them of his Christmas

152

treat, 'B' Company had pre-empted him by arranging for 50 of their men to go on leave over Christmas. Vexed as he was at being thwarted in his endeavour to 'make the men very happy', Coco-Oscar was powerless to do anything: the accommodation had already been booked.

The day before we left Ipoh, with all the packing completed, there was still time to fit in a deciding football match with the Gurkhas that evening. With some of the better Tac HQ footballers already *en route* to Batu Pahat, I was again called upon to play, and we ran up a 3-0 lead in the first 15 minutes. Thereafter, the super-fit Gurkhas ran us ragged, and we held out for a 3-3 draw. With honours even we bade farewell to Suvla Lines over a few post-match beers with our new-found sporting friends before an early night.

After my last waiter-served breakfast with the REME crew on the morn of departure, it was off to the GPO for the final mail collection before drawing my rifle and parading with the rest of Tac HQ ready for the move. I was in the road party which left Ipoh at 10:30 am, leaving the rail party to wait for the night train. Initially, the road journey took us through typically rugged jungle-covered Malayan terrain, passing through Gopeng, Kampar, Tapah and Trolak on the way to Batu Cantonment, a large Malaya Command base and transit camp on the outskirts of Kuala Lumpur where we overnighted.

Continuing our journey next morning we headed south through Seremban and on to Tampin. After a roadside stop for a picnic lunch, we passed through Cha'ah, Yong Peng and Ayer Hitam, finally arriving at Batu Pahat around dusk. Our first sight of the infamous Bull Capital as we waited at the gate was not at all assuring. The camp comprised a maze of whitewashed structures of varying styles enclosed by whitewashed fences. Any other fixed objects that were not whitewashed were painted in maroon and green regimental colours. The armoury, where we handed in our weapons, was also whitewashed on the inside with the rifle racks highlighted in regimental colours. Welcome to the Bull Capital!

Sergeant Kaz, who had travelled by train, showed me to the Int Section accommodation, a wooden building on stilts, which also housed the control signals set, the RSO's office, the Int Section office and the IO's office. The telephone exchange and SDS centre were located directly opposite. Needless to say, the building was whitewashed.

After a quick shower I headed off for tea and then on to the NAAFI for my first taste of the 'spirit' of Batu. There was none. After first being gripped for not having my jacket tucked into my trousers and sleeves rolled down, I joined Patto and Tiss. No sooner had I joined them than the two of them, both corporals, were told they couldn't drink with me and were moved on to the Corporals Mess. Moving on to the 'Quiet Room' I found a group of Orderly Room lads, including Filly, the Post Corporal. As we began comparing notes about Batu and Ipoh, the NAAFI Orderly Corporal ordered Filly out of the Quiet Room, and into the Corporals' Mess. Class distinction was alive and well in Battalion HQ. Even in their free time, the lower orders were segregated from friends they had trained with — in disgust I headed for my scratcher, already loathing Batu Pahat.

Matters didn't improve in the morning. Entering the mess hall, I was again gripped for not having my jacket tucked into my shorts. When Patto and Tiss, used to the freedom of camp life in Ipoh, again joined me at breakfast they were promptly moved on to the corporals' section of the mess hall by the Orderly Sergeant. (How does enforcing segregation between junior NCOs and Other Ranks foster esprit de corps?)

The first morning at Batu the RSO, adhering to Ipoh custom, held an informal Paludrine parade for Tac HQ personnel on the Tac HQ veranda. This enabled us to avoid inspection by appearing on the HQ Company Muster/Paludrine parade. Our escape was short-lived. That same afternoon, the recently arrived Ipoh contingent was assembled on the parade square for a 'Welcome to BHQ' pep talk from the CSM, WO2[63] Twort. He stood a little over five-and-a-half feet short and was a ball of energy and invective — often entertaining if you were not on the receiving end. He had swept back dark hair, an immaculately manicured moustache and an accent that came from a long way south of Notts & Jocks recruiting territory. He wasted no time in laying into us.

'You bloody men from Ipoh, you're in the peace-time army now and you're in BATU PAHAT, ON TERRA FUCKING-FIRMA, not running around the fuckin' hilltops in the *ulu*. When you've been here a bit you'll wake up in the middle of the night screaming — ABOUT ME!

---

[63] Warrant Officer 2nd Class

To emphasise his point, he informed us that there would be a Company Commander's inspection the following morning, and every day after that, except on weekends, but there was a catch: this coming weekend a CO's inspection had been scheduled on Saturday morning as well — bull was now creeping into the weekend. On inspecting the Tac HQ ranks Twort gripped me for the tattered and faded green square of fabric behind the badge on my beret, and for my moustache which, during the bull-free days in Ipoh, had strayed well beyond acceptable Army bounds. Pointing to his own precisely pruned upper lip adornment, he said,

'You're not in the fucking *ulu* now so get that 'tache trimmed before I clap eyes on you again'.

Thursday night was spent bulling for the OC's inspection next morning, when we were to be dressed in best boots, hose tops and puttees. Our jungle boots and other kit were to be displayed on our beds in a specified order and there was even a specified layout for kit stored in our lockers. Fortunately, at that stage, Tac HQ personnel did not have lockers so we were able to stuff our spare kit into our kitbags. Immediately after the Friday morning inspection, Trev, Sammy and Osbert had to get bulled up for Guard-mounting practice, while I was left to restore order to a huge pile of unsorted maps.

At the guard mounting practice, Trev and Sammy, who had done no drill since we left Worcester, copped a blistering tirade from Twort but later survived the formal guard-mounting without being charged. Seven of the other newly arrived Tac HQ, lads, including Osbert, were all charged for various faults in their turn-out or arms drill.

Friday night was another bull night in preparation for an inspection by Coco-Oscar himself in the morning. With the green fabric patch on my beret replaced at my own expense to avoid being jumped on again on the Saturday parade, I was gripped by the Provost Sergeant for a dirty cap badge (which I had cleaned meticulously when re-attaching it to the newly sewn green patch) and for un-polished boots which, being new, did not have the bene-fit of a year's spit and polish. The day didn't get any bet-ter, because this time I was rostered on guard duty and Saturday morning saw me engaged in even more bulling of kit and rifle-cleaning to avoid any charges on guard-mounting. Together with other Tac HQ lads from Ipoh, we were subjected to more of Twort's invective at guard mounting practice.

'Robinson, you jumped-up-never-come-down streak of piss, get a hold on that fucking rifle. You're six foot tall and that rifle weighs nine pounds and you handle it like it's nine hundred fucking pounds. Do you want seven days?'

'No, sir,' was the reply.

'Course you don't,' countered Twort. 'You need four-teen fucking days!' and charged him for being 'idle on parade'.

'When you lot were in Ipoh,' he continued, 'you may have thought "Fuck Batu, fuck the whitewash, fuck the bull, fuck the guard duties, even fuck me", but I've been fucked so many times that I'm immune – and I'm still not pregnant, so get a fucking grip of yourselves.'

So, this was the peace-time army! Mercifully I only had another nine months to endure.

I survived guard-mounting without charge and with Henry Ford in charge of reliefs I got the best 'stags'. Guard duty enabled me to have a nocturnal nose around the camp itself. It was a hotch-potch of brick buildings with tile roofs, wooden huts on stilts, corrugated iron go-dolphins and rattan bashas, all dispersed around the camp, with no semblance of order, separated by areas of long grass dissected by monsoon drains. The layout was so haphazard that neither Leonardo da Vinci nor unlimited quantities of whitewash highlighted with regimental colours could come close to making it pleasing to the eye — the place was simply a dump populated by bull-happy NCOs enforcing class distinction, even among the lower ranks. On top of that the food, which we had (falsely) been led to believe would be at least palatable, was in a word — shite! Life in a temporary operational bush camp with leaking tents and dig-your-own monsoon drains was far preferable. Word was that the town was no better, it had four bars, three cinemas and was crawling with RPs and a diligent civilian police force.

As we were assembling for Muster Parade on Monday morning, the start of our first full week in Batu, we saw the entire Signals Platoon out doing early morning PT. This was another of the RSO's initiatives which enabled the signallers to evade the morning Muster/Paludrine parade. Later that day we learnt that the RSO also permitted his platoon to engage in sport every afternoon except

Fridays. Naturally, since the Int Section too had also recently returned from operational duties, we pressed Sergeant Kaz allow us to join in the Signals Platoon afternoon sports activities instead of sitting in our office pretending to be busy. Kaz was his usual negative self — to him no change was a good change. Fortunately, Captain Pavior came in during our entreaties and was all in favour of us joining the Signals Platoon for morning PT, playing badminton, tennis or football every afternoon and joining the occasional swimming parties organised by the RSO for his platoon at the Kluang Garrison swimming pool.

This enabled us to kill three birds with one stone. First, by doing PT we missed the morning Muster Parade every day but Friday; second, playing sport in the afternoon provided an escape from the office; and third, I was able to improve my fitness which, for someone with ambitions of playing Varsity rugby after demob, was a big plus. Rugby though was still a neglected sport in the battalion, even though there was rugby kit and balls in the sports store. With too few players to raise a team within HQ Company and with the rifle companies dispersed in satellite camps, organising a rugby team was all too hard for Lieutenant Nickelhead, the sports officer.

A week after we arrived in Batu, Dan re-joined us after his three weeks of bliss in BMH Cameron Highlands recovering from weeping tinea. Fortunately, when he returned, Osbert had already been sent on an NCOs cadre leaving a spare bedspace in our compact quarters.

Even so, Dan bitched about our Batu living space even more than he had when he re-joined us in Sungei Cesspit following his leave in Penang. His tinea was still active and, within a day of his arrival back in sea level humidity, he developed a severe sweat rash causing the MO to refer him to a specialist at BMH Singapore — this raised Dan's hopes that he might be Medevac-ed back to England if it did not clear up.

With no PT on Friday, we were condemned to appearing on Muster Parade where I was again gripped by WO2 Twort, this time it was my hair, curling out from beneath my beret (but not a patch on the Z-craft skipper).

'Your bloody hair is curling,' he snarled. 'The only people in the Army who can curl their hair are the WRACs (Women's Royal Army Corps), and you ain't no WRAC, you know why? Cos you ain't wearing a skirt. Get your fucking 'air cut before I clap eyes on you again!'

That same morning, we were subjected to a lengthy lecture on sexual hygiene. There had been over 60 cases since we arrived in Malaya — two or three a week. Coco-Oscar was finally taking notice and had become sufficiently alarmed to arrange for the Padre an the MO to lecture all ranks on the immorality and health risks of consorting with prostitutes. This was something he should have done right after our arrival when the first cases were diagnosed, rather than simply writing memos to Company Commanders instructing them to warn their men of the risks of unprotected sex. The Padre took a more worldly approach to the joint disquisition than the MO who, surprisingly for a doctor, seemed somewhat embarrassed by the topic, approaching it in more formal medical terms unfamiliar to most of the lads. Both, however, stressed the importance of using condoms, which were freely available from the MI Room (if you weren't too embarrassed to ask).

The following day, Saturday, was my birthday, so Henry thought it was a good occasion to escort the birthday boy, Dan, Trev and Johnny for our first visit to the town. The prices soon drove us out of the South Seas Bar, reputedly, the best bar in Batu. Not a good introduction. Henry then took us to the Palace Bar, where prices were more to our liking so I ordered a bottle of rum to celebrate no longer being a teenager. This was soon gone following the arrival of Filly and several of the Orderly Room lads. With the bottle finished, we headed to Lulu's Bar, renowned as Batu's last resort for lonely, sex-starved and dispirited soldiers. We tried to inject some life into the place by buying another bottle of rum and launched into a sing-song. This provoked the lonely and dispirited-looking Band Sergeant, drinking quietly in the corner, to phone the Guard Room. Soon afterwards a Land Rover arrived bearing both the BOS (Battalion Orderly Sergeant) and COS (Company Orderly Sergeant) to put a stop to our choir practice.

'Time to go,' said Henry at the sight of the red sashes so he, Filly and I disappeared out through the back of the bar. The others were too pissed to get the message and were returned to camp in the RP Land Rovers. Fortunately, they escaped charges but were kept standing to attention outside the Guard Room for a whole hour waiting to receive a bollocking from the Orderly Officer. After a few more drinks Henry, Filly and I later made our way back by taxi. Hearing voices in the Tech Stores, we found the REME mechanics jugging up on beer surreptitiously sneaked out of the NAAFI. Naturally, we joined in to conclude a memorable birthday which came with an equally memorable hangover in the morning. Fortunately, it was Sunday, the best day in the Army — sod all to do and all day to do it — ruined only by being woken up by the bugler who, every morning since our arrival, had stood outside our *basha* to blow Reveille, Sunday included.

Having now sampled the delights of the town we decided, 'To hell with Christmas in Batu,' and submitted our names for Christmas leave at Sandes Home in Singapore. Like 'B' Company, the Quartermaster had already pre-empted Coco's festive 'Christmas-in-camp' plans by arranging block bookings for BHQ personnel at Leave Centres in Penang and Singapore. Coco-Oscar's Christmas ambition to 'make the men very happy' had been totally undermined.

Monday evening, was the lead-in to Coco-Oscar's festive fun in the form of a concert performed by the Regimental Band. As I described it at the time:

On Monday evening we had the Band Concert, which included numbers from My Fair Lady, *a bit of Rogers and Hammerstein, Irving Berlin and a few 'trad' numbers murdered by a group going under the name of the 'Dixie Group', then a medley of the* Evening Hymn *and the* Last Post *as a finale. After that, Coco-Oscar got up and said the appropriate thanks and then, instead of 'The Queen' to close with, we had the Regimental March, with the tall elegant Coco standing stiffly to attention with little fat Major Rocky at his side doing likewise, as were all the other officers. The sight of Coco and Rocky side-by-side was so ludicrous that I had to make a supreme effort not to laugh out loud. The concert only proved one thing. The Band is in the running for the biggest waste of man-power in the FARELF. Also, if that was the start of Coco's jolly Christmas for the lads in camp, then thank heaven that I am going away, because it was positively dead.*

Thursday was pay day and, on discovering a hair-cutting stoppage from November had been deducted from my pay, I immediately disputed the deduction.

'I was in Sungei Kuang on that date, sir, and there wasn't a barber within miles. You must be mixing me up with my namesake in 'A' Company.'

I won my point and collected the full $54 — my biggest-ever pay, being two weeks' pay plus ration allowance for our leave. Pay Parade was followed by Rocky's Christmas leave lecture.

'At this festive time, I'd like to wish you all a jolly good Christmas, chaps. For those of you going on leave by all means enjoy yourselves but for the sake of the reputation of the Regiment (was he aware of the Regiment's repu-tation after the Jubilee incident?), I do not want to hear of you getting drunk and being charged by the RMP. Re-member, you have the good name of the British Army to uphold.' (Hear! Hear!)

On Saturday morning, after putting in my leave pass for signing, I was on my way to the NAAFI when I was but-tonholed by Johnny who told me he was driving the MO to Singapore for the weekend and would I like to come, semi-officially, as an escort? Officially, escorts were no

163

longer needed in central and south Johore, which had been declared a 'White Area' only days before. Naturally, I agreed, raced off, got changed, threw a few essentials into a bag and took off with them. It was only after we had crossed the Causeway into Singapore that the Doc revealed he was not returning to Batu Pahat until Tuesday morning. This placed me in a predicament. I would be in Singapore without a leave pass, not on official duty and with no means of getting back to Batu before Monday morning. The Doc was no help, saying he'd assumed I had made my own arrangements to get back to Batu, so the problem was pushed to back of mind for the time being. We drove to the home of Major Harris[64], a huge mansion in Selerang Park, where Johnny and I were invited to share a marvellous lunch with the two Docs and the Harris family.

After lunch, we were delegated to keep Doc Harris' kids amused while the two Docs attended to work matters. Later in the afternoon, the MO drove with us to Selerang Barracks, home of the Cheshire Regiment, and arranged accommodation for us, but I was still without a means of getting back to Batu Pahat. My problem was solved the following day when I accompanied Johnny to the RASC depot on the other side of the Island to collect some items for the 2i/c. After a leisurely Sunday morning drive across Singapore my luck was in, on arrival at the depot I spotted a Notts & Jocks' three-tonner being loaded ready to return to Batu that afternoon and managed to

---

[64] Major Harris was a dermatologist temporarily attached to our Battalion doing research into skin conditions experienced by the troops.

cadge a ride. Not quite the weekend Johnny and I had in mind but, at least I had averted the drama of not appearing for PT on Monday morning and being declared AWOL.

Arriving back in Batu, I was regaled over tea with the story of Coco-Oscar's driver, Thommo, who had headed into Batu the previous night and got utterly stocius in Lulu's Bar.

'Fuck off, and leave me alone.' was his response when the town patrol tried to remove him from Lulu's Bar and he was promptly arrested. Back at camp he was put into the makeshift cell adjacent to the Guard Room to sober up, where for some reason he removed all his clothes. Soon after midnight he'd had enough of the cell so, stark naked, he manhandled a stretcher through a shutter opening before easing himself off the bedhead and sliding on his backside down the stretcher to freedom. Poking his head around the main Guard Room door, he told the Guard Commander what he could do with his cell and pelted down the road out of camp. The Guard Commander set off in pursuit of the naked runner, but rapidly lost ground.

Returning to the Guardroom he called out the guard to search for the escapee. They searched monsoon drains along the road and anywhere else Thommo might have hidden, all without success. By this time, the Orderly Officer had taken over and decided that further search was futile. Assembling the Guard on the road ready to march back to camp, he noticed an unclothed figure emerge from the darkness and attach itself to the rear rank.

'There he is!' he exclaimed, pointing at Thommo, 'Grab him.'

Before anyone could react, Thommo was off again. This time, however, he was caught and taken back to the Guard Room where he was placed under close arrest, to appear on orders the following Monday. I'd done a few escort duties with Thommo and never for a moment imagined he had this mischievous and rebellious streak in him.

Christmas mail was rolling in and, to our surprise, the Int Section received a card from Captain Pavior and his wife, so we had to act smartly to get one back to him in that day's mail. As for my mail, I received more Christmas cards from home than ever I expected, some from unexpected sources including a long-past girlfriend, an uncle, and the father of a long-time friend, both of whose sons had avoided National Service by deferment to attend university or by being in a reserved occupation. Both of these cards enclosed ten-shilling notes. Did this surprising generosity reflect a degree of guilt that their sons had escaped National Service — or was I being overly cynical? Even so, being so far away from any vestige of a 'White Christmas', the number of cards I received certainly lifted my morale, conveying, as they did, a spirit of Christmas totally absent in the shithole that was Batu Pahat.

During our early days in Batu Pahat perhaps the most astonishing incident was when one of our wireless operators, manning the control set in the Signals Office, picked up the last distress signal from a Shackleton of 205 Squadron, based at RAF Changi, shortly before it crashed into the South China Sea near Sin Cowe Island, with all crew lost. Amazing to think that an infantry wireless operator picked up this signal on a set intended for short range communications. Further confirmation, perhaps, that the high opinion of the Notts & Jocks' Signals Platoon held by the Royal Signals Rear Link operators in Ipoh was not misplaced.

That night Dan and I joined REME Smudge and Arthur Booth[65] from 'D' Company who were having their final demob bash in the NAAFI. Along with several others, we got a good sing-song going until the Orderly Officer came in at around nine o'clock to make sure everything was under control. After being greeted by *Why was he born so beautiful?* he deemed all was well and left us to it. Shortly afterwards, the Provost Sergeant, made an appearance and immediately closed down the session in a needlessly unpleasant fashion, so he too got the full *Why was he born so beautiful?* treatment.

After the following morning's Muster/Paludrine parade, the Provost Sergeant kept the Tac HQ personnel back after the parade had been dismissed. Evidently, we had got up his nose big time the previous night and he proceeded to berate us for taking the piss, for some reason directing most of his ire at me.

'I've had enough of you blokes taking advantage of demob parties and birthdays to 'ride' me and the other RPs.

---

[65] Arthur hailed from Bulwell, where I went to school and where my grandfather kept a pub which Arthur knew well.

We will not stand for it in future, especially at the Christmas party, got it?'

After that little tirade, we had to get ourselves into the frame of mind to enjoy Coco's Christmas jollities that evening with the self-same Provost Sergeant and his RP bully boys.

Days to do were getting few, 261 days to push with Christmas in Singapore to come.

CHAPTER 8
Christmas In Faraway
FARELF

As unlikely as it sounds, given our first three weeks experience in Batu, the Christmas Party for BHQ and attached personnel was surprisingly enjoyable. Proceedings kicked off with Sid Twort giving us a cautionary word of warning regarding behaviour before he opened proceedings with a few risqué, bordering on crude, jokes. The party came alive when 'Boy' Burden strolled onto the stage wearing a white suit and, to everyone's surprise, looking genuinely sophisticated. 'Boy' was widely regarded as being as daft as a brush; he lived in a fantasy world telling everyone he was having an affair with Coco-Oscar's wife and that he had played strip poker with Coco-Oscar and the Adjutant. He was clapped and cheered all the way as he proceeded, in his own fashion, to 'sing' and soon had everyone in fits. After 'Boy's performance Sid Twort called up the next performers, and thereafter each performer nominated the person or group to follow them.

It didn't take long before it was the Int Section's turn, and Dan, Sammy, Trev and I performed an all-action rendition of *Ring the bell Verger* to great acclaim. Of course, we couldn't resist calling up the RPs to perform next but, by this time, the Provost Sergeant and newly promoted Corporal 'Piggy' Gitt had disappeared and, to loud jeers, the other two RP Lance-Corporals had nothing to offer. Instead, 'Boots', from the RAPC, entertained us to some 'rock and roll' riffs on his guitar which got Sid Twort jiving with one of the Band before taking over the double bass, strumming it and twirling it around like a hot jazz player, all but climbing it.

By this time the invited officers had arrived, and Sid called each of them up do a turn — all bar Captain Toff, the Adjutant, and Major Little, the 2i/c, both of whom melted away before Sid had chance to call them. Coco-Oscar led off with a joke about a 'bastard file' before saying his little Christmas piece.

'Chaps, I'd like to wish you all a very happy Christmas, even though you are all so far away from home. In particular, I'd like to er . . . to thank all the Tac HQ personnel who did such a good job (really?) when we were in Ipoh on operations, especially the Signals Platoon and the Int Section (loud cheers). Thank you all so much. Now, please carry on and er . . . enjoy the evening. For those going on leave, remember that you er . . . have the proud reputation (the what?) of the Regiment to uphold. Merry Christmas, and thank you all.'

The remaining officers and senior NCOs followed; some were excruciatingly bad, like Lieutenant Nickelhead's attempt to recite a 'naughty' poem. Some, though, were exceptionally good, such as Doc Drew's conjuring act, a hard act to follow, but the RAPC Sergeant, was up to the task with his own composition about the rigours of Batu. He used the occasion to take digs at his own boss,

Captain Potts, the Adjutant (who was no longer there to enjoy a few home truths) and Major Rocky, the HQ Company Commander, who was. Finally, it came the turn of the Padre who was spared having to tell any risqué jokes when the Band launched into *Silent Night*. Everybody joined in, and this passed as the Padre's turn. After a few more jokes from Twort, he called on 'Harry the Horse' from the Band to recite *Eskimo Nell*. Harry went through it faultlessly, with many accompanying actions and contortions and had everyone reeling.

That was the close of the entertainment, after which we went through to the adjoining room, where a superb buffet had been laid on – chicken, ham, prawns and all manner of savoury delicacies, all well prepared and displayed. How in hell's name could our woeful cooks have put on such an appetising looking spread? Trev, whose blood/alcohol content had reached his aggro level, couldn't resist having a dig.

'Why can't you put on meals like this every day?' he asked the Brummie cook.

'Don't get the same ration indent every day,' replied Brummie-boy, confirming our suspicion that the buffet ration allocation been supplemented by funds from the PRI.

'You got the same ration indent as the Loyals cooks in Ipoh and they could cook decent meals,' Trev went on.

'That's only your opinion'

'Ah, leave it, Trev,' interjected Dan, surreptitiously helping himself to more prawns while Brummie-boy was distracted.

During the buffet break the officers made themselves scarce before we returned to the main bar where the music was hotting up and the beer continued to flow until close to midnight but, in an instant, the atmosphere changed. With half empty beer glasses lying around on tables the Int Section, who else, began tossing abandoned beers over one another. Inevitably, a misdirected aim from Trev splashed Lance-Corporal MacGuire, one of the precious RPs.

'Get your heels together and apologise,' he snapped.

'Bollocks!' replied Trev, whereupon MacGuire ordered him outside, saying he was going to march him to the Guard Room.

At this point SSI (Staff Sergeant Instructor) Jeffrey our APTC (Army Physical Training Corps) instructor, stepped in telling MacGuire to drop it. Minutes later MacGuire started 'coming it' again with another lad for some trivial or imagined misdeed. This time he was immediately jumped on by Sid Twort, who kicked him out of the bar with a few choice words, as only Twort could. Those of us who were left had a quiet nightcap standing round the bar thanking 'Schoolie' Cobb, the Education Sergeant, and SSI Jeffrey, who had manned the bar all night when, before I knew what was happening, I found Sid Twort's arm wrapped around my shoulder as he wished me 'A Merry Syphilis and a Happy Gonorrhoea'. Stunned, I returned the compliment and then he was gone.

Following this bizarre embrace, I headed back to our *basha* with Dan and Trev reflecting on what a surprisingly good party it had turned out to be. In no small way this had been due to Sid Twort; his excellent compering, his jokes and good-natured words of warning to the few blokes threatening to get out of line.

Unable to face a cookhouse breakfast the following morning I resorted to the *char-wallah* for a cup of hot sweet tea and an egg banjo, which I struggled to keep down during the ride to Kluang Station aboard a three-tonner. Life improved after a swim at Sandes Soldiers Home followed by an appetising dinner in the magnificently decorated dining room, with a realistic snowy Nativity scene at one end. By this time, I was feeling fit enough join Dan at the Union Jack Club, from where we headed to the Brit Club. With three Royal Navy ships in port, the Brit was overrun by matelots so we decided to move on.

Despite it being Christmas Eve, there was little evidence of Christmas spirit. It was more like Guy Fawkes Night, with people letting off Chinese crackers in the streets and in almost every bar, and lads lobbing them into trishaws. With the streets full of servicemen and all the noise from firecrackers, it seemed as if the city was under siege.

After these frolics the previous night Christmas Day at Sandes was celebrated with a substantial, but not especially tasty, lunch, each course washed down with glasses of orange squash in this alcohol-free Christian home-away-from-home. Not even a drop of alcohol for the Loyal Toast. After our 'dry' Christmas lunch, we set out for the Union Jack Club where we learnt from Dan that the food there had not only been plentiful and tasty, but the beer had flowed freely. We then headed off to watch the first half of the Christmas Concert. The star performer was the 'Elvis Presley of Singapore', who had all the moves of the man himself. At the interval, we'd had enough and having decided to head off to see Brigitte Bardot in *The Night Heaven Fell*. We hadn't gone far before we were stopped by a Military Police patrol.

'You the lot that's been letting off firecrackers?'

'Not us, Corp, we've come straight from the concert at the UJ Cub,'

'You carrying any firecrackers?'

'No, Corp, but we're in a rush to see the Brigitte Bardot film.' I replied truthfully.

Thankfully, our innocent sounding intention dissuaded them from conducting a search because they would have discovered a few crackers in Dan's possession. The film was not great, but enjoyable nonetheless; for the air-conditioning, the comfortable seats and, not least, *la belle Brigitte*!

We met Dan again on Boxing Day morning and investigated Change Alley for the first time to see if there were any true bargains to be had there. Johnny and Trev each invested in 'bargain' pairs of trousers, but the rest of us remained sceptical of the proclaimed discounts being calculated with great dexterity on abacuses which, at the end of each deft calculation, did not seem to amount to much at all. At this point, Trev left us to obtain an entry form for the Carlsberg Beer Drinking Contest being run in conjunction with the film, *The Vikings*.

Re-joining us later at the Union Jack Club, he brought the news that entries for the beer-drinking contest had closed on the 18th, so that was us out of luck for free beers – you've got to be in it to win it! Disappointed, we moved on to a bar that Trev had discovered on his way to enter the Carlsberg contest; a congenial, dimly lit little joint with some alluring hostesses but our stay was short-lived — the drinks alone were beyond National Service pay level and the cost of the company of a hostess was off the chart.

The following day we headed off to Changi Beach at the eastern tip of the island for a swim. On arrival we found it to be surprisingly deserted and it didn't take us long to spot two gorgeous looking bikini-clad English girls. Having not seen a white girl in months we were drawn like moths to a flame.

'You'll have no luck there, mate,' was the advice of a group of RAF lads sunbathing nearby, 'Prick-teasers, the pair of them — officers' daughters.' Nonetheless, they were easy on the eye — and didn't they know it.

Returning from Changi, we got into the steaks at the Union Jack Club, where we learnt that three of the four teams in the Carlsberg beer-drinking contest the previous night had failed to appear. So, we headed off to secure a place on the rails ready to step in if there were any no-shows that night. Unfortunately, all teams made their appearance so we had to be content to spectate. The format took the form of a 'Boat Race', with four to a team. Each team member had to drink a pint of Carlsberg out of the bottle, holding the empty bottle upside down to show it was empty before the next drinker could pick up his bottle. There were four teams, three mixed Asian teams and one comprising an Aussie, an Englishman, and two Singhalese, presumably off a merchant ship. The multinational team won easily having only downed two bottles before all the Asian teams had been disqualified for spilling their beers or not emptying their bottle ahead of the next man starting. Backing up, they won the final against the previous night's winner and were rewarded with half a dozen bottles of Carlsberg apiece. With Henry in our team, we would have romped it.

On Sunday, after lunching at the Union Jack Club we headed to the station for the return journey to Kluang. Typically, on arrival at Kluang there was no transport waiting, but the Notts & Jocks trucks rolled up only ten minutes late. We returned to a malodorous *basha* inhabited only by Osbert, who had returned to Batu after his NCO cadre, and his now skeletal, stinking, lice-infested dog. We had not shared accommodation with Osbert since he had left Ipoh in November and we all fervently hoped his dog had not taken to sleeping on any of our beds during our absence.

'Osbert,' said Dan 'don't you think it would be better if your dog slept on the veranda? There's five of us in here now in a room intended for four. It's already too crowded and your dog stinks'

'I like her inside so I can keep an eye on her,' replied Osbert.

'Well, we don't.' I said, and there, for the moment, the matter was left.

After that exchange we turned in early to prepare ourselves for the resumption of regimental life, the Bullshit Pahat way.

Leave over, with another 256 days to push — little did I know what those days had in store.

CHAPTER 9
BACK TO BULLSHIT PAHAT

The Monday after Christmas saw Captain Pavior back on duty, and he briefed us on what had been happening in Johore State over our Christmas break. As I knew from my bogus escort duty accompanying the MO to Singapore, Central Johore had been declared a 'White Area' on 8th December. Also, six of the remaining eight terrorists, known to be in the Pengerang peninsula, east of the Johore River, had surrendered shortly before Christmas, leaving only two known CTs at large with the might of two Gurkha battalions hot on their tails. Consequently, all civilian food and curfew restrictions had been lifted and the Notts & Jocks would not now be required to resume operations.

Instead, we were to remain in Batu Pahat until March, before returning to an 'upgraded' Burma Camp at FTC Kota Tinggi, where we were to re-train for a SEATO (Southeast Asia Treaty Organisation) exercise on Borneo with the US Marines. This was to be an amphibious exercise, in May or June, lasting around six weeks. Whatever it entailed, it would certainly be a welcome change from the regimental regime in Batu, and a great opportunity to observe how Coco-Oscar's Battalion measured up alongside the might of the US Marine Corps.

The NAAFI was quiet on New Year's Eve so an impromptu decision saw us head into town wearing an assortment of clothes: me in a pair of borrowed OG drainpipes with a civvy shirt and Dan, even though excused boots, was wearing civvies with ammo boots. We did the rounds, making ourselves unpopular, first at Lulu's Bar and then in the South Seas Bar, before being rounded up by the BOS and the town patrol and driven back to camp in time to welcome in 'Demob Year' with a raucous rendition of *Auld Lang Syne* outside the BHQ office.

Thankfully, Coco-Oscar had declared New Year's Day a holiday, giving me time to work off my murderous hangover and hang my new *Punch* demob year calendar showing 252 days to push. The less good news was discovering I was on guard duty again the following night.

Back in the office the following morning the news broke that the boredom at 'D' Company had taken a deadly turn and the Notts & Jocks had sustained their first fatality. This had nothing to do with terrorist action. Two corporals had driven into Cha'ah on New Year's Eve to celebrate. On the way back, after more than a few beers, the driver rolled the car and was killed. The passenger was thrown clear and survived with barely a scratch. The truly tragic aspect of the incident was that the wife of the driver was, at the time, aboard TT *Nevasa* on her way to join him.

The uninjured passenger turned out to be 'Big Ned' who had been rewarded with two stripes and made section commander after proving to be a capable leader on jungle operations. After the accident he had been taken back to 'D' Company camp where, on arrival, he took

179

umbrage at being told he was to be placed in detention. Still sporting his shaven Yul Brynner hairstyle, the 6' 3", well-muscled Ned reacted by laying into members of the Guard before being overpowered and bundled into a cell. Appearing on Orders on the Friday after New Year, he was stripped of his two stripes for assaulting the men on guard duty and placed on open arrest pending the outcome of the inquiry into the road accident.

Over a few Sunday evening beers in the NAAFI, a core group comprising Johnny, Dan, Trev, Gerry (with whom I'd played schoolboy rugby), Murph, the armourer, and myself vowed to dedicate the New Year to getting fit – cutting back on the beers and starting a rigorous weight training programme, as well as taking advantage of every badminton, tennis and football opportunity we could. The rugby players amongst us, having learnt that Staff-Sergeant Swain was keen on rugby, resolved to once again press Lieutenant Nickelhead, the Sports Officer, to organise a BHQ/HQ Company rugby team. We were particularly pissed off after learning that 'A' Company in Kota Tinggi had already formed a team, and, not only that, but my mate Chesh was playing for a civilian club in Johore Bahru and had even had a trial for the Johore State team.

The round-ball footballers were even more pissed off after learning that the 13th/18th Hussars, who had arrived in Malaya four months after us in October, had not only entered a team, but had reached the semi-final of the All-Malaya Army Inter-Unit Cup. In the Fed since June, the Notts & Jocks had not even got around to entering a team. This was about to change. On the first Monday of the

New Year, a football match between BHQ and the Signals Platoon provided the first inkling of the footballing talent within the Battalion and, unknown to him at the time, the start of Coco-Oscar's journey to his only FARELF success.

As for Osbert and his dog nothing had changed. Instead, he had found a new hobby — entomology. Equipped with a newly purchased butterfly net, corkboard, various pins and display containers, his spare time was spent out with his net, catching all manner of butterflies and beetles, while continuing to neglect his sickly dog. Every time we found it in the *basha* we chased it out. With what he had spent on his new hobby, we had assumed his latest plan to buy himself out of the Army, announced when he re-joined us after Christmas, had been abandoned. Not so it turned out: with Lucy now forgotten, his current scheme was to try to persuade the Army to pay to bring his 'fiancée' out from England to marry him — never short of ideas, Osbert.

A week into the new year came an exponential upturn in 'flaps' around the Int Office with the return of Sergeant Kaz from leave. Luckily, when he showed up, I had acquired a new job and was busy stencilling titles onto file folders and was able to tell him where to stuff his make-work jobs. Soon the Int Section's neatly labelled files attracted the attention of Coco-Oscar. He wanted all the Orderly Room files to look equally 'nice', so I was lumbered with labelling them too. Word of my drafting skills soon spread and, by Wednesday I had been press-ganged into drawing a diagram of the workings of a Sterling

SMG for the Adjutant — surely a captain should know how an SMG works?

On his first Saturday back Kaz decided to conduct an inspection of our *basha*. Since we now had now been issued with lockers and were no longer able to simply stuff surplus kit into our kitbags, he was intent on picking on us for non-conforming locker layouts but failed to find fault. It was during this inspection that we took the opportunity to get into Kaz's ear about Osbert's dog,

'Sarge, can you tell Osbert to keep his snotty-nosed dog outside on the veranda. It stinks and we don't like the thought of it kipping on our beds when we're not around,' I said.

'Do you know it sleeps on your beds,' he replied.

'No, but we don't know it doesn't either, and it's unhygienic to have a mangy dog living in our room anyway. We're already overcrowded with five blokes and only four bedspaces.'

'Not my problem, sort it out yourselves with Lance Corporal Osbert,' was his typically unhelpful response.

That night in the NAAFI over a few beers, with our request having fallen on deaf ears, we mulled over what action we should take. The upshot was that we left the NAAFI early, went back to the *basha* and, with Osbert and Sammy absent in town, took their beds and lockers out on to the veranda. Here, to the extent that the space on the veranda permitted, we positioned their beds and lockers to conform with bedspace requirements, made their beds and rolled down their mosquito nets. We locked the double doors onto the veranda to stop the dog nosing them open and left the door on the opposite side of the room closed, but unlocked.

Osbert and Sammy returned after lights-out to find their beds on the veranda. Osbert promptly went to fetch the Guard Commander, Sergeant Holland. Without ascertaining whether the room could be accessed via the back door, Holland ordered us to unbolt the double veranda doors and move the beds back inside. Addressing Osbert before he left, he said,

'I'll leave it up to you if you want to take any further action on this, Corporal.'

After Holland had gone, Osbert said that he would take no further action if we put everything back in place by morning.

'Only, if you promise to keep your stinking dog out of the *basha*,' was our unanimous response, to which there was no reply so Osbert, Sammy and the dog slept on the veranda that night.

Nothing changed on Sunday and eventually, during teatime, Sammy moved his bed and locker back inside. Osbert remained obdurate and slept another night outside with his dog. On Monday morning, during our absence at the Signals Platoon PT session, the odious Osbert, like a fart in a bath, bubbled us to WO2 Morgan, the new CSM (Sid Twort having been promoted to Acting RSM). Morgan escorted Osbert to the *basha* to view how we'd laid out his kit on the veranda. Having displayed the evidence, he moved his belongings back inside. When we returned from PT Osbert jubilantly informed the three of us that the CSM wanted to see us immediately. On reporting to the Orderly Room, Morgan advised us that Osbert had laid a charge against the three of us and that Sergeant Holland, the Guard Commander, and Sammy would appear as witnesses.

We had foreseen that it might come to this and, in our defence, we advised CSM Morgan that both Osbert and his dog stank and that, despite raising this with him on numerous occasions and reporting the matter to Sergeant Kaz, Osbert had done nothing either to improve his own personal hygiene nor the condition of his dog.

Well, didn't that stir things up? Morgan went off to confer with Major Rocky, the Company Commander, who in turn called in Captain Pavior. The upshot was that Dan, Trev and I were ordered to appear on Company Orders at 9:30 am. According to our Orderly Room sources the Adjutant and RSM Twort had also been consulted. Together, they had checked our disciplinary records and our release dates, and whether we had booked out on Saturday night, and, if so, could be charged with 'causing a disturbance after lights-out.' No success there so they settled for charging us with 'causing a disturbance in the barrack room.'

At 9:30 sharp, we were 'tapping the boards.' The three of us were marched into Rocky's office at the double.

'Heft ri', heft ri', heft ri', heft... Mark time! ... keep those knees up! ... **Halt! Left turn!**' which we did, slamming our heels into the floorboards.

Major Rocky opened proceedings by calling on Osbert to give his evidence.

'When Private Sammy and I returned to our . . .' he began, before I interrupted,

'Sir,' I said, addressing Major Rocky, 'we'd like the evidence to be given on oath, please.'

'Surely that's not necessary for a matter like this?'

'We would prefer the evidence on oath, sir,' I replied, knowing from experience that, to Osbert, the truth was whatever best served his purpose. I also knew from boning up on Queen's Regulations while on night duty in Ipoh (checking to see how far we could push our luck), we were quite entitled to ask for evidence on oath. Rocky demanded a Bible be found. His anger mounted as almost ten minutes of fruitless searching failed to locate a bible until someone had the bright idea of asking the Padre. Bible obtained, Osbert swore that his evidence would be, 'The truth, the whole truth, and nothing but the truth.'

'While Private Sammy and I were in town these three,' he said, pointing at us 'piled all our stuff out on the veranda and locked us out of the *basha.* I had to fetch the Guard Commander to get them to open the doors and, still they refused to move our beds and belongings back into the *basha.'*

When asked to give his evidence. Sammy repeated Osbert's account of events almost word for word.

Following this Sergeant Holland, the Guard Commander, was asked to give his version of events. He commenced his evidence by saying,

'When I arrived at the scene of the crime …,' and carried on in that vein.

Anyone would think there had been a murder.

'Is this true?' enquired Rocky, addressing the three of us.

I was the first to respond.

'First, sir, I'd like to contradict Corporal Osbert's statement. We did not "just pile their beds and belongings out on the veranda", we placed their beds and lockers as close as we could to conform to regimental regulations in the space available. Second, we did not "lock them out". We locked the double veranda doors to stop the dog from pushing them open with its nose but left the other side door closed but unlocked. The reason for our action is that the dog smells and it has lice and ticks and, despite our frequent requests, Lance-Corporal Osbert refuses to keep it outside on the veranda.' I was into my stride and fairly laid it on, 'when I was a boy my family bred prize-winning cocker spaniels and, judging from the state of the dog's eyes and nose I reckon it probably has distemper. Our quarters are barely adequate to accommodate five men, let alone a dog and it is unhygienic for Lance-Corporal Osbert to allow the dog to sleep on his pillow and, for all we know, sleep on our beds when we are not there.'

'So why did you move Private Sammy's bed and locker outside as well.' demanded Rocky. Here, Trev got a bit creative and, taking a few liberties with the truth, replied,

'Private Sammy had been complaining there's an ants' nest under his bed so we moved it and spread insect repellent around his bedspace. To spare him from sleeping in a miasma of the insect repellent, we put his bed out on the veranda as well. Not wishing to inconvenience him we made his bed for him and rolled down his mozzie net.'

Dan then got onto Osbert's personal hygiene and body odour.

"It's not only the dog that smells, sir, but so does Lance-Corporal Osbert. We have only seen him take a shower once in the six weeks we've been in Batu Pahat.' Of course, Dan omitted to mention that Osbert had been away on an NCO's cadre for three of those weeks, but why let a detail like that get in the way?

Dan also backed me up, stressing there was nothing to prevent Osbert and Sammy entering the room via the un-locked back door.

Our defence did not go over well. Rocky was seething; not quite to inkstand slamming level, but not far off.

'You cannot take the law into your own hands,' he blus-tered, 'especially where NCOs are concerned. You must complain through the proper channels …' Here, Trev jumped in,

'We reported the matter to Sergeant Kaz, sir.' (You're pushing our luck here, Trev, I thought, dragging Kaz into it).

'These matters take time,' continued Rocky, but Trev wouldn't let it go.

'Sergeant Kaz wouldn't do anything about it. He said we had to sort it out between ourselves.' (For fuck's sake, back off, Trev!)

'Well, that's what you should have done. In a small section you should get along swimmingly, you must work together. This is the Army not playschool… blah … blah … blah . . . to do such a thing to an NCO is unthinkable … blah … blah … blah!' and so he went on.

Since our 'offence' was more of a protest than a breach of discipline punishable by detention, he stopped each of us five days' pay. Given the number of officers and senior NCOs involved in determining the charge, I suspected that we may well have been within our rights to object to Osbert keeping an animal in the barrack room, but not in the way we did (pity I didn't check that out in Queen's Regs when in Ipoh).

Some consolation was drawn from Osbert being called in by Rocky after Orders and ordered to get a kennel for the dog, keep it outside and look after it properly. Rocky also told him that if there was any truth in what we had said regarding his own personal hygiene he should improve his ways. Typically, Osbert took the easy way out and had the dog put down — probably the kindest act he had ever done for it.

Besides losing pay the three of us, quite coincidentally of course, were put on ammo fatigues that night loading ammo boxes into the armoury. Another outcome of this episode was that Osbert and Sammy, who had now become big mates, were renamed 'Bubble' and 'Squeak' — Osbert, for putting the 'bubble' in and getting us charged, and Sammy for 'squeaking' up in support.

Subsequently, we complained officially to Kaz about Osbert's personal hygiene and suggested Kaz should initiate a 'Bath Book'. This sent him running off to the IO, who had been busy on Courts of Inquiry and Audit Boards since his return from Christmas leave. After first pumping Kaz, Osbert and Sammy over what had been going on Captain Pavior called us into his office to hear our grievances. We restated what we had said on 'Orders' and he quickly identified the growing rift between 'the Three Musketeers' (as he described us) and the other members of the Int Section. As I recorded at the time, Captain Pavior summarised the situation as follows:

Since we had been in Batu with nothing at all to do there was greater likelihood of trouble being caused out of idleness than on ops, when we were bound in some loose manner by work and conditions. He admitted that, whilst we had responded quite well to easy discipline on ops, it was different here and he was partly at fault for not keeping us occupied, and that he had now organised, or rather got Sergeant Kaz to organise, an Intelligence training programme for the next fortnight, during which we should stop baiting Lance-Corporal Osbert, Private Sammy and Sergeant Kaz. After the cadre, he might send two of the 'Musketeers' out to the rifle companies to do intelligence work, both for our benefit and to split us up and try and calm us down a bit. He also hinted that our escapades from the early days had been gone into and he realised that we had generally got out of hand.

To us, this final comment was further evidence to support our view that our punishment exceeded the amount merited for the 'misdeed' for which we were charged, and it really was a cumulative punishment to try and make us knuckle under. Nevertheless, I think the IO did far more good this morning by treating the matter

*logically and calmly and admitting that there were
points on both sides, which had gradually led to so much
ill-feeling being aroused. More good than Rocky, with
his pay stoppage, Morgan, with his threats, and Kaz with
his raving could ever do.*

Notwithstanding the proposed training programme, the
IO said we could continue to play as much sport as we
could fit in, but warned us that, if we did not toe the line
in every respect, he would come down on us like a ton
of bricks. As an officer who had our respect, Captain
Pavior's intervention did much to clear the air but, now
we were no longer on Ops, we had no sense of purpose
and our relationship with him began to change.

Following our interview with the IO, Thursday brought
the first welcome event of the week — Pay Parade, the
first since our pay stoppage. Marching briskly up to the
paymaster's desk, I acknowledged receipt in a loud voice,

'Five dollars and 25 cents. Pay and pay book correct,
Sir!' and, maintaining a dead pan face, gave him an im-
peccable salute, much to the amusement of those present.

At tea that night I found myself sitting at the same table
as Big Ned. Having seen him on the defaulters' parade
when on guard duty the previous week, I was aware he
had been transferred to Batu from 'D' Company to be
under the direct control of the Provost Sergeant while
awaiting a decision from GURDIV on whether he would
be court-marshalled over the car crash on New Year's
Eve. Despite his reputation, Ned had a benign grin as if
butter wouldn't melt in his mouth, and during the course
of the meal he inquired mischievously,

'Anyone fancy going downtown tonight?'

Knowing he was confined to camp, most of the lads assumed he was joking. I wasn't so sure and might have been tempted but, having that day received a miserable $5.25 to see me through the week, I thought better of it. Not so 'Nog' Norris, a Lance-Corporal with only five days to do in FARELF. Nog fancied himself as something of a hardman and rumour had it he'd ask lads hold up fire buckets for him to practice his 'Liverpool Kiss'. That night, when Big Ned was absent at roll call and nowhere to be found in camp, the Provost Sergeant and the Orderly Sergeant, set off downtown. Here they encountered a trishaw driver holding his bleeding head.

'Big soldiers no pay, bash me,' he said, pointing in the direction of Lulu's Bar and continued cursing away in Cantonese. Here the two Sergeants found Ned and Nog and attempted to place them under arrest.

'Fuck off unless you want a dose of webbing rash,' was Ned's response.

'On your feet, now!' said the Provo only to cop a blow to the head from Ned's fist wrapped in his webbing belt. After a bit more argy-bargy during which the Provo got panned again, the Orderly Sergeant, the bucolic 'Farmer' Wardle, adopted the psychological approach.

'Look lads, why don't I send the Provost Sergeant back to camp in the Land Rover, we'll have one for the road and I'll take you back in a taxi.'

This solution seemed to placate the pair, the Provost Sergeant made himself scarce and Wardle, Ned and Nog had another beer apiece before taking a taxi back to camp.

On arrival at the Guard Room, Ned took umbrage at the Guard Commander's order to stand to attention while he was being formally charged and promptly thumped him. Bursting into the Guard's sleeping quarters he lifted the tea urn from the table and hurled it across the room. At this, all the off-stag members of the Guard scrambled out of the open windows, leaving their rifles behind. Fortunately for Dan, Trev and Squeak, who were on Guard that night, all three were out on stag while this was happening. Ned lashed out at the Guard Commander again before 'Farmer' Wardle, once more playing the 'good cop', managed to coax both Ned and Nog into the cell, now secured by surrounding coils of barbed wire following Thommo's recent escape.

Once inside the cell the pair dismantled the bedframes and tried to batter the door open with a bedhead. The Guard Commander had a Land Rover driven around to the Guard Room to light up the scene of the mayhem with its headlights. By this time the Orderly Officer had been called out. To try and stop the continual battering at the cell door he mustered the Fire Picquet and ordered them to turn the fire hose onto the cell. Concurrently, in case the miscreants did manage to batter the cell door open, the off-stag Guards, armed with pick handles, were posted around the cell, remaining there for the rest of the night.

The mayhem abated until around one thirty when Nog tried a new ploy. Using a bedhead, he dislodged a section of the corrugated iron roofing and climbed onto the roof looking for an escape that way, only to be met with a full blast from the fire hose. Undeterred, he tried, with Ned's help from below, to haul a bedstead onto the roof to lay over the barbed wire to enable them to escape. Eventually, the constant drenching proved too much and Nog retreated back into the cell where the pair resumed their onslaught on the door. The stand-off continued all night, with intermittent bursts of hammering. This was the circus that Coco-Oscar had brought to Malaya to combat hardened jungle fighters — hard pressed to prevent its own prisoners escaping from custody.

The morning after the fracas the hungover Ned and Nog were roused early and despatched under escort to the Army Detention Centre in Singapore and Nog's berth on the *Empire Fowey* was cancelled. Collateral damage from Ned's rampage also came to light. On being released, the poor prisoner who had been occupying the cell when Ned and Nog were incarcerated was sporting two black eyes. According to him, when Ned saw the state of him that morning, he had said,

'You look in a bad way, mate, what happened to you?'

'You laid into me last night!' he'd replied.

'Sorry, mate,' said Ned 'I must have thought you were one of those bastards trying to bang me up.'

As for the off-stag guards who had fled the flying tea urn, consideration was given to charging them for leaving their weapons behind, but the matter was not pursued. Nevertheless, the repercussions for Dan and Trev were more dire. With no sleep at all the previous night, they skipped *tiffin* and went for a quiet gonk in the *basha* and missed the afternoon Muster Parade. After Muster Parade was dismissed, I dashed to the *basha* to wake them but it was too late: their absence had already been reported to Sergeant Kaz. Triumphantly, he stormed into the *basha* and, finding all three of us there, marched us to the Company Office at the double and charged us all for being absent from Muster Parade.

When I pointed out that I had been on the parade Kaz rushed along to the Int Section office to confirm this with Squeak who, to his credit, corroborated what I had said. When Kaz returned to the Int Office after taking my name off the charge sheet Trev, still incensed over the charge, shot his mouth off.

'For fuck's sake, Sarge, what sort of arsehole are you? We got no sleep on guard last night, got drenched into the bargain guarding the fuckin' cell and you charge us for having a quick gonk.'

Unfortunately for Trev, his outburst was overheard by the RSO, in the adjoining office.

'Sergeant!' he called through 'Charge that man with insubordination and you can call me as a witness.' Kaz hotfooted it once again to the Company Office, obviously relishing the chance to nail Trev on an extra charge.

With the pair on Orders on Monday morning facing the prospect of jankers[66], Saturday night was a big gibbering night but, before heading to the NAAFI, I found myself

---

[66] Confined to barracks and required to report numerous times a day to perform tedious tasks and be subjected to frequent uniform and kit inspections.

the combatant in one of Henry's 'friendly fights', where you belt seven bells out of each other with flip-flops. The problem with Henry was that he never knew when to stop, so the 'fight' went on until we were both exhausted, almost wrecking the room in the process. This exercise worked up a giant thirst and, fortunately, on arrival at the NAAFI, the other lads, acknowledging the dire financial straits of the 'Musketeers', kicked in our contribution to the kitty.

'Well.' I proclaimed, with my first Anchor in front of me, 'fuck this for a game of soldiers, why don't we apply for some leave and get out of this shithole for a couple of weeks?

The idea was unanimously supported and, by the end of the night, Filly the postman, Johnny, Murph, Trev, Dan and me had all decided to bung in leave applications.

The following morning Henry was nowhere to be seen. Turned out that that during our flip-flop fight the previous evening he had chipped a bone in his elbow and damaged some ligaments and had been taken to hospital at Kluang to have his arm X-rayed. Returning with his arm in plaster and a Cheshire-cat grin on his face he triumphantly declared,

'No more fucking regimental duties for me, this plaster stays on until I head home next month.'

Monday morning also saw Dan and Trev tapping the boards again. They were jumped on heavily, with Dan confined to barracks for seven days by Rocky for missing Muster Parade, and Trev placed on CO's Orders for his insubordination.

Confining him to barracks for 14 days, Coco-Oscar asked Trev if he had anything to say for himself — didn't he just?

'What do you expect, sir? We have a lazy prat of a sergeant who is never around when there's any work to be done. He wouldn't support us over Lance-Corporal Osbert's mangy dog and it cost us five days' pay to get anything done about it. Even when there's nothing to do, he refused to let us go on afternoon sport until the IO over-ruled him. How does that build team spirit, sir?'

His outburst did him no favours. An infuriated Coco laid into him and Trev was lucky not to get another seven for answering back. Some good did emerge from the episode though because, according to our Orderly Room spies, the RSM hauled Sergeant Kaz over the coals for failing to maintain discipline in his section. While the views of a mere National Serviceman like Trev might not carry much weight, the episode could not have enhanced Kaz's promotion prospects.

That week saw discipline in BHQ and HQ Company tightened even further, and it was a bad time for Dan and Trev to be on jankers. There were more frequent kit checks and a big bull drive was initiated in preparation for the Brigadier's visit the following Tuesday, with everyone kept busy bulling until after dark. The bull drive escalated even further on Thursday when, out of the blue, it was announced the GURDIV Commander was paying a snap visit next morning. The MT lads were so jacked off with the painting and polishing and labelling, and tidying all spare parts into symmetrical rows that they all put in for a transfer on the morning of the General's visit. As I wrote at the time, the General's visit was hilarious:

Officers were peeping around corners to see where he had got to on his tour of the camp, and everyone was crashing to attention and saluting 13 to the dozen. The General asked to see Captain Sherry as he had served with his now deceased, father. Sherry flapped like mad, running from the PRI office, fixing his Sam Browne as he went. I am sure the bloody officers cannot know what idiots they look panicking at the arrival of any brass. They really zoom to astronomical heights in order to create a good impression, and bow and scrape like humble mediaeval serfs paying homage to their liege lord.

As part of this latest 'bull drive' all personnel had their classifications re-checked. This was another farce. The educational records of Bryn, the Orderly Room typist and a cadet journalist prior to call up, and Dan had been lost and Rocky was all for sending them on an Army 3rd Class Education course. Even better, Rocky got it into his head that, Murph, a REME-attached craftsman who was one of our armourers, had no trade certification and therefore was not entitled to tradesman's pay. Not only had Murph completed an apprenticeship at the Royal Ordnance Factory, Fazackerley before he was called up, but he had also undertaken a further four months trade training at Gosport after call-up.

With all the emphasis on bull, the meals continued to get worse, except for the days when brass-hats were visiting when, miraculously, appetising food could be produced. The Saturday following the General's visit, the food was so diabolical all I could bring myself to eat at *tiffin* was

197

half a dozen chips and a piece of cheese and, on Sunday, only an orange. Until they found a way to get under the peel, our cooks could not spoil oranges. This was the beginning of my reliance on NAAFI food to sustain myself.

The one good outcome of the week was that all our leave applications were approved. Amazingly, Kaz had raised no objection to Trev, Dan and me all going on leave at the same time — probably glad to see the back of us for a while — and it got him off the hook over developing further material for our intelligence training, which he had started that week. The three of us comprised almost half the Int Section, a good indication of how little we had to do; little surprise therefore that Captain Pavior raised no objections either, probably thinking it was a good idea to get shot of the 'Three Musketeers' for a couple of weeks.

The week of the visits by the brass-hats saw further stirring of the Notts & Jocks football ambitions with a trial match between BHQ and the Band. Even fielding a scratch team, with people still on leave, the BHQ performance provided further evidence of the footballing talent within the battalion, exemplified by a spectacular headed goal by Dan from a corner.

Concurrently, Johnny and I continued to persevere with trying to get the oval ball game started as well. We'd identified 26 men who either played the game or wanted to learn, so we continued to hammer away at Lieutenant Nickelhead, the Sports Officer, to establish a rugby team.

To demonstrate the level of the support for rugby, we organised our first unofficial practice for the last Friday of the month only to be thwarted by the MO who scheduled our first polio shots that afternoon. This meant cancelling the practice as we were all placed on light duties after our jabs. Further evidence that inoculations were deliberately scheduled on Fridays so, if anyone had a bad reaction it was on their own time over the weekend. These jabs may have protected us from polio but they presaged the death of rugby in BHQ/HQ Company. The following week seven of the core rugby enthusiasts disappeared off-camp; Johnny on a medical course in KL, Clem to FTC, Gerry on an NCO cadre, and Dan, Trev, Murph and myself on leave.

The week before I was due to start my leave the Regimental Band was scheduled to give a concert on the Batu Pahat *Padang* on the Tuesday evening. That morning on Muster Parade the RSM called for volunteers to go to support the band. Not a single hand was raised. Apart from the unwritten Army rule of never volunteering, going into town in any official capacity meant dressing in best kit and exposing oneself to inspection before departure. This, in turn, could result in being charged for some item of attire not being up to scratch. Undaunted, the RSM ordered Acting Sergeant Brannock to take the names of all the volunteers.

Brannock proceeded to move along the front rank, writing everyone's name on his clipboard. Soon he was standing before me, pencil poised,

'Name?'

'Bramley,' I muttered,

'Spell it!'

'B–R–A–double N–O–C–K, Sarge,'

199

'That's my name,' he blurted,

'You want to go don't you, Sarge?'

The suppressed mirth around me was palpable and I could almost hear the cogs grinding in Brannock's head as he licked the point of his pencil. On the spectrum of thickness, he ranked marginally above pig-shit. The only reason he had never achieved substantive rank as a Sergeant was his inability to pass the 3rd Class Army Education Certificate, a feat not beyond the ability of most 15-year-old school leavers. He was clearly grappling with how stupid he might look if he charged me and having to detail his grounds for the charge. The dilemma was evidently too much for him and he moved on to the next man. Never would I have dared to pull that stunt with any other NCO, but with Brannock the temptation was irresistible.

Thursday was a much better day, with a bumper Pay Parade, including two weeks leave pay in advance, my biggest pay day ever. That night, the eve of my departure on leave, called for a triple celebration. First, the return to solvency of the 'Three Musketeers', with Dan and me (Trev was still on jankers) shouting drinks for those who had subsidised us during our pay stoppage. Second, was Murph's lucky escape that day from a truck roll-over from which he had emerged unscathed and, third, an early-bird farewell for Henry, who would be sailing for Blighty while we were in Penang.

Friday brought the first of the newly introduced daily kit checks but, fortunately for me and Filly, we were heading off to Penang that morning and had already checked all our kit into the store. Before our departure we picked up on the latest Orderly Room gossip. Subsequent to the Divisional Commander's inspection the previous week, he had followed up with a stern letter to Coco-Oscar regarding the high incidence of VD in the Battalion. After only seven months in FARELF, the Notts & Jocks topped all British units in terms of VD infections and were second only to the Aussies – a dubious distinction for Coco-Oscar to bear.

Leave ahoy, with 202 days to push.

CHAPTER 10
RESPITE IN PENANG

As the kit check took place, Filly and I were being driven out of the gate to Kluang Station for our fortnight's respite in Penang. Our stop in Kuala Lumpur gave us the opportunity for a quick look around the capital of Malaya: a compact town with some imposing buildings in the city centre, which melded into rundown shophouses and more ramshackle structures the further we strayed from the centre. A few pints at the NAAFI Club, and it was time to board the night train to Prai, arriving early in the morning after a good night's gonk in our reserved sleepers.

After arriving at Prai a half hour ferry crossing took us to Penang Island where, unlike at Batu, transport was waiting to take us Sandycroft Leave Centre in time for breakfast. Situated on Batu Ferringhi Beach, a beautiful stretch of palm-fringed sand, lapped by crystal-clear water, Sandycroft, the Golden Sands Hotel and the Australian Army Leave Centre were the only evidence of human presence[67]. For the first couple of days, we stayed in the

---

[67] Unlike my next visit in 1976, by which time the beachfront was wall-to-wall hotels and the sea was beginning to take on the characteristics of a sewage lagoon.

Centre simply enjoying the beach, the views, the luxury and the comfort of our light, pleasantly decorated, fan-cooled rooms, the excellent food and service, and freedom from the constant barrage of orders. There were facilities for tennis, football, cricket, putting and swimming, with a diving board on stilts a little way out to sea. There was a palm-shaded bar and a beer garden overlooking the beach, where we discovered a new flavoursome Aussie brew: Melbourne Bitter.

Monday turned out to be Chinese New Year (Gong Hei Fat Choy to the locals), so we decided to go into Georgetown to experience the festivities, sharing a taxi with couple of Loyals lads. As it turned out, the Lunar New Year festivities were to be decidedly low-key so, after a couple of drinks at a rooftop bar, we headed to the cinema to see *The Vikings*, (but no associated beer drinking contest in Penang) only to discover that every cinema in town was booked out due to the Chinese New Year holiday. Our other option was the Peach Blossom Revue, which we assumed to be a strip joint but, before watching some not especially beautiful girls performing not particularly polished striptease routines, we had to endure a long and tedious Chinese play. The Chinese in the audience seemed to enjoy it, so it could not have been too bad if only you understood what it was all about.

On Tuesday, we went on a tour organised by the WVS (Women's Voluntary Service). It was a hair-raising drive around tortuous hairpins, with sheer drops on some of the mountainous sections. A picnic lunch at a small waterfall cascading into a fair-sized pool enabled us to have a swim in the invigoratingly cold water at the foot of the falls — I'd never been in such cold water since leaving Blighty. Returning to Sandycroft, we stopped at the Snake Temple. As a spectacle it was disappointing, being dingy, dull and shabby, with none of the snakes particularly active, seemingly doped up by the aroma of incense.

On Wednesday we welcomed Trev, and introduced him to Melbourne Bitter at the evening barbecue where we strived, without success, to join the ladies who were there on leave. Thereafter, I was oblivious to the night's activities which included, according to those who had any recall of the night's events, the sight of me running along the beach chasing a dog and bellowing out the words of Elvis Presley's *Hound Dog*.

The morning after my canine antics the others forced me to join the day's outing to Penang Hill despite my death-like state — and I was glad they did. We rode to the summit on the funicular railway, an impressive piece of engineering, built on a gradient averaging 1:1.96. The coaches were built step-like to match the gradient and were hauled up the rail by a cable. There was a lower section going up to nearly 1,300 feet, at which point we transferred to cars on the upper section which took us to the top of the hill, 2,600 feet above sea level. The panorama from the gardens at the top was spectacular, taking in the view across the strait between Penang and the mainland, the big water supply reservoir for the Island and the town of Georgetown occupying the peninsula jutting out into the strait. Compared with sea level the temperature at the top was refreshingly cool.

Murph arrived the following day just in time to join our day trip aboard the RASC MV *Uriah Heep* (a name sounding like something out of Dickens or the Goon Show). After cruising from Georgetown Harbour along the coast we went ashore on Tiger Island, where we enjoyed a hilarious game of cricket on the beach, using a flotsam barrel as a wicket, the stalk of a big palm frond as a bat and coconut shells for balls. After a picnic lunch, we made our way across the island to the other beach for a swim. Re-boarding the good ship *Uriah Heep* we returned to Georgetown after a truly enjoyable and relaxing day out.

That evening, after a few grogs, we headed off in search of some female company at a dance organised at the RAF Leave Centre but to no avail. Sadly, the WRAFs (Women's Royal Air Force) all seemed much more interested in RAF types than we brave but impoverished National Service *ulu*-bashers. After this rebuttal we turned our attention to a group of shy looking Chinese girls[68] who were more willing to engage with us, but not in the kind of activities we had in mind.

---

[68] Many years later when visiting my father, by then living in Italy, he introduced me to Mary, a Malaysian Chinese woman from Penang, who lived in the next village. She told me that because of discrimination against Chinese Christians in Penang, Chinese girls were desperate to marry foreigners. Mary was one of six sisters, and in her case, had married an Italian engineer working in Penang laying the undersea telephone cable from the mainland; two others had married Australians based at RAAF Butterworth; another had married a Frenchman and lived in Paris, and only

After Friday's exertions, Saturday morning saw the arrival of Dan and, finally, all the gang were together except for Johnny, stuck on his medical cadre in KL. We spent the morning sightseeing around the Waterfall Gardens and feeding the scores of surprisingly well-mannered monkeys, before we visited a Hindu temple (shoes off before entering) to watch rather grubby looking priests in loincloths performing their midday ritual accompanied by banging of drums and ringing of bells.

That evening we introduced Dan to the town, with a visit to the Green Parrot Cabaret where partners could be hired for the night for $12, plus their extortionately priced drinks. What you did after the cabaret closed, and at what cost, was entirely between you and the girl. Not for us — those prices were way above our NS pay scale. In any case we were there far too early, and the place was dead so, after one expensive drink, we left and headed for Georgetown's 'Boston Bar' and enjoyed a few beers with a mob of Aussies, who delighted in calling us 'Pommy Bastards' and introducing us to other expressive Aussie slang.

Sunday was a day of rest for most of the gang, but Murph and I took some exercise by hiring bikes. The highlight of our sightseeing ride around Georgetown was the Buddhist temple (another barefoot entry). The temple was large, airy and clean: the outstanding feature being a huge dais in the centre of the temple, on which reposed numerous ornate bibelots and statues, with Buddha

---

two remained in Malaysia. Mary was only a little younger than me and may well have been at that RAF dance.

himself as the centrepiece. The rest of the temple was equally ornate and a fascinating contrast to the incense-reeking Chinese and Hindu temples. Returning mid-afternoon, between mealtimes, was when we first took an interest in the food stalls we had seen on the beach. This was my introduction to the spicy delights of Penang hawker food. Previously, apart from a couple of meals in the *kampong* at Telok Sengat, we had steered clear of street food, due to concerns over the dodgy hygiene – potentially even worse than the Notts & Jocks' cookhouse. However, after our initial taste, we soon acquired an appetite for *nasi goreng*, *mee goreng*, *char kway teoh*, *satays* and other noodle dishes.[69]

Monday saw the Notts & Jocks contingent, with REME support from Murph, challenge the rest of the Leave Centre to a game of six-a-side football which, under the captaincy of Dan, we won 7-1. This display of football talent inspired the Camp Sergeant-Major to organise a match against the Royal Engineers from Butterworth and a team was selected following a trial match the following afternoon. That night, squally weather drove everyone from the beer garden into the crowded shelter of the bar, where an Aussie bombardier, known fondly as 'Bastard' to his mates, joined our darts school. Strangely,

---

[69] I next tasted Penang hawker food in 1975 at the Merlin Hotel in Kuala Lumpur during 'Penang Week', where hawkers from Penang set up their stalls in the hotel dining room. Above each stall was an extractor fan connected to an air-conditioning hose that vented the charcoal fumes out through window openings sealed off with duct tape. Penang hawker food in air-conditioning – now that was living!

he was wearing uniform. Earlier in the evening he'd rashly accepted the challenge from a WRAC to join her for a fully clothed swim in their civvies. Keen to see her nubile figure shown off to advantage in a clinging wet dress, he had rushed into the sea, but she didn't follow — hence his uniform. We played an inter-Commonwealth challenge of 'Killer'. Bastard the Bombardier and I were the last two left and, by sheer fluke, I won — the first and last time I ever won a darts competition. But it costs you to win against Aussies: only after buying pints for all the contestants was I declared the champion. Thereafter, the beer continued to flow and the singing began. Introducing us to the (im)proper words to 'Waltzing Matilda', Bastard got as far as, *Once, a jolly bombardier caught a dose of gonorrhoea* ... before being abruptly cut off by some RAF 'Sir Galahad' pointing out the presence of women in the bar.

The Aussies stocked up on beers to keep the session going outside after closing when we all returned to our blustery perches in the beer garden, where I surreptitiously helped myself to a bottle from the Aussies' stash — big mistake!

'Where's my fucking beer gone? exclaimed Bastard.

'That Pommie bastard half-inched it,' replied another pointing at me and soon I was confronted by half a dozen angry Aussies. At this point, the sizeable form of Dan stepped in as peacemaker, returning the missing bottle to its rightful owner, thus defusing the situation. Shortly afterwards, Trev and Dan had to take Murph away for a chunder and put him to bed leaving me at the mercy of the Aussies, and they wasted no time in taking their revenge. Four of them grabbed a limb apiece and dumped me, fully clothed, into the sea. Ocean-bound, I had managed to discard my specs and was faced with the task of finding them after I emerged from the sea. It was a pitch-black night, but, after crawling around in the sand in my myopic state, I finally found them and was relieved to discover they had survived with no further damage than the already missing arm, broken off during my flip-flop fight with Henry. Honour satisfied, the Aussies invited me to share the rest of their beer stash but the squally weather and chill of our wet clothes quickly brought proceedings to a close.

Thursday was the day of the big football match against the Butterworth Sappers. Dan scored an early goal, but soon afterwards limped off with a sprained ankle, followed by another of our better players with a gash over his eye requiring stitches. So, with only 8½ men (the half being the portly, slow-moving Filly), Sandycroft crumbled to a 5-1 defeat.

The following morning, after counting what little money I had left after shouting drinks for my darts victory, I decided a trip to Georgetown was required to exchange my last emergency British one pound note, received at Christmas, for Malay dollars. Not one of the money-changers would accept it due to its unusual colour resulting from my involuntary dip in the ocean which had caused the dye from my wallet to run.

For Filly and me Saturday was our last day and, after sharing a few farewell beers with the remaining lads, we were driven to the ferry terminal for the crossing to the mainland. After claiming our sleepers at Prai Station, we set off on our overnight journey to KL. I slept well, only waking as we were passing through Ipoh — perhaps I had disturbed some ghosts from the recent past?

After a hearty breakfast in KL, we re-boarded the south-bound train. True to form, on arrival at Kluang, transport from every unit bar the Notts & Jocks, was waiting to collect arriving passengers. A phone call, an hour-and-a-half wait, and three beers later, our transport finally showed. Returning to camp, Batu proved to be the same hellhole we had left but with even worse news awaiting us. No longer on operations we now had to pay for re-placement kit, weekly drill parades had been introduced, and there was a new Army treat to look forward to — shooting reclassification on the rifle range.

Twentynine more days of Batu Bull and days in the Fed will be down to 171.

CHAPTER 11
LAST RITES IN BATU

Monday morning and there was no mistaking being back in the Bull Capital: a return to having my sleep shattered at 6:00 am by the bugler blowing Reveille directly outside my *basha*. Oddly enough, inside the *basha,* there was no sign of Bubble and Squeak. It was over breakfast I learnt that they had gone to Singapore for the weekend on 48-hour leave passes and, having not returned by six o'clock, were now officially AWOL.

I picked up a few other morsels of good news over breakfast. The date of our move back to Burma Camp in Kota Tinggi had been set for the 21 March and the provisional plans for the joint exercise on Borneo with the American Marines had been received. The exercise was scheduled to start on 1 June 1959 and last for a fortnight — something to look forward to because, after that, it would soon be August and the voyage home.

News of the sergeant-slugging Big Ned and his mate Nog was that they had been sentenced to six months detention at a District Court Martial. 'Butch' Martello, the unlicensed child-killing road menace, had been found guilty of manslaughter and fined $150 in the civilian court — an unbelievably light penalty for killing a child while driving unlicensed, but no doubt substantial compensation had been paid.

For Dan there was good news and bad news; the good news was he had been selected to play in a trial for the Combined Services football team later in the week, the bad news was he was still in Penang nursing a sprained ankle.

Later that morning, as I was about to leave the office unattended to report sick with my broken glasses, who should show up but Bubble and Squeak, three hours overdue. Luckily for them Sergeant Kaz was still on leave and Captain Pavior was engaged in a planning meeting for an upcoming IS drill in Singapore. Their absence therefore went unnoticed and charges were averted — what a shame! The MO effected temporary repairs to my specs with some remarkably good glue and, after asking how long it had been since I'd had my eyes tested, booked me an eye test appointment at BMH Singapore.

But the real bombshell gossip of the morning was that Coco-Oscar was scheduled to return to the UK for a couple of months for an Infantry Commanders' Conference and for some home leave. How he would go about gilding the lily about the battalion's combat performance at the conference would be worth listening to with the battalion's operational record reading:

Terrorists killed – 0

Terrorists captured – 0

Terrorists surrendered – 0

Civilians killed – 1

Battalion fatalities – 1

Musical instruments captured - 4

VD infections – lost count!

I was more than a little curious about how Coco-Oscar's operational report would be received at the War Office. Having recently read excerpts from *Monty's Memoirs* serialised in the *Sunday Times* while in Penang, I discovered that, in stark contrast to Coco-Oscar who, in my presence, had dismissed the private soldier as having 'no personality', Monty cared deeply for the troops under his command. He strived to forge collective confidence between all ranks, believing that morale was the greatest single factor in winning battles. In turn, he maintained that it took leadership of the highest order to rally troops to a common purpose and inspire confidence; and that's what he focussed on, leaving the detail to his subordinate officers in whom he placed great trust. Notably, most of Monty's personal staff were not professional soldiers but were former civilians who, according to his memoir, were highly proficient.

None of these qualities or practices were discernible in Coco-Oscar's circus. Instead of delegating he was obsessed with inconsequential detail; he had little regard or respect for his men and, in the absence of any inspired leadership, morale was low. His subordinate officers could not even ensure his men were fed palatable meals, or that adequate hygiene standards were maintained in the cookhouse. Observing them grapple with routine administrative tasks was akin to watching a one-armed man wrestling an octopus. With Monty's judgment in mind, it was striking that the most proficient officer in the battalion was the RSO, a former National

Serviceman who had only re-enlisted after being unable to find suitable civilian employment.

One aspect of Batu life that remained unchanged on my return was the pigswill standard of cookhouse meals, despite the arrival of a new Cook Staff-Sergeant — but perhaps my expectations had been raised too high at Sandycroft. After my first breakfast comprising of a cold hard-boiled egg, grey on the inside, a cold leather-skinned sausage, supplemented with two pieces of bread and margarine and a mug of grey liquid described on the urn as coffee I determined I had to do something — but what? My first option was to resort to NAAFI food, but the Batu NAAFI did not offer a satisfactory alternative. Apart from being poorly managed, the food in the Batu NAAFI was well below the standard of the NAAFIs at Nee Soon and Colombo Barracks and, of course, the cost of NAAFI meals came out of my own pocket.

Rostered for guard duty on the coming Tuesday night I wangled a great skive after being informed that my eye appointment at BMH Singapore was on Wednesday morning, which entailed catching a pre-dawn train from Kluang. Since this encroached into my scheduled period of guard duty I reported the matter to the RSM. His solution was for me to replace Squeak as 'Waiting Man', with Squeak taking my place on the guard. An eminently satisfactory outcome; I got off guard duty, Squeak lost a night's sleep and my 'Waiting Man' duty still counted as a guard duty on the roster.

At BMH Singapore, a young optometrist put me through the eye tests and concluded that my vision was little changed. Even so, he prescribed new lenses to go into my new frames. After this consultation I had the rest of the day to myself in Singapore. Starving after my early start I headed for the Union Jack Club for a budget lunch due to my dire post-leave financial circumstances. Chatting to a Singapore-based squaddie he told me I had missed seeing the Duke of Edinburgh sailing out of Keppel Harbour that morning on the Royal Yacht *Britannia.* He also told me that the bull inflicted on the Singapore garrison for the Duke's visit had been horrendous — lucky we were in Batu: who knows what Coco could have come up with to impress the Duke?

After a post-lunch siesta in the UJ Club, I tried, again without success, to return to solvency by exchanging my stained one-pound note. Again, not one money-changer would touch it. Consequently, still penniless except for an essential 30 cents, I headed to the Britannia Club to kill time in the cool of the Reading Room until it was time to return to the railway station. As expected, on arrival at Kluang the Notts & Jocks duty truck was nowhere to be seen, even though my pick-up had been pre-booked. Recalling Osbert's impatience at Ipoh Station, I waited. Ten minutes went by, twenty minutes, and finally, on the half hour, it came time to make use of my last 30 cents. I phoned Batu to request the duty truck to come and collect me. The call was transferred to the Guard Commander who, taken by surprise, flapped around, humming and hawing, before suggesting I ring back after he had checked with the Orderly Officer and MT clerk to authorise the pick-up.

For fuck's sake! Sergeant or no sergeant, I let rip over the phone,

'I've just returned from BMH Singapore, the fucking pick-up has already been authorised by the MO and pre-booked with the MT Clerk, and I have no cash to make another call.' I told him and rang off. Eventually, my wheels turned up and I arrived back at Batu after mid-night, only to learn from Dan, newly returned from leave, that I was due on the range at seven that morning — for fuck's sake, once more!

On the range, where WO2 Morgan, the new HQ Company CSM, was in charge of firing practice, I managed to zero on both rifle and Bren even wearing my old, mackled-together glasses. Returning to camp I cleaned my rifle before strapping Dan's sprained ankle for him prior to his departure for Cha'ah to join the 'Jockstrap Platoon' for football training.

That afternoon it was back to the standard Int Section routine of trying to look busy: that was until Captain Sherry, the QM, breezed in. He handed me the outline movement order for the transfer to Kota Tinggi and a messy-looking sketch of the Grand Master Plan for Burma Camp. These he wanted drawn up into big charts that could be understood by officers and senior NCOs — some challenge that, I thought — and to be completed by Monday!

Thursday afternoon did bring some compensation in the form of my first pay day since returning from leave, ac-companied by a second polio jab for good measure. Cashed up again, I headed to the NAAFI along with Trev, who had returned from Penang that afternoon, to finish re-paying our various debts. Here, we learnt that Squeak was seriously considering signing on and had collected the forms and information sheets from the Orderly Room. Apparently, he seemed taken in by all the promotional garbage in the Army advertisements: *'A great career'*; *'See the world'*; and, most importantly for Squeak, *'Good pay'*, his real motivation. Since he had been knocking around with Bubble he was constantly short of readies trying to match Bubble's extravagant ways. As a National Serviceman, this was understandable, but not to warrant signing on for six years. Rather than trying to talk him out of it, I tried to discourage him by resurrecting the signs we had used in Ipoh when Sergeant Kaz signed on for the full 22 years — 'If you're thick, sign on quick!'

Most of my Saturday was spent on the Grand Master Plan, with a short *tiffin* break — one taste of the congealed 'curry' and it went straight into the slops bin. That evening I joined birthday celebrations for Tiss, who was turning twenty. During the evening Trev harangued Squeak over the idiocy of signing on, aided and abetted by a Signals Corporal who was himself a regular soldier. By the end of the night, their anti-Army arguments seemed to be outweighing Squeak's need for immediate cash to keep up with Bubble.

The following week saw the start of weapons training every morning except Wednesday, a day reserved for the Company Drill Parade. This training included 'pokey drill' [70] under the polished direction of Staff-Sergeant

---

[70] A set of drills designed to improve shooting proficiency, involving rotating the rifle from hand to hand, passing it

Jeffery, the Battalion APTC instructor and proved to be a surprisingly enjoyable form of exercise. By this time, I had completed the draft Grand Master Plan, and was drawing up individual unit movement plans for the transfer. Concurrently, Trev and Squeak were marking up the Burma Camp site plan indicating the areas to be occupied by each company, no doubt to enable the powers-that-be to identify who was responsible for any unswept paths, unpainted posts and railings, uncut grass, unemptied water containers and mete out suitable punishments to the delinquents.

Murph had returned from Penang on the Monday night somewhat worse for wear after smashing the record for the longest ever wait at Kluang Station for Notts & Jocks transport to arrive — 14 hours! Fortunately, he had the good sense to go to the MP Post, where he met up with a fellow Scouse and was liberally supplied with free beer all day. Next morning , still hungover, he was rushed off to Cha'ah to join Dan in the Jockstrap Platoon for football training. The battalion's footballing ambitions were taking shape.

Wednesday saw me on Sick Parade again to have my new glasses fitted — most opportune, as I missed the weekly Drill Parade. However, my jubilation was dented by being rostered on Fire Picquet that night. The newly promoted Corporal 'Piggy' Gitt, the most obnoxious of all the RPs, was in charge.

---

around the back and holding it at arms' length to strengthen wrist, forearm and shoulder muscles.

'Defaulters, shun!' he barked.

We all took exception to being addressed as 'defaulters' and not a man moved. Gitt repeated this order twice more and still got no response. Eventually, Trev enlightened him.

'We're the Fire Picquet, Corp, not defaulters.'

The light bulb finally came on. Thereafter he addressed us as the 'Fire Picquet'. A moral victory which Trev later clinched by refusing to call Gitt by his rank when answering questions about our duties. Addressing Trev, he inquired 'How many hydrants are there on the camp?'

'Three,' replied Trev.

'Three what?'

'Fire hydrants.'

'Fire hydrants, what?'

'Three fire hydrants on the camp.'

Clearly exasperated by failing to obtain acknowledgement his new rank, 'Piggy' gave up — one up for Trev!

Saturday night brought the long-awaited CSE[71] Concert, starring Lita Rosa, a sultry Mersey-sider who had sung with the Ted Heath Band before going solo. She was supported by comedian Ken Roberts, conjuror Ossie Noble (the poor man's Tommy Cooper), pianist Jeff

---

[71] CSE – Combined Services Entertainment, a registered British charity that was the official provider of live entertainment to the British Armed Forces.

Saunders and violinist, Shelagh Williams. The show took place in the hall of the Batu Pahat High School. The whole Battalion was present in best dress, most of them well lubricated. Judging by variety shows I had seen at the Nottingham Empire, this was a second-rate line-up, but who was going to complain?

Most acts went down well with the performers attracting a flood of wise-cracks from the audience especially Ossie Noble. In the manner of Harry Secombe when he missed a note and re-started a song, whenever any of Ossie's tricks went wrong (deliberately or otherwise) he gave a loud 'Harrumpf', tapped the side of his nose, and started the trick again. It did not take long for the audience to start mimicking him. Undoubtedly, the star of the show was Lita Rosa, playing the cynical, hard-faced vamp, quite at ease among a horde of sex-starved squaddies. One poor lad's request for one of her hit songs, *Who is my Jimmy unknown?* was rejected with the cutting reply,

'Well, it's not you!'

Later, in response to the audience reaction to a sultry ballad, she broke off and, in her huskiest tone, whispered into the microphone;

'Hmmmmm, you've obviously been out here longer than I thought.'

The concert was the highlight of our time in Batu and much appreciated by all. After the show the entertainers were whisked off to be entertained in the Officers Mess where, mess staff reported later, the younger officers clustered around Lita Rosa like flies round a dung heap.

R A (BRAM) BRAMLEY

Sunday's *tiffin* again went into the bin. Close examination had revealed there was some meat attached to the lump of gravy-covered fat that had been dumped over slices of tinned beetroot and covered with a dollop of mash – but at least the jelly at tea-time was edible. That was the night when it became clear that I wasn't the only one jack of the food so, once again, it was a case of what to do about it? At a gripe session in the NAAFI, it was agreed it was a waste of breath complaining to Orderly Officers on their cookhouse rounds. With few junior officers in HQ Company at Batu, Orderly Officer duties were shared by senior NCOs. Of the officers, only the RSO, attempted to effect improvements, but they were usually short-lived. Complaining to Lieutenant Nickelhead, who chaired the weekly Messing meetings, was a waste of breath. The more we saw of him, the more he seemed to be one brick short of a load and, reportedly, even Coco-Oscar had suggested he should get out of the infantry and find some backwater job in one of the service corps. As for complaints to senior NCOs they were an even greater waste of breath.

'Well, you know what Army food is like, nothing I can do about it.' was the standard response.

'Food this bad in the Sergeants' Mess?' I asked the Drum Major on one occasion trying to stir him up but, as usual, was ignored.

Complaints were supposed to be raised formally at weekly Messing Meetings at which the Int Section was represented by the Orderly Room Corporal but nothing ever changed. To reinforce our discontent, the Int Section nominated Bubble to attend the weekly Messing

Meeting armed with our list of our complaints. At his first meeting he was told that all of our complaints had been raised before and been dismissed. The poor quality of the meals was attributed to either the inadequacy of the ration scale (which had been cut back after we came off operations), the poor kitchen equipment (but with the promise that kitchen facilities at Burma Camp would be much better), or the poor quality of the provisions supplied by local civilian contractors. It was never the fault of the cooks. Their standard fall-back excuse was the inadequacy of the reduced ration scale now we were no longer operational. This was determined by the War Office which, as we all knew, was infallible.

The Messing Meetings were presided over by Lieutenant Nickelhead or, in his absence, by the ACC Staff-Sergeant in charge of the kitchen (talk about Caesar judging Caesar). According to Bubble he became enraged when asked how the cooks could always produce excellent meals when brass-hats from Brigade or Division were visiting but not the rest of the time. On the rare occasions that complaints were considered serious enough to refer to Coco-Oscar, they were usually dismissed by him as 'unnecessary' (choice of tea or lemonade at *tiffin*) or 'too expensive' (greater choice of vegetables) — so much for Monty's philosophy on morale and *esprit de corps*.

The week after the CSE Concert, every morning was devoted to weapons training. This involved not only weapon-handling, but undertaking re-classification on the range. This new classification involved firing our rifles from the standing, kneeling and sitting positions, none of which we had done before (having passed out at the end of basic training as fully trained soldiers having only fired from the prone position). Nickelhead made us snap-fire in these positions (two rounds in six seconds) at figure targets rather than the large target boards with concentric circles which were all we had shot at previously. The scores were pitiful. My best was seven out of 20 and even Trev, the best shot in our intake, scored only nine out of 20: and he had been classified as a marksman in basic training. Our performance was not improved by the heat and humidity making it difficult to grip our rifles firmly with sweaty hands, especially the drill involving doubling onto a firing point and firing within a set time. In my case, a further handicap was sweat clouding my new glasses.

It was that week when, for the first time since volunteering to teach on the troopship, I broke the ironclad Army rule and volunteered once more. This time it was to be driven to FTC Kota Tinggi, along with the other volunteers, to support the Battalion football team against the Cheshire Regiment in the Far East Army Association Football Cup competition — the first test for our team. On arrival we found there had been a colossal storm over Kota Tinggi: the pitch was flooded and the match had been postponed. Arriving back at Bullshit Pahat after our goal-less 180 miles round trip, we found that no arrangements had been made for a late meal — what a surprise!

The following day marked my completion of 18 months service – only six more months to push — but no sign of my 18 months' pay increase on pay parade that day so I resolved to skive out of all drawing work. Instead I set about clearing the office of all the 'gash' stuff we would not be taking to Burma Camp and dumping it. The next day we escaped Kaz's Int Section office chores once again, joining the other 'volunteers' being driven to FTC to watch the re-scheduled football match.

In true 'hurry up and wait' fashion we arrived early which gave us time to look over our next home before the match started. Generally, the accommodation looked pretty good, but there was a vast, forbidding-looking parade square on the hilltop and our new office was also much too close for comfort to those of Coco-Oscar, the Adjutant, and the RSM.

The Notts & Jocks won the match 2-1 in a close-fought, end-to-end battle. This victory proved to be first step on the way to the Battalion's only success during their Far East tour of duty. After the match I had chance to catch up with Chesh, who was already based at FTC with 'A' Company in Nyasa Camp. Gleefully, he told me he had scored the only skive going in a rifle company — that of Company Clerk. As he told it, on the first parade after the Company arrived at Nyasa Camp, the CSM asked,

'Who's got GCE?' There were three of us in a platoon of 30-plus. The platoon sergeant looked at me and said: 'Right, Cheshire, Company Clerk!'

It wasn't a completely cushy number, but at least it kept me out of the jungle until my return to the UK. Towards the end of my service, the CSM convinced the Company Commander that it was essential that I stayed behind in the office to help train the new clerk. As a result, I missed the ship taking the rest of my Intake back to the UK and subsequently flew back to London, arriving with only five days to do before demob.

After a couple of pints with Chesh, it was back to Batu, this time sitting in the cab with the driver, 'Wyatt' Earp, who I had known at primary school. Astonishingly, after Wednesday's fiasco, we were served a tasty late supper on our return. The cooks were primed to be on duty but, not knowing our arrival time, they were unable to start cooking until we arrived. For once, the meal was served straight out of the pans and was hot and appetising, begging the question: 'Why can't these so-called cooks produce meals this good all the time?'

The big news that weekend was from the Orderly Room confirming that Squeak had abandoned his plans for signing on — sanity had prevailed. Left for another week in Bubble's company, it would have been six years before the Colours.

The following week, the last before the move to FTC, I continued my new work-avoidance resolution by becoming the Section's self-appointed handyman, avoiding all drawing work that Sergeant Kaz tried to load onto me on the pretext of completing numerous repair tasks in preparation for the move.

'Got to repair these packing cases and replace the lids, Sarge, otherwise they'll fall apart.'

These jobs kept me out of the office until Wednesday when Kaz finally collared me for the urgent task of tracing and colouring American badges of rank for the Borneo exercise from the one chart that had been supplied to the battalion. Each company and, of course, various other self-important officers, all had to be supplied with coloured copies of their own. Why more of the charts could not have been provided by the Americans was

225

known only to Coco-Oscar and/or the Yanks who, I'm sure, would have had plenty of them. As a result, the whole Int Section were conscripted to trace and colour a dozen or so copies. In my case, in the absence of the IO who was acting Adjutant, I followed Kaz's example. Every time Kaz disappeared into the IO's office for a smoke and to read a comic, I downed tools and read my own book.

Thursday dawned to the news that, on Wednesday night, our favourite Provo, Piggy Gitt, after getting above his station and grogging up with a couple of Sergeants in Batu, returned to camp and, for no reason, laid into a couple of NS Lance Corporals in the NAAFI. The guard was called and he was escorted to the Guardroom where he broke free, headed for the QM stores, tipped the ration storeman out of bed and laid into him. After being subdued by the camp butcher and the Guard he was dragged, none too gently, back to the Guardroom. Appearing on CO's Orders that morning he escaped with no more than a 'severe reprimand' for 'causing a disturbance'. No mention of striking an inferior rank, of breaking out of close arrest, or of drunken-ness that might have exposed his off-camp boozing with a couple of Sergeants. To keep the Sergeants out the picture, the RSM and Provost Sergeant squashed the whole matter. Talk about double standards: Big Ned and Nog Norris were sentenced to six months in the glasshouse for much the same offences!

Thursday also saw Pay Parade come and go but, again, with no sign of my scheduled 18 month pay increase. This failure to commence my pay increase on time

reinforced my resolution to skive out of every task I possibly could in the run-down to demob. My resolution
was further reinforced after 'Boots', one of the RAPC
Pay Clerks, confirmed that my 18-month service increase of nine dollars had been approved and I had been
promoted to three-star Private entitling me to another
three dollars a week on top of my 18 month increase.
This meant my pay would be hitting $30 a week - but it
was still to be published on Part 1 Orders.

With all our stores packed, Friday saw us loading for the
big move. The Band and the Int Section had been allocated six lorries between them for the move and that
morning the lorries were drawn up nose-to-tail.

'Get those fucking lorries loaded, now!' barked the
Drum Major.

'Can't' was the reply, 'they're too close together and we
can barely get the fucking tailgates down, let alone load
beds and packing cases.'

With typical Notts & Jocks efficiency, the drivers had
parked the lorries nose to tail and disappeared. After
wasting almost 20 minutes trying to convince the Drum
Major that it wasn't practical to load the lorries as they
were, the drivers were rounded up and the lorries were
moved apart. Finally, loading began.

The convoy departed for Kota Tinggi early on Saturday
morning with Kaz, Bubble and Squeak aboard with the
advance party. A serious miscalculation on their part
meaning they would have to do all the unloading at the
other end. Meanwhile, after the ridiculously early Reveille to get the advance party on the move, Trev, Dan

and I spent most of Saturday morning catching up on some lost shut-eye, having conned the RSM into believing we still had loads of work to do to finish cleaning out the Tac HQ offices and making all doors and windows secure before the lorries returned. During this final clean up, I discovered a book by Louis Golding, *No News from Helen*, regarding the Japanese invasion of Malaya, which revealed that many people had been slaughtered by the Japanese in Batu Pahat, quite likely in the older part of our camp, once part of a Japanese barracks.

My final night in Batu was spent in town with the RAPC lads reminiscing over a few farewell drinks, about this out-of-the-way hell hole that we hated so much. Little were we to know that Kota Tinggi would prove to be an even more dedicated temple to the great god, 'Bull'.

Sunday morning, and another pre-dawn Reveille soon saw us on the move to Burma Camp, but not before Trev and I had yet another stand-up row with the Drum Major, the exact same bastard who, on our initial move to Kota Tinggi, had moved us out of our comfortable *basha* into a tent. His current beef was that we had put our beds on one of his lorries. Off he had gone bleating to the RSM that he had only been allocated four lorries for the band and he had no space for Int Section beds. Naturally, Twort took his side but neither of them could think how else we were to get our beds to Kota Tinggi so the beds stayed aboard the Band lorry. Rather than travel with them Trev, Dan and I scrounged a lift on one of the Sergeants Mess trucks, gonking on a pile of mattresses.

'Goodbye Batu' and good riddance! Only 171 days to push.

CHAPTER 12
SILVER CITY RE-VISITED

On arrival at Burma Camp we handed in our rifles, unloaded beds and, in pouring rain, manhandled them to
our billet, where we remained, trying to avoid any more
unloading in the rain. Having been on the first Advance
Party to FTC the previous June, we had seen enough not
to get caught up in another Notts & Jocks removalist fiasco, but our luck didn't hold. We were sprung by Sergeant Kaz who had us working until mid-afternoon unloading and storing BHQ gear. From that moment it was
full-on for the rest of the week trying to get everything
unpacked and in place before the upcoming Easter weekend. The access road ran along the top of ridge with HQ
Company on one side of the ridge and the rifle companies on the other meaning all gear, including beds, tables,
chairs, officers' furniture and equipment had to be carried down flights of steps and along terraced pathways
to their final destination (and sometimes not so final destination).

Trev and I again found ourselves on fatigues next day,
while the two Int Section 'brown noses', Bubble and
Squeak, helped Sergeant Kaz set up the office out of the
rain. Rather than lugging kit down steps from the road,
our task was the reverse — heaving concrete kerbstones
up two flights of steps in the rain to delineate parking

spaces in the Officers Mess car park (must have 'nice' designated parking bays for Coco-Oscar's return). Following this, we were assigned to the Band work party unloading all the officers' paraphernalia.

Sherpa duties continued the following morning, this time unloading the Sergeants Mess furniture, the prize job being man-handling a huge icebox down 45 steps to the Sergeants Mess kitchen. This shit of a day was capped off when I found out I was rostered on for guard duty again that night. Still being Advance Party days, there was no formal Guard-mounting and we turned up in whatever kit we could find that was dry. The Burma Camp Guard Room was a far more intimidating looking place than the one at Batu, situated, as it was, up a flight of 28 steps at the entrance to the camp. Moreover, the cells looked far more escape-proof than those at Batu — but later events were to prove otherwise.

Having had next to no sleep overnight, a little judicious volunteering enabled me to escape from the Band work party the following morning. Rather than helping to hump 90 beds, 240 chairs and 60 tables from the road down to a mid-slope storeroom in the rain, I spent the day disturbing a legion of ants, cockroaches, and chit-chat lizards stripping softboard off the inside walls of another vacant hut for the Int Section to use as map boards. Fortunately, I managed to spin this job into a second day cutting the softboard to size thereby avoiding being returned to the Band work party which was greeted with the news that the hut in which they had placed the furniture the previous day had been re-allocated for soldiers' quarters. Consequently, they had to transfer all the furniture to another store room — lucky I'd taken the soft(board) option.

That afternoon, we were graced with the arrival of our esteemed Company Commander, His Mustachioed Corpulence Major Rocky. He had us assembled for a briefing on progress, stating how well the Advance Party had worked, but emphasising that there was still much to be done. The cookhouse was still unfinished, and swarming with local tradesmen completing the improvements promised at the last Messing Meeting in Batu. Likewise, the NAAFI was also still a work in progress, being half NAAFI- half warehouse. Not only that but the ablution and toilet blocks were incomplete, with only four washbasins, two sinks, two showers, and two bogs to serve HQ Company's 170 men.

Rocky informed us that he would inspect the camp in the morning and, if our re-occupation was sufficiently advanced, we would be granted leave over the Easter holiday weekend. Returning to the Int Office, we were greeted by the Adjutant accompanied by the Padre looking for an office of his own. To accommodate him, we had to move everything out of our newly organised map store into an adjoining vacant office. Why the Padre could not have occupied the already vacant office remained a secret known only to God, the Padre, and the Adjutant.

Thursday morning saw the first stirring of homage to the Army deity, the great god 'Bull'. It began with the first full-on Batu-style Muster Parade, taken by the RSM. He made it clear that we should get used to a future of 'regimental soldiering' and all that went with it — no more of that 'sloppy soldiering' we had enjoyed on operations (wasn't that what we were here for?). To make his point, he gripped me yet again over the length of my hair, and I was forced to engage the services of a new camp barber who damned near scalped me.

After the parade, the mighty Rocky conducted his room inspection which resulted in yet another accommodation reshuffle. The accommodation on the HQ side of the ridge consisted of long blocks subdivided into small rooms, each accommodating three men — much better than Batu. Trev and I had already occupied one room, keeping a space for Dan when he returned from his latest Combined Services football match in Kuala Lumpur. But this did not suit Rocky's tidy little military mind and he decreed that all of the Int Section should be in adjacent rooms and, likewise, all the HQ Company clerks. To achieve his 'tidy' accommodation solution, he ordered Trev and me to change rooms with two of the HQ Company clerks whose room was next to that of Osbert and Sammy. Of course, it was no surprise that the bookshelves I had installed in our original room did not fit the equivalent space in the new room and had to be sawn shorter. But up they went, along with my trusty *Punch* calendar, denoting the countdown to demob was now 169 days.

On returning to the Int Office, Captain Pavior informed us that, regardless of Rocky's intentions about Easter leave, the Int Section office set-up was sufficiently advanced that we could have Easter off. Then, turning to Trev and me, he inquired how long we still had to serve,

'One hundred and sixty-nine days, sir,' we replied in unison.

Apparently, the reason for his interest was not just to check how much longer he had to put up with us but to ascertain how long he had to identify possible replacements from future drafts. Apparently, the strength of the 5717 Intake had already been submitted to GHQ (General Headquarters) for troopship bookings so, finally, the wheels were in motion for our release. Coupled with my news from 'Boots' before we left Batu regarding my imminent 18 month pay increase, news that our passage home was being booked was cause for real celebration — an end date was within sight. With the Borneo exercise coming up in June to break the drudgery, it was beginning to feel like demob was within reach.

However, to put a dampener on this good news, the IO also informed us that Coco-Oscar was due back from UK after Easter, and would inspect the camp the following Saturday. Here we go again, I thought, all the regimental overkill that goes with peacetime soldiering: more 'Stand by your boots with your beds in your hands!' and all that bullshit. The prospect drove me to the, as yet, unfinished NAAFI for more than a few beers with the REME crew, several of whom, including Murph, were also due for demob around the same time.

After a leisurely Good Friday, Saturday saw us head for Singapore, where the city was teeming with sailors from eight or nine British, Australian and New Zealand warships, all enjoying shore leave. Trying to get a drink in the Britannia Club was like being in the middle of a rugby maul so we moved on. A wise move because, later, an almighty brawl broke out between the Brits and the Anzacs.

Returning to Kota Tinggi on Easter Monday we were greeted by the start of the promised bull blitz in preparation for Coco-Oscar's return. Ceremonial Guard-mountings incorporating Advance in Review Order were introduced and there was even talk of introducing tap drill[72]. Full kit and locker layouts were also back. And that night, to celebrate this joyful Easter news, we were served warm beer in the 'work-in-progress' NAAFI.

The bull drive continued throughout the week following Easter and, by Friday morning, it had become evident that some elements within the Battalion had already had more than their fill. On the road outside the BHQ office, in large white letters, was painted the message: '**DOWN WITH BULL & THE CO & THE ADJT**'. On Muster Parade, Rocky was fuming, keeping us standing to attention in the scorching sun for three-quarters-of-an-hour, waiting for the road painters to own up. None did, of course, so the 'Rock' set off on his tour of inspection not in the best of moods. When he got to our billet, he

---

[72] 'Tap drill' is when a series of drill movements is initiated, not by word of command, but by a single tap on a drum. As the 'Advance in Review Order' involves the whole Battalion marching forward 14 paces and halting without an order and continuing the succeeding movements at the tap of a drum without vocal orders and is an impressive display if mastered.

wanted to know why my spare boots were not on show as they should have been. On producing them he charged me for not having any laces in them (the reason they were not on show). Fortunately, I got off with a reprimand because the QM Stores had no spare laces in stock.

Saturday, the day of Coco-Oscar's scheduled inspection, dawned to the revelation that the anti-bull vandals had struck again. The HQ Company signboard had been pushed over and scattered down an embankment, the flagpole had been uprooted and the pride of the Pioneer Platoon, the huge Regimental sign on the road outside the camp, had also been pushed over. If this was the new regime of 'regimental soldiering' promised by the RSM on our first formal Muster Parade at Burma Camp, it was clearly causing seething discontent among the troops.

With Coco-Oscar due to inspect the camp that day, this further vandalism invoked dire threats of disciplinary action and suspension of weekend passes. Once again Major Rocky was fuming. All the damage had to be rectified before Coco-Oscar's expected arrival but, as it turned out, all for nothing — he failed to appear as scheduled. Instead, the acting CO, Major Little, the RSM and Rocky himself conducted the inspection. Fortunately, by the time everything was back in order there was only time to inspect half of HQ Company lines and the Int Section escaped scrutiny.

Monday morning, it was panic stations again, this time due to a scheduled visit by the Major-General from GURDIV. The only benefit for us was an exceptionally good *tiffin* (in case the General should visit the cookhouse) of roast pork, apple sauce, peas, tomatoes, chips and boiled spuds, followed by trifle and fresh fruit. Normally, we never had anything approaching that standard, and it was usually either fruit **or** a pudding, not both. Amazing what our cooks could produce at the mention of 'brasshats' — and in a kitchen still undergoing renewal.

The same week, Captain Pavior was confronted by Osbert's latest domestic drama. While he was on leave in Singapore, a telegram had arrived from his 'fiancée' in England advising him that she was expecting a child by another man, who was either unknown or was unwilling to marry her. Essentially, she was asking whether Osbert would agree to marry her if the Army would fly him home. The telegram had been forwarded to him at Toc H[73] in Singapore, which he and Sammy had declared as their leave address. This declaration was somewhat wide of the truth as both of them were staying with the family of Osbert's latest Chinese girlfriend, for which they had no authorisation. Consequently, the Toc H manager had returned the telegram, advising that no person of that name was staying there.

When Osbert returned to camp, not only was he faced with a domestic dilemma, but both he and Sammy found themselves on 'fizzers' for stating a false leave address (for the second time in Osbert's case). There was talk of the fiancée's parents buying Osbert out of the Army if

---

[73] Toc H – Talbot House was a soldiers' Rest and Recreation Centre known by the abbreviation Toc H. 'Toc' signified the letter 'T' in the alphabet used by the British Army in World War.

he returned to England to marry their daughter. After speaking to the Padre, Osbert — ever the optimist — indicated that he would be prepared to do so if the Army flew him back to England. Realistically, his chances of being flown back to Blighty at Army expense were no better than me being promoted to colonel. More to the point, the Battalion had been requested to fill a vacancy for a Lance-Corporal Intelligence Clerk at 63 Brigade, and Osbert was in the frame for the job. This posting offered the Coco-Oscar a convenient way of ridding himself of Osbert and his attendant problems.

The upshot was Osbert and Sammy ended up on Company Orders with Sammy getting seven days' jankers. Osbert was remanded for CO's Orders next day when he was given a severe reprimand. Given his previous record of staying in unauthorised accommodation in Ipoh, he was extremely fortunate to escape so lightly. He should have been busted back to private but, in view of the upcoming vacancy at Brigade, it was clearly more pragmatic to reprimand him and allow him to retain his rank.

After enduring 18 months of my gripes about the Army, my father, who had ended his wartime service as a Captain in the Seaforth Highlanders, had obviously become extremely irked by my 'puerile bellyaching about Army discipline' in letters home, pointing out to me that 'the British Army had been winning wars for countless years and that bull had always been an integral part of a good unit.' This, I felt called for a reasoned response and I wrote:

Operationally this battalion got out here at the wrong time and under the wrong man. The places where we were put on operations were not areas where great success could be expected and the men in general soon could not care less. Now we are off operations and not likely to start again. This had been known for long enough, and that we were having this place (Burma Camp, Kota Tinggi) as a permanent camp – and what happens when we get here? We immediately undergo a bull blitz. It was not confined to getting the camp into shape but bull for bull's sake, and we are gradually getting more and more twists to it. This camp, which was to be really modernised to serve as a permanent garrison barracks, is just in a transition stage. The cookhouse, which was going to be the best in Malaya, still produces poor food; the improvements promised at Batu only materialised for one meal when the Major-General came. The Army has been catering for units of our strength for countless years yet still we have lengthy queues – and that is with a good proportion of the lads going to the NAAFI for all meals or to the char wallah's, where, at dinner time, the queues are just as long as in the cookhouse. The washing up water is generally not hot, contains no detergent or soap and has a thick scum on top. We have complained to the MO and he has gripped the cooks, but any improvement only lasts a day or so.

There is a lavatory near our accommodation which often smells terribly at night. We have complained to the MO who diagnosed a blocked sewer and reported it – without any results yet. The roofs of our office and our accommodation leak in numerous places and when it rains, we have to send someone down to the rooms to shuffle the beds around to avoid the leaks. We have complained to the CQMS 'through the proper channels', as Rocky might say, and they will be mended once the REs have done an inspection of the camp. How long will that be? The roofs are asbestos and intensify the heat when it is hot but there are no fans in the rooms although most others have them. Unless it is bright sunlight the rooms – offices and sleeping – are poorly lit as the wall with the large windows faces onto a steep bank and the wall looking out over the hill possesses only a door and minute 'cell type' window. At night all we have are two 60W bulbs for light which is inadequate with the walls being black with preservative and offering no reflection and you can't get bigger bulbs.

One still has to queue for a shit, shower or shave due to the hopeless inadequacy of the washing and toilet facilities for most of HQ Company. Despite these things this camp is considered a good modern army camp of a permanent nature. We aren't experiencing any difficulties due to operations as there aren't any.

These I consider genuine complaints, and nothing has been done about them, or to improve the NAAFI. On April 2nd a new draft arrived out here. When their documents were checked, it was found that one of the draft was due for demob in May. Useful sending him out here. At Ipoh Sammy made two letter trays for Captain Pavior's desk out of wood he'd scrounged. When the CQMS came around he put them on our office inventory as 'traps, letter, wooden', and I suppose now, if they are lost, someone has to pay for them. Soon you will have to be careful leaving personal stuff about or you will find it on an inventory as WD property.

Since arriving here all No 5 rifles have been equipped with bayonets – we did not need them on Ops, but we need them now for drill and ceremonial guards. All the rifle companies have FN rifles which cannot be used for drill, so they have now been given a proportion of inferior No 5 Lee-Enfields for drill. A retrogressive step in the cause of bull and drill. Why can't they accept that the No 4 & 5s are out of date and it is sheer stupidity to keep on using drills evolved for them years ago? Why can't they take the big plunge and accept that the FN is being made the standard infantry rifle and adapt their 'traditional drill and ceremonial' to keep abreast of advances in weapons?

I am sure there is considerable justification in my adverse opinions of the Army going by this unit. Two Loyals we met on leave, both National Servicemen, lapped the life up in the Loyals but, of the regular and NS men (in the Notts & Jocks) below the rank of sergeant, including many blokes with considerable length of service in this shower, you would be lucky to find 10% with any respect for the regiment, or the life in it at present. That includes old sweats of the 'Acker' type who, although not too reliable themselves, did at one time lap up life in this battalion. (In fact, sergeants might be included too, quite a few will, in conversation, admit that they don't think much of this battalion at present.)

As it turned out, I received no response to my diatribe because, by the time my father wrote again, my army life had taken a far more dramatic turn.

On his return from England that week, Coco-Oscar celebrated Hari Raya, by introducing his latest and greatest

240

innovation on the bull front. Posted on Battalion Orders was a list of explicit instructions on how to wear a beret correctly, carrying with it the sentence of wearing a steel helmet for three days for anyone who did not comply — what on earth do they teach them at Infantry Commanders' Conferences?

The camp soon appeared as if it was on alert for an air raid, especially around the MT park, where the REME vehicle mechanics, who spend half their time with their heads in engine compartments or under vehicles, regularly breached Coco's new beret edict. We were, however, granted some compensation for the 'tin hat' regime by being given the following Saturday morning off in lieu of Badajoz Day[74] which had fallen on the previous Monday (April 6th). By rights we should have had a full day holiday for Badajoz Day and also for Hari Raya the previous Friday, a declared military holiday throughout Malaya. Conveniently, the half day holiday enabled officers with families in Singapore to enjoy a three-day weekend. Meanwhile the poor squaddies were stuck in camp because it was too late to book leave accommodation due to the late notice of the Badajoz half-day

---

[74] This commemorated the Anglo-Portuguese victory over the French at the siege of Badajoz in 1812 during the Peninsular War. It is one of the most illustrious Battle Honours of the 45th (Nottinghamshire) Regiment. Reputedly, following the French surrender, a member of the Regiment had hoisted a red coat on the flagpole, a tradition that the Regiment still upheld, albeit on this occasion five days late.

holiday. The simmering discontent that pervaded the camp prior to Coco-Oscar's return had now become palpable.

Despite this discontent, there was a lift in morale on the Monday with news that the Battalion football team had defeated the Royal Signals in the quarter-final of the Far East Army Association Football Championship, with Dan and Murph again starring. This victory enabled the Jockstrap Platoon to continue their unmolested life; no muster parades, no guard duties and no fire picquets to interrupt their preparation for the semi-final in Seremban the following week.

The week also saw the first appearance of Americans around the camp in connection with the forthcoming Borneo exercise, one of whom by all accounts had a square foot of medal ribbons bedecking his chest. The US liaison officers were not allowed across the Causeway unless accompanied by a British officer, due to the Malayan Government's neutral policy of not appearing to support the Americans. Consequently, our officers and senior NCOs had to go to Singapore to be trained for the amphibious landing before returning to Kota Tinggi to train our ORs — another recipe for disaster!

Come Friday, it was time for another shooting reclassification and, following a pre-dawn Reveille, we were on the range early under the direction of Captain Sherry. Once there, we twice went through a new and complicated classification course run by CSM Morgan. The whole shooting show was over by three, by which time we had only received our first practice scores. Dan and I were initially graded second-class and, ironically Murph,

R A (BRAM) BRAMLEY

one of our armourers, failed to qualify due to his weapon having numerous stoppages.

It was around this time, banking on my yet-to-be-received 18-month pay increase, that I finally decided to give up on the camp cookhouse as a source of sustenance. Instead, I began to subsist on an egg banjo and a mug of tea from the *char-wallah* for breakfast and a *nasi goreng* or something similar in the NAAFI at night, only visiting the cookhouse at midday for *tiffin* on the off-chance there might be some fresh fruit or any other edible looking source of sustenance.

The following Tuesday we were back on the range for Bren classification. It was a scorching, sunny day but, thanks to an efficient butt party and surprisingly efficient management on the firing point, we completed our classification by early afternoon. After failing the first practice classification miserably, I managed a First-Class classification on the second round which, CSM Morgan gratuitously informed me, made me eligible for another star and another seven shillings per week in real money; an increase I had been eligible for since my previous classification at Batu Pahat on 12th March, but had yet to see — it was now the 21st of April.

Just to add to my discontent I found myself on guard duty again the following night. With the whole Battalion now together, why had the HQ Company guard roster not yet been updated? With a full complement of nearly 200 men in HQ Company (excluding attached personnel and those in essential occupations who were excused guard duty), why were they were still using the Advance Party roster and why was I doing my third guard duty in

243

three weeks? According to Henry Ford's replacement, the Monk, none of the later HQ Company arrivals had done a single guard since arriving at Burma Camp.

On the upside when I handed in my rifle after guard duty next day, I was chuffed to be told it was to be re-assigned to a rifle company to be re-fitted with a bayonet so they could continue their antiquated practice of doing arms drill with obsolete Lee Enfield .303 rifles — finally I was off the hook for rifle cleaning! Returning to the office, I discovered that, having already been re-located once to satisfy Rocky's sense of order, the Int Section was on the move again to a new billet. This time we were being re-located over the hill to 'D' Company lines on the far side of the camp. The reason was to enable officers' batmen to be accommodated closer to the Officers' Quarters.

Despite the inconvenience of having to move again we liked the new location; it was nearer the cookhouse (for what that was worth), nearer to the NAAFI, the Medical Centre, the barber, the *dhobi-wallah* and the *char-wallah* — and well out of the way of HQ Company office and the scrutiny of Rocky and the RSM. The only downside of the move was that we again had to share a room with Bubble and Squeak, but this was offset by the abundance of washbasins, showers and lavatories in 'D' Company lines — a real luxury not having to queue for a shit any-more. Needless to say, before moving, we were made to endure another maddening inspection of our old billet by Major Rocky — why, when we were packing up and moving to new quarters later that day?

The week brought even more evidence of the clueless-ness of the Battalion's command structure. The renovations done to adapt the camp to be a permanent base for the Battalion had been a complete cock-up. Apparently, M$500,000 had been allocated for these improvements but there was little to show for it. Much of the money appeared to have been spent on the Officers Mess and officers' quarters. For example, ceilings had been installed in the officers' quarters to stop creepy-crawlies falling from the rafters onto the heads of our precious officers. The former Gurkha Sergeants' Mess had been panelled and decorated, but fond hopes that was going to be turned into a reading room or an annex to the NAAFI were dashed when Coco-Oscar decreed it should be reserved for use as a lecture room. So, while we had a newly decorated but seldom used lecture room, ORs had to make do with an unimproved and undersized NAAFI.

Healthwise, the MO was pulling no punches in his health returns to GHQ regarding poor hygiene standards. His reports caused a stir at GHQ, resulting in another visit from the GOC. On his tour of the camp, the General indicated he could see no sign of any improvements since his previous visit — evidently, he didn't inspect the officers' quarters. Coco-Oscar's attempts to explain away the inadequacy of the HQ Company toilet and ablution facilities and account for how little there was to show for the money spent, were not well received. A black mark for Coco-Oscar.

As it was, half of HQ Company still had to make do with two sinks, four washbasins, two showers and still only two toilets. Not only that but a load of attap, delivered for the purpose of building an additional washhouse for

HQ Company, had been used to build a screen between the officers' quarters and HQ Company lines — can't have the officers' quarters exposed to the eyes of these frightful Other Ranks.

That wasn't all: the cookhouse, which we had been assured in Batu would be among the best equipped in Malaya, resembled a semi-permanent field kitchen. The level of hygiene and the quality of the meals that came out of it were still appalling, as was well illustrated by the abnormally high rates of gastro-enteritis and diarrhoea in the Battalion since arriving in Kota Tinggi, all of which was diligently reported by the MO in his monthly reports to GHQ. Another black mark for Coco-Oscar.

The Battalion's reputation suffered a further blow with the cancellation of the Divisional Rifle Meeting. Apparently, this was one of the biggest events on the Malayan Army social calendar, and only FTC had both the range facilities and accommodation capacity to host the event. As the largest single unit at FTC the responsibility for organising the meet fell to the Notts & Jocks. However, having barely settled into Burma Camp, and with training for the Borneo exercise about to commence, it was all too much for Coco-Oscar and his circus clowns. The Rifle Meeting was cancelled. Yet another black mark for Coco-Oscar.

This overall mood of discontent did not appear to affect MT 'Smudge', who had recently bought himself a huge Hudson Hornet limousine, in which, for a nominal contribution to petrol costs, he took swimming parties to Lombong Falls on weekends. The limo was black, with

R A (BRAM) BRAMLEY

reputedly the widest front seat of any car in production, comfortably seating four across in the front plus another four or five in the back. With its high waist and relatively small side windows, it had the appearance of an American gangster-mobile.

Early on the Sunday morning following the Int Section's latest relocation, Dan rolled in from Seremban bragging about the battalion team's victory in the semi-final of the Far East Army Association Football Cup. The Battalion was now only one win away from actually achieving something in Malaya, even though it had nothing to do with ending the Emergency. Later in the day, to celebrate, we took off on one of Smudge's swimming parties. As we returned from the falls, I felt a splitting headache coming on that subsequently kept me awake all night. I had been feeling off-colour for most of the week with an upset stomach and had been very relieved (no pun intended) to move into our new accommodation and no longer having to queue for a shit.

On Monday morning, still with a splitting headache, the overnight codeine obtained from Johnny having not helped, I reported on Sick Parade along with 59 other Monday morning malingerers. With my temperature of 103°F, the Doc decided to send me to the MRS (Medical Reception Station) at Majedee for further examination. However, in case any more patients needed to be transferred, I had to wait until Sick Parade was over before the ambulance was allowed to depart. During this time my head felt like bursting every time I moved it. Eventually, after waiting almost four hours, I was the only patient to be transferred, but not without a further delay.

247

All set to go, I climbed into the back of the ambulance with my small pack, so what could possibly go wrong now? The ambulance wouldn't start — water in the petrol. Why was I not surprised?

Unbeknown to me, with 136 days push, I was about to embark on a medical marathon.

CHAPTER 13
HOSPITALISED

As the effects of a hefty dose of codeine wore off and I returned to consciousness, the pain in my head felt like a thousand kettle drummers were beating a tattoo on the outside, and Big Ben was boinging away on the inside in time with my heartbeat.

Tentatively opening my eyes, I took in the rust-tinged cream underside of a vehicle roof. The vehicle proved to be an ambulance and I was lying on a stretcher. There was no sign of the kettle drummers, who turned out to be monsoonal rain pounding on the roof of the vehicle. Big Ben in my head proved to be the mother of all headaches, far exceeding the pain of my worst hangover. Turning my head slowly, since any sudden movement caused intense pain behind my eyes, I noticed a uniformed person sitting on the bunk opposite. It was a RAMC medical orderly, who informed me that we were on the way to the Medical Reception Station at Majedee, where a doctor would examine me on arrival.

The medic got out to talk to the driver who had pulled off the road onto the laterite shoulder due to the storm, which had cut visibility to near zero. Left alone, I squirmed around trying to move my head into a position where it did not hurt. In so doing, I put my hand between the bunkhead and the back of the cab and grasped what felt like the barrel of a gun – a rusting Sten gun, no less.

'This yours?' I asked the medic when he returned.

'Fuck, no,' he replied. 'Where'd ya find it?' I pointed.

'Best put the fucker back,' was his response. It was nothing to do with him, and he wanted to keep it that way. So much for weapons security.

When the kettle drummers eased off, I heard the driver start the engine and attempt to get back on the road. Wheels spun, the back end of the ambulance slid down the shoulder towards the storm drain and we were bogged. Luckily, a passing tractor from the nearby rubber estate towed us back onto the road.

On arrival at Majedee, I was issued pyjamas, given more codeine and had my temperature and pulse recorded, assigned a bed and told a doctor would see me soon. 'Soon' turned out to be 20 hours later, when the resident doctor showed up for his regular morning rounds.

'Best take a look at that bloke first,' urged the patient in the adjacent bed 'Bastard kept us awake all night with his moaning and groaning.'

By this time, my headache was worse, if that was possible. I had also developed a rash, my back ached and my whole body felt stiff and tender. After examining me, the doctor dispensed yet more codeine and immediately dispatched me to BMH Singapore. On arrival, I was subjected to numerous blood tests and, when I could finally produce any, had to submit my dainty turds for examination. The real treat, though, was the lumbar puncture.

Preparing me for this, the less than sensitive male medical orderly told me with great relish:

'The Doc's going to stick a sodding great needle into your spine with no local anaesthetic so you'd better pray he hits the spot first time, or you can look forward to some real pain.'

Thankfully, the doctor was on the money first time and spared me any additional agony. My spine duly punctured, nine medicos (four lieutenants, four captains and a lieutenant-colonel) assembled at the foot of my bed but, in the manner of doctors the world over, told me nothing other than that I was 'a very interesting case and it would be interesting to see what the virologist discovered.'

The virologist's diagnosis was that I was a victim of *Aedes aegypti*, and had contracted dengue fever which, in turn, had brought on aseptic meningitis (inflammation of the membrane covering the brain and spinal cord). The outcome was that I was prescribed total bed rest to minimise the risk of inflammation of what passed for my brain, supplemented by regular aspirin and pethidine injections. The upside was the alluring bevy of QARANC (Queen Alexandra's Royal Army Nursing Corps) and civilian nurses at my beck and call, attending to (almost) my every need. Even the male orderly who had prepared me for the lumbar puncture showed a little more empathy when he removed the dressing from my back enabling me to enjoy the luxury of a hot bath for the first time since Christmas.

'Gonna come and scrub my back?' I invited the nurse who delivered my bath towel. No response: caring as

251

they were, the nurses were immune to salacious advances from impecunious National Servicemen.

In the week that followed I lay in bed diligently obeying orders by exerting myself as little as possible and enjoying the meals brought to my bedside which, compared with meals back at camp, were gourmet standard. Gradually, the rash subsided, the overall aches and the severity of the headaches began to diminish and the pain behind my eyes became less acute. During this time all I had to do was lie there, partake in the bedside NAAFI service to the extent my meagre funds would allow; be gracious to the kindly WVS ladies who visited the ward offering to play (respectable) games with patients; and, when my headaches subsided, borrow books from the Red Cross library trolley.

My first weekend in hospital, I was surprised to have a visit from Dan and Sammy the Squeak, who gleefully informed me that I would be on a fizzer when I got back.

'How come?' I asked.

'Malaria, mate, self-inflicted illness, not been taking your Paludrine tablets.'

'I don't have malaria, Sammy, I've got dengue fever. Paludrine doesn't work against dengue, so you can tell Rocky or whoever where they can stick their charge.'

Enquiring why Trev wasn't with them, I was told he had reported sick the day after me, with a stomach upset much like I'd had initially. The following day, after becoming feverish and vomiting, he too had been sent to the MRS.

Another luxury in the ward was the headphones that enabled me to listen to the wireless whenever I pleased, without disturbing others. This allowed me to listen late at night to the commentary of the FA Cup Final won by my home team, Nottingham Forest[75]. As soon as I could concentrate sufficiently to write a letter home, I offhandedly mentioned that I was in hospital with meningitis, quite oblivious to how serious it could be (despite the pain I had suffered). Little did I know the alarm and consternation this would cause on the home front. The first I knew of parental distress was seeing Pop Homan, whom I had not seen since my early days at FTC, striding along the ward accompanied by his wife.

'How on earth did you know I was in hospital?' I asked.

'Your father sent us a telegram asking us to check up on you,' said Mrs Homan.

'Well, you can tell them I'm over the worst of it and on the mend,' I said, trying to downplay how sick I had been, but no doubt they'd heard the full story from the doctors.

'Can we bring you anything?' Pop asked.

'A few Tigers (beers) would be good,' I said. Pop laughed.

---

[75] In that pre-substitute era, Forest was the only team to ever win the FA Cup after losing a man to injury, holding out for a 2-1 victory over Luton Town after losing Roy Dwight with a broken leg in the 33rd minute.

'I'd never get them past the Matron,' he replied. Suitably re-assured after a catch-up conversation, they left to re-port back to my parents.

Later, I discovered via 'Sputnik', one of the Orderly Room clerks, who paid me a surprise mid-week visit when he was at the hospital for a medical appointment, that my father had also contacted his pre-war rugby team-mate, the self-same Colonel of the Nottingham TA Battalion who had orchestrated my 'compassionate leave' to play rugby during basic training. He, in turn, contacted the CO of the Regimental Depot who tele-grammed Coco-Oscar, urgently requesting news of my state of health. According to 'Sputnik' the telegram gal-vanised Coco-Oscar into action.

'Who is this man?' he had demanded, bursting into the Orderly Room, and waving the telegram in the face of the Company Orderly Sergeant, evidently having forgot-ten he'd had almost daily contact with me in Tac HQ during the time we had spent on operations.

'Bring me his service record,' was his next demand.

Given his opinion that 'the private soldier has no person-ality', it was no surprise that I had failed to register on his consciousness. Nonetheless, once having ascertained my identity, he was on the phone to BMH Singapore de-manding details of the condition of one of his valuable soldiers.

Suitable reassurances were transmitted back home from the Homans, who had witnessed that I was still extant, and from the CO of the hospital, as confirmed to me by the civilian ward sister. Eventually, Coco-Oscar added his own authoritative confirmation that I was receiving good care and recovering well, so it had to be true. The Sister in charge also assured me that meningitis was no longer as serious as it once was, and that I'd had only a mild form, with no danger of permanent after-effects. She also advised me that the following week I would be transferred to the cooler, higher altitude Cameron Highlands for convalescence.

Much as I was enjoying my sojourn in female company — such a fantastic change after so long in an all-male, military environment — the downside was no beer. To remedy this, I had to become an 'up-patient', which entitled me to a free daily bottle of beer. However, despite being denied beer, my spirits were lifted when, after ten days in hospital, I received my first pay in almost three weeks, delivered by the Padre on a pastoral visit. Apparently, it was only when the hospital sent for my medical and pay records that it came to light that my 18-month reclassification pay rise, effective from 12 March when we were still in Batu Pahat, had yet to be posted on Battalion Orders. It was now mid-May and, with the gee-up from the hospital, my reclassification was finally posted, so not only did I receive two weeks' pay but also my pay increase, back-dated to March. Having handed over this largesse, the Padre then had the hide to tap me up for a donation to some army charity. He was out of luck.

'I am a charity case,' I told him.

After two weeks I was deemed healthy enough to be declared an 'up-patient' in preparation for my transfer to the Cameron Highlands. On the way to the hospital admin office to get my transfer papers signed, I bumped

255

into Satch who told me that, after three days bedrest in MRS Majedee, Trev had made a full recovery and was back at camp, fit and well.

The day before my transfer to the Cameron Highlands Captain Kelly, my primary doctor, discussed my condition with me advising that my latest blood test and stools were normal, and that the hospital CO had again written to my parents confirming this. Up early the next morning I boarded a bus to RAF Changi along with matelot from the same ward was also being transferred. At Changi, we boarded an RNZAF (Royal New Zealand Air Force) Bristol Freighter, a twin-engine workhorse fondly known as the 'Bristol Frightener'[76] and sat in rear-facing canvas seats. Minutes later the Captain and First Officer boarded, both wearing one-piece coveralls open to the navel. 'Flying time to KL a bit over an hour, weather clear all the way, but just keep your seat belts fastened,' was the cryptic pre-flight briefing from the captain as he passed us on his way to the cockpit.

We taxied to the end of the runway, where the captain wound up each engine in turn. The plane rattled and shook as if it was on the point of falling apart, the noise deafening and the fumes toxic. But this was nothing compared to when both engines were powered up together and we set off along the runway. This was my first experience of flying, and I was having serious doubts as

---

[76] Bristol Freighters were still in service with the RNZAF until 1975, when the New Zealand High Commissioner was flown out of Vietnam on one on the last flight out of Saigon in April 1975!

to whether we would get airborne. Eventually we did, labouring up to our cruising altitude as if we were flying through cotton wool rather than cloud. Reaching cruising level, the noise was still ear-splitting and, even though we scarcely seemed to be moving, we actually arrived at KL in 'a bit over an hour' as predicted. Here we picked up a few more patients and, after another hour's flying, I was back in familiar territory, Ipoh.

From the airfield we were taken by bus to the railway station to pick up a group of Aussies and Kiwis recently arrived by train from BMH Taiping before setting off for the Cameron Highlands. The winding mountain road was a succession of tortuous hairpins and Z-bends with sheer drops on one side and cliff-faces on the other — great ambush country.

On arrival at the hospital, we were served tea before drawing our hospital clothing. By the time we had changed, it was time for dinner, overseen by a most prim and proper matron who recited 'Grace' before allowing us to be seated. We were served by Malay waiters and, apart from having to make our beds and bump the floor every morning, it was little different from staying in a hotel. To us the food was Michelin standard, even better than hospital food in Singapore. Unlike the surly, 'couldn't give a stuff' attitude of our regimental cooks, the hospital cooks took great pride in their cooking and, every mealtime, the Cook Corporal came around to check that everything was satisfactory. Portions were generous and the quantity of meat in the mixed grill served for *tiffin* on our first Saturday equalled, if not exceeded, our total meagre daily meat ration at Kota Tinggi.

Unlike BMH Singapore, where 'up-patients' received a beer each night, this hospital was totally 'dry', in that we were not allowed any alcohol, and were forbidden to drink when we went into the township, which we were encouraged to do. Despite it being a hospital, Paludrine seemed to be optional with tablets left on the dining table in a jar along with salt tablets — perhaps *Anopheles* mosquitoes were not endemic at this elevation?

Situated nearly 5,000 feet above sea level, the weather in the Highlands was several degrees cooler in the day and much less humid than at sea level. In the evening the drop in temperature came as a surprise and the sweaters issued to us were definitely needed. Five blankets were none too many, and the early mornings were like waking up on a chilly autumn morning in England. The vegetation too was more characteristic of temperate rather than tropical climes and, with many of the houses built of brick or stone, the settlement almost had the aura of the English Lake District. The hospital itself overlooked the main township and had been a convent before being converted into a military hospital by the Japanese during World War II.

After feeling pretty creased the day after our arrival, I had more energy on the second day and, together with my new Royal Navy mate, Roy, with whom I had travelled up from Singapore, we began exploring the environs. The main settlement was quite small; a dozen or so cafes and assorted stores and, being something of a hill station holiday destination, there were several gift shops. Numerous bungalows and a few hotels were dotted around the hillsides for holidaymakers, and there was an

R A (BRAM) BRAMLEY

Army Leave Centre in the village. Afternoon walks soon
became the routine because, if you stayed in the hospital,
the nurses would constantly chivvy you out into the fresh
air anyway. Roy and I soon teamed up with an Aussie
and a Kiwi for our walks. Bert, the Aussie, had only a
month to push and was totally demob-happy. Wattie, the
Kiwi, was Maori and led our search for an out-of-the-
way bar. Out together in our varied headwear; Roy in his
naval rating's round hat, Wattie in his Kiwi cap, Bert
wearing his slouch hat and me in my beret, we were
readily identifiable and styled ourselves the 'Fearsome
Foursome'. Between us, the illnesses we were recovering from were just as diverse as our headwear – scrub
typhus, tinea, jaundice, dengue fever and meningitis.

But it wasn't our headwear that gave us away when the
temptation of an illicit beer got the better of us, it was
our white hospital shirts. Before we had even finished
our first clandestine beers we were startled to see a Military Police Land Rover pull up outside. Out jumped the
Hospital Provost Sergeant.

'Right lads, on your feet, hop in the back of the vehicle
and I'll take you back for a nice cup of tea — after I've
charged you!'

How the hell had they got onto us so fast? Unbeknown
to us, what we thought was an out-of-the-way bar was
on the Hospital Commandant's route from his home to
the hospital. On his way back to work that afternoon, he
had spotted our white hospital shirts as we were being
served our first beers. Parading on Orders in the morning
we pleaded ignorance, claiming the relevant page of the
dog-eared copy of Hospital Regulations which we had

259

been given was missing, and escaped with being admonished. Thereafter, the 'Fearsome Foursome' tried to keep a low profile: Bert, because he was so close to demob and Wattie, who didn't want to ruin his chances of being granted leave when he returned to his unit by having a charge recorded on his hospital record.

As for the other patients, the Aussies and Kiwis were all sports-mad and spent most of their days using the tennis and badminton courts within the hospital grounds or out golfing or horse-riding. For hospital patients, they all seemed to be remarkably healthy and, it transpired, not without ingenuity. It was the golfers who cracked the solution to the drinking ban. They bought bottles of rum in the village, secreted them in their golf bags, and bought bottles of chilled Coca-Cola at the golf clubhouse to take around the course for refreshment.

In the evenings entertainment consisted of card games, table tennis or snooker or the cinema. Here, even the films took on an Aussie flavour with the showing of *The Shiralee* starring Peter Finch. After the cinema it was a glass of Ovaltine and off to bed — a truly sober and temperate life.

Over the two weeks I learnt a little more about some of my fellow patients. Roy, the matelot had joined the Navy at 15, served on eight different ships in seven years and had certainly been around — visiting many European countries as well as Cyprus, Ceylon, Singapore, Hong Kong, Japan, New Zealand and Australia. He had served in the Suez crisis and was aboard the last British warship to leave the Canal Zone before the UN Force took over, almost being impounded by the UN for overstaying in

Port Said as they waited to pick up a missing Army officer.

Another compelling character I came to know was Corporal Rangi Tataura (Sam) Christie, a Maori, on his second tour of Malaya after also serving in Korea. Sam was a huge slab of a man[77] who had skippered the 1NZR team I'd watched defeat 3RAR in the Merdeka Cup final in Ipoh. It was our shared interest in rugby that brought us together, especially with the British and Irish Lions about to tour New Zealand. He was a tough nut: after running away from home at the age of ten, he had lived with his grandparents, did a spell in Borstal, and had been a fisherman, farmhand and sheep shearer before joining the Army and, according to the other Kiwis, was quite possibly the unluckiest man never to have pulled on an All Black jersey[78].

The start of my second week saw the arrival of 'Yorky', a six-foot-three New Zealand Military Police Corporal, who was scarcely sober from the moment he arrived with

---

[77] Sam was recuperating from malaria and, according to another Kiwi, had walked ten thousand yards out of the *ulu* after contracting the fever.

[78] He had played Ranfurly Shield-level rugby for several provinces. Early in his career he'd missed an All Black trial due to a broken leg. He missed playing against the 1950 British and Irish Lions due to what he described as 'a bung knee'. Finally, in 1957, having been selected to skipper the Maori XV in an All Black trial match, he was prevented from playing because his battalion was due to sail for Malaya a few days before, and his CO would not release him to play.

a bottle of rum stashed in his backpack. His attempt to convince the Australian Sister that he was affected by the altitude rather than by rum was met with total ridicule on her part.

Following the arrival of Yorky, the illicit drinking, especially by the Kiwis, stepped up appreciably. After the golf club manager had banned them for drinking on the course, they resorted to local bars and were charged after being caught drinking in the village two days in a row. Appearing on orders next morning, Yorky baffled the presiding officer, a British Sergeant-Major, with the finer points of New Zealand Military Law and somehow got them all off.

Despite the amount of grog the Kiwis put away, none of them ever appeared unduly drunk. Possibly, this apparent tolerance for alcohol could be attributed to the infamous 'six o'clock swill', then current in New Zealand and Australia, when the bars closed at six every night and men had to squeeze in as many drinks as they could between leaving work and closing time. The Fearsome Foursome were not exactly innocent regarding illicit grogging either. On the second Monday of our stay our circumspect approach was abandoned when Bert spotted a couple of sergeants from his battalion, who were taking a few days leave. They invited us back to their hotel[79], where I was introduced to another excellent Aussie brew – Fosters Export.

---

[79] In the Notts & Jocks, or any other British regiment for that matter, it was quite unthinkable that a pair of sergeants would invite ORs to share a drink with them in their hotel.

That was the start of a ruinous afternoon's drinking. When we returned to hospital in our drunken state, the lovely, and normally solicitous, Sinhalese Night Sister revealed her less lovely side. On her rounds next morning the puritanical Matron gave us another severe tongue lashing. Realising that our escapades had ruined any chance of extending our stay in the Highlands — bed numbers were limited and in great demand — we stayed off the booze that day.

The morning prior to my scheduled return to Singapore I underwent my final medical checks which revealed that I had returned to health and had regained most of the weight lost while bedridden in Singapore. That afternoon the Foursome set off on our final stroll together. On our way to the river, we passed the Kiwi 'Scenic Appreciation Society', innocently sitting in a park shelter, quietly sipping Cokes and admiring the view. Not so innocent was the rum in the Cokes they were drinking, obtained from a nearby bar. Soon after we had seen them, they were spotted by the MPs. Their Coke bottles were checked for alcohol and they were charged again. Due to appear on Hospital Orders the following morning, Yorky was again primed to plead their case but, with an early departure, I never knew whether his defence stood up a second time.

Departure day saw us transferred by truck to a waiting bus for our ride down the mountain to Ipoh where Roy and I shared a couple of farewell drinks with Wattie before flying back to Singapore. After landing at Changi, we were transferred back to BMH Singapore, and re-admitted for a period of observation and more blood tests.

Despite having felt so healthy the previous day, once more the journey had utterly drained me and, after barely sleeping that night, I woke with a headache when roused for up-patient duties, and was still feeling sickly when examined by Captain Kelly later that morning.

'I'll run some more blood tests,' he said, concerned over the recurrence of my headache following the journey, 'but, if they're normal, you'll be discharged on Tuesday and confined to Light Duties for two weeks when you return to your unit.'

It turned out that my return to Singapore coincided with a momentous week in Singaporean history. The 1958 Constitution, had vested full internal governing powers to the Singapore Government with the exception of matters of internal security and defence. Saturday, 30 May 1959, was the first General Election in which all members of the Singaporean Parliament were to be elected by Singaporeans (rather than a minority being appointed by the British government).

In view of the vocal anti-British and anti-colonialist rhetoric of David Marshall, the former leader of the Labour Front, and the vehemently anti-Communist campaign of Lim Yew Hock, leader of the Singapore People's Alliance, unrest and even rioting, was anticipated. Virtually every military vehicle on the island had been augmented with anti-riot mesh over all windows and around the backs of lorries. As it turned out these precautions proved to be unnecessary as the election was conducted in an orderly manner, with the People's Action Party (PAP) winning a landslide majority of 43 of the 51 seats, but with a less decisive majority of the votes.

264

The Monday after the election, the Governor, Sir William Goode, invited Lee Kuan Yew to form a government. On Wednesday, 3 June, Lim Yew Hock resigned as Chief Minister and the 1958 Constitution took full effect by proclamation of the outgoing Governor, Sir William Goode. Following that, Goode was sworn in as the first Yang di-Pertuan Negara[80] and, in this new capacity, he installed Lee Kuan Yew[81] as Singapore's first Prime Minister on 5 June 1959.

Post-election Sunday was a quiet day in the hospital, but not so outside, where election victory celebrations were in full swing. Sunday also saw the arrival of the Notts & Jocks in Singapore, prior to embarking for the Borneo exercise the following day. Meanwhile, across the Causeway, equally momentous events were taking place with the death of the Sultan of Johore and the declaration of three days mourning throughout the State.

Around this time I learnt a little about the ship that would carry the Battalion to Borneo from an American patient. A sailor from the USS *Lenawee*, a World War II vintage ship, he told me that the bunks onboard were six tiers high and the sleeping quarters were like an oven. Not a pleasant prospect, especially as Uncle Sam's Navy was 'dry'.

---

[80] Yang di-Pertuan Negara (literally Head of State), was constitutionally only the **de facto Head of State.**

[81] This was to be the beginning of unbroken PAP rule to this day and the Lee family dynasty with Lee Kuan Yew and his son, Lee Hsien Loong, serving as Prime Minister for a total of 45 years.

The other news was that the lads had been put through intense training for the exercise at the end of which Coco Oscar had given the Battalion one of his morale boosting pep talks, telling them how much tougher they were than the US Marines and how they were going to show the Americans what real soldiering was. Reportedly, Coco's pep-talk only succeeded in causing mirth among our lads and raising the ire of the American Marine Demo Team who were within earshot. Not one of the crew-cut 'all-American' Demo Team was less than six feet tall and all were solidly built compared with the scrawny build of many of our squaddies, like Joe Belly. That is not to say our scrawny blokes might not have been better suited to spending four days living in cramped trenches right on the Equator when they arrived in Borneo.

By Monday morning my headaches were no better (and could no longer be attributed to nauseous fumes of the Bristol Freighter). Captain Kelly cancelled my discharge and said that if there was no improvement, he would have to order more blood tests and, joy of joys, another lumbar puncture, which he duly did.

By Wednesday, I was still an up-patient but continued to feel unwell with an elevated temperature and pulse rate, so I took to my bed once again. Here I remained until the following day, not wanting to get up and trigger another bout of headaches. Unfortunately, this was the day when the hospital CO did his weekly rounds. On finding my most recent blood test and lumbar puncture results were normal, he ordered my discharge on Saturday. This came as a shock as I felt nowhere near as well as I had when I left the Cameron Highlands but, as far as the hospital CO was concerned, if my results were normal, how I felt was not going to change anything — he was not having any malingerers in his hospital. My hospital sojourn was over.

Come Saturday, Nate, one of our signals corporals and I spent the morning being given the run around trying to get our discharge clearance forms signed. Being the weekend, officers with the necessary authority were thin on the ground and it took until after midday to collect all the requisite signatures and arrange transport back to Kota Tinggi.

Back to Burma Camp with 55 days left in the Fed and an ocean cruise to survive.

CHAPTER 14
DEMOB HAPPY

With the Battalion still in Borneo, Nate and I arrived back to an almost deserted camp. Dan and Murph, who been spared Borneo for football training in the lead-up to the FARELF Army Cup Final, were the only mates to be found. Being Saturday, I had to scour the camp to find a storeman to open the unattended Company Stores to retrieve my kit and draw some bedding. Luckily for me Dan managed to round up a REME mechanic with a car to ferry me and my kit back to the *basha* because I was breathless just hauling my mattress up the steps to the road.

News from the BHQ *wallahs* in the NAAFI that evening was that the long-promised Britannia demob flights back to Britain were unlikely to commence for some months so the troopship sailing programme up to early August was unchanged. This meant that the 5717 Intake would not be flying home as we'd feared but would depart on the TT *Empire Fowey* on 31 July. Returning to the *basha* that night I updated my *Punch* demob calendar, now down to double digits — only 55 days and an early breakfast left in the Fed.

On Monday, I had the office to myself and was able to skive unmolested all day. With the MO in Borneo, it was not until Tuesday that I was able to go on Sick Parade to report my discharge from hospital to a hungover-looking Major Harris who seemed to have been enjoying Mess life more in the absence of Coco-Oscar and his syco-phants. After skipping through the hospital report he dis-missed me without, as I was soon to learn, entering my Light Duties status in the Sick Book.

CSM Morgan, however, had been alerted to my return because the following day I was rostered on for guard duty. Right after Muster Parade, I hot-footed it to Mor-gan's office to inform him I was on Light Duties and therefore excused guard duties.

'Not in the Sick Book,' he said, 'too bad!'

This sent me scurrying back to the MI Room. After ex-plaining the situation to Doc Harris, he signed a note cer-tifying that I was on Light Duties for 14 days dating it that day rather than the date I was discharged from hos-pital. This gave me an extra five days on Light Duties — how lucky that proved to be only became apparent later. With only 100 or so personnel in camp from which to select the Guard and Fire Picquet, an irate Morgan had no alternative but to take me off guard duty, but had his requital by rostering me on the Fire Picquet instead.

With no choice, I paraded at 7:45 am next morning to find two of the rostered picquet were out of camp on other duties and four of those remaining, including me, were on light duties. We all refused to roll out hoses so the fire drill was a total farce. How big a farce became apparent later that morning: a series of violent thunder-storms overnight with deafening thunder and lightning and near-cyclonic winds had damaged the camp's elec-trical system putting the fire pumps out of action and disabling two of the camp's water-supply pumps. Ironically, in the midst of this torrential rain, water restrictions were imposed throughout the camp due to the damaged water pumps, but at least the storm had reduced the temperature and the humidity.

Being on Light Duties I quickly learnt that, in the eyes of officers and senior NCOs, Light Duties was regarded as nothing more than a skive, even if you had been in hospital for six weeks. Consequently, it was a constant battle to assert my medical status and be excused regular duties. Although I felt well enough generally, I had no stamina at all and, after the Cameron Highlands, I found the heat and humidity at sea level totally enervating. The first few days back at camp had been extremely hot, and walking up the hill to the cookhouse left me breathless: a trip that was hardly worthwhile anyway because the food had not improved in my absence, so I reverted to my diet of *char-wallah* egg banjos for breakfast and NAAFI- *gorengs* at night.

Other changes I found on my return were that Sid Twort was no longer acting RSM but his rank had had been officially confirmed; Major Rocky was moving on, and Nickelhead was to be seconded to an interim posting with the Singapore Military Forces[82] — lucky them! I also learnt of the current panic sweeping the officer ranks: the belated discovery that most of the Battalion's National Servicemen were coming up for demob. All but five of the Signals Platoon were due for release before the end of the year, 13 of them from the 5717 Intake due

---

[82] Predecessor of the Singapore Armed Forces

to sail on 31st July. In response to this crisis, Coco-Oscar instructed the RSO to speak to all the National Service-men in the Signals Platoon and encourage them to sign on. Well aware that there was no more committed band of demob-conscious conscripts in the whole battalion, the RSO did not waste his breath.

The following Monday the Borneo warriors returned, full of American slang and loaded with Yank cigarettes, rations and souvenirs. It turned out that the exercise had been so simple that even the Notts & Jocks were able to complete all of their assigned objectives on the day they landed. With three days allotted for these assignments, more tasks had to be conjured up on the spur of the mo-ment. As for the US troopship accommodation, the sleeping decks were sweltering as predicted by my American hospital companion, but the onboard food more than made up for the heat. Copious quantities of chicken, ham, steak and freshly baked bread, liquid ra-ther than powdered milk, even grapefruit juice and strawberries were freely available. In addition, there were Coke machines onboard and coffee and iced water was on tap day and night, unlike the Notts & Jocks cook-house where it was lemonade **or** coffee at meal times only.

According to Trev, American equipment, mobility and efficiency were streets ahead of ours. Despite British mockery at the apparent laxity of American discipline, the Americans had a bulldozer and crane ashore and had built a road up the beach before our Gurkha RE Squad-ron had landed their bulldozer on the beach. When the exercise concluded, the Yanks, using 16 helicopters, transferred a battalion of US Marines out to an aircraft carrier in a little over an hour. Their landing craft and tanks were well designed, fast and well protected in contrast to the British equipment — but the one thing the Yanks did have in common with the Brits was griping about their officers.

So simple had been the exercise that even the Notts & Jocks had failed to stuff it up but, according to Gerry, who had succeeded Acker as Coco's wireless operator, this did not prevent Coco Oscar getting into frequent flaps. Gerry also recounted that, in order to impress the Yanks, Coco would take his wireless set off him and carry it himself every time he approached a US Command Post or detachment. Once out of sight, Gerry got the wireless set back again. This added credence to the tale told by Coco's batman of him carrying a battery-less wireless when leading his first route march after taking command of the battalion in Germany.

After the exercise, the US Admiral sent a message declaring the joint exercise a great success and that 'the US Marines would be honoured to serve beside such a fine fighting force under their outstanding CO anytime, anywhere.' This message was posted on Battalion Orders, along with a congratulatory message from Coco himself, declaring that all the returning participants could have the day off as a reward. What he failed to say was that day was a military holiday throughout Malaya in honour of the King's birthday[83]. Not surprisingly, with the

---

[83] Malaya (later Malaysia) is a constitutional monarchy with a monarch, the King, or Yang di-Pertuan Agong,

exercise having been a 'dry' event, the NAAFI was well patronised that night.

This free day was followed by a black day for me. In preparation for taking command of HQ Company on Rocky's departure, Captain Sherry was carrying out an accommodation inventory and I was the bunny given the task of fetching and delivering the keys to different huts. The first couple of times, I slung him up a smart salute which passed without any kind of acknowledgement. On both these occasions the keys the storeman had given me to deliver were the wrong ones. By the time of my third key delivery Sherry was beginning to get exasperated so, when I failed to salute him, he snapped.

'Don't you salute your officers, Private?'

'I already did, sir,' I replied, 'twice.' (big mistake, I was in a hole)

'Don't backchat me!' he thundered.

'I wasn't, sir.' (the hole got deeper)

'And don't contradict me. You salute an officer every time before you address him.'

Keen to escape his presence, and genuinely wanting to appear helpful, I replied,

---

elected as Head Of State by the nine rulers of the Malay States and is one of the very few elected monarchies in the world.

'Righto sir, is that all, sir?' I'd expressed myself poorly and Sherry took my answer the wrong way. (I'd reached the bottom of the pit)

Turning to the corporal with the clipboard accompanying him, he said, 'Corporal, charge this man with insubordination.'

Turning back to me he barked, 'Now, **you**, fall out, take these useless keys back to the QM store and **bring me back the right ones**,' as if it was my fault that I'd been given the wrong keys.

'Yes, sir!' I replied, saluting snappily, and fell out.

On Orders before Rocky the following morning Sherry gave evidence, saying I was arrogant, insolent, slovenly, idle and always looking for trouble. Coming from him that was rich. Even in the best of moods he was a bombastic, arrogant, conceited bully. That morning, he was in a particularly foul mood. Despite pointing out in my defence that I was still recovering from six weeks in hospital and was still on Light Duties, I was sentenced to seven days jankers. The one compensating factor was that, thanks to Doc Harris post-dating my period of Light Duties, they covered the whole seven days. This meant the Provos couldn't run me around at the double in full kit, or put me on work details, all I had to do was show up five times a day, with both myself and my kit looking immaculate. For once, this justified the cost of paying for private *dhobi* to get my best OGs starched and pressed to the point where they almost stood up on their own. The second bad news of the day was that our sailing date had been put back five days, so days to do in the Fed had jumped back up from 44 to 49.

Although not a great day for me, my first day on default-ers coincided with a red-letter-day for the Battalion. The football team had won the Final of the FARELF Army Association Football Cup, defeating the RAPC after extra time in Singapore. Coco-Oscar was beside himself, at last the Battalion had achieved some kind of success — nothing whatsoever to do with defeating Chin Peng and the MNLA, but what did that matter? According to Dan, Coco did his utmost to appear in all the team photographs with the Cup but, annoyingly for him, he did not appear in the photo published in the *Straits Times* the following day.

Not to be denied being photographed with his victorious team, the players were reassembled after Dan returned from playing for the Combined Services in Kedah. More photographs were taken with both the FARELF Army Cup and the 17 Gurkha Division Cup on display, with Coco-Oscar seated front and centre. That was the pinnacle of his Battalion's accomplishments during its Far East tour of duty and there was no chance of an encore the following season. The team's eight National Service-men were due for demob by year's end and the remaining three Regulars early in the new year. At one fell swoop the Jockstrap Platoon was disbanded and the players went back to their regular duties — the jubilation was over.

On his return to camp after the football final, Murph was not a happy boy. Originally scheduled to sail with us on the *Empire Fowey* on 31 July, the delayed sailing date meant he would not arrive in Britain before his demob date. Fearing that he would be flown home, and therefore condemned to an extra three weeks in Burma Camp, he was overjoyed when the REME secured him a berth on the TT *Nevasa*, due to sail on 10 July.

My week on defaulters was not without its moments. The first night on Staff Parade, Lieutenant Duff-Cannonier, the Orderly Officer, ordered the duty Provo to 'Parade the criminals on the veranda!' (who did he think he was, the Governor of a gaol?) On my last night the Orderly Officer was Captain Pavior in an extremely picky mood. On Staff Parade he ordered all 16 defaulters to parade in the pouring rain on the road under the newly installed lights, so that he could examine both us and our kit in a better light. Inspecting my kit Pavior ordered me to display the contents of my 'housewife'[84] which was found to be lacking any cotton thread.

'Where's your sewing cotton?' he demanded (all used up sewing buttons on greatcoats, if you must know). Desperate to avoid another charge, I recalled my 'boots without laces' incident during Rocky's inspection back in April and took a chance.

'QM's got none in stock, sir.' I replied, fervently hoping this was the case should he check — charge averted! Barring any unforeseen calamity, this was my last ever defaulters' parade.

Having been barred from the NAAFI for seven days whilst on jankers, I was looking forward to a couple of beers the following night, especially as it was pay day. CSM Morgan had other ideas. He had diligently noted

---

[84] Housewife – soldier's sewing kit.

my Light Duties ended the exact same day I came off jankers and he rostered me on guard duty the following night. Still troubled by occasional headaches, this called for another attendance on Sick Parade. No joy there: the MO did not extend my period of Light Duties, only dispensing more aspirin for my recurring headaches.

During my enforced absence from the NAAFI, a new record had been added to the jukebox – *Everyday*, by Buddy Holly – and already the opening lines had become the demob theme for the 5717 Intake:

Everyday it's a-gettin' closer,

Goin' faster than a roller coaster . . .

If the song was not playing when a member of the 5717 Intake entered the NAAFI, it was obligatory for the first arrival to select it.

The day after my guard duty, I wasted no time heading to Singapore for the weekend. Dining with the Homans on Sunday evening, I caught up with post-election politics in Singapore. Despite the fears of the pessimists, there were no signs of Singapore becoming a police state. The Government was continuing its efforts to avoid showing any overt allegiance to the West, adopting the prevalent 'sitting on the fence' attitude of other post-colonial countries like India. The PAP government seemed anxious to promote goodwill with the Federation, and there was much talk of greater cooperation between the Singaporean and Malayan Governments.

Domestically, the new Government appeared keen to set its own house in order, with big drives against gangs and secret societies and, more especially, the dreaded

'Yellow Culture' — long hair on men was banned, as were pornographic publications and films, striptease shows and rock 'n' roll music. This included juke boxes, which had been banned everywhere even in the Union Jack and Britannia Clubs. Concurrently, the government was seeking to promote healthy cultural activities focusing on forging a stronger common Peranakan[85] culture.

Returning to camp after the weekend the hot news was that the accelerating rundown of National Servicemen between July and Christmas was now causing serious alarm among the senior ranks. Of the 39 men of 5717 Intake who had been posted to the Battalion, 30 were in specialist jobs in HQ company, 13 of them wireless operators, and there were no Regular soldiers in the new drafts trained to replace them. The Signals Platoon would be reduced to 11 men by December, 35 below strength, and even some of those were due for demob early in 1960. The MT Platoon was not much better off and would have only 16 drivers by the year end. The QM and PRI had requested that their key men (mostly from the 5717 Intake) be held back as long as possible as 'essentially employed', and only flown home immediately prior to demob.

Already one man below strength since Osbert's transfer to 63 Brigade, Captain Pavior would need three new Intelligence clerks by early August but, for reasons that

---

[85] The Peranakans, or Peranakan Chinese, are a sub-ethnic group defined by their genealogical descent from the first waves of Chinese settlers in the Malay Peninsula and Indonesian Archipelago.

became obvious later, he showed no inclination to hold me and Trev back to help train newly arrived Regular soldiers. He did, however, detail me to try my hand at technical drawing, to provide a scaled, cross-section of a 120 mm Mobat[86] round for an upcoming Anti-Tank Cadre. This was my final, crowning masterpiece in the Int Section. It required great care to avoid smudges from sweaty forearms and dripping perspiration in our stinking hot, fan-less office, taking three days with ample breaks to allow ink to dry. I thought it looked most impressive but, no, it wasn't good enough. More colour was needed and more stencilled detail so it was back to the drawing board.

Although my drafting skills were showing promise, my writing skills apparently did not conform to Army requirements. On a release form I had signed I had failed to confine my signature within the 'box, signature for the purpose of'. Kaz, of course, couldn't resist berating me for this act of non-compliance.

'They should make the box bigger, Sarge,' I said, trying to wind him up but he did not bite.

Wednesday that week, however, proved to be a momentous day. On Battalion Part 1 Order No. 126, appeared the following order:

5.   *R.H.E. PERS EMBARKING ON TT "EMPIRE*
       FOWEY"

---

[86] The Mobat was a 120 mm calibre recoilless anti-tank gun

The following pers will depart this location on 5th August 59 on movement to U.K. for release, Move Order No 2 will be complied with:

23418855 PTE BRAMLEY, R. (+ 38 others)

('Hoo-fucking-ray!')

Friday brought more welcome news that all personnel sailing on 5th August should report for pre-release medicals on 9th July. The release process was finally under way and I was summoned to be measured up for my going-home battledress.

After that, it was off to Singapore on a 48-hour leave pass to celebrate Murph's last weekend in FARELF. On the drive back to Kota Tinggi our driver, 'Brummie George', was stopped by the MPs for speeding. This came as no surprise since George was 'Ton-up Trev's' closest challenger for the title of the Battalion's craziest driver. George's greatest claim to fame though came during the following week, not for his driving but for his command of the English language. Having set off for Singapore early in the morning on the ration run, he returned on foot an hour or so later. Walking into the MT yard, he was accosted by the MT Sergeant:

'George, where's your fuckin' lorry?'

With admirable brevity, using only different forms of a single word, George replied,

'Fuckin' fucker's fucked, Sarge.' (what further explanation was needed?)

For Trev and I our first priority back in camp on Monday was to confirm our final leave, scheduled to begin the following Friday. I trotted along to the Orderly Room to see the Monk, another of the 5717 Intake who, despite Henry Ford's antipathy towards him, had certainly picked up a few tips on how to fiddle leave records. According to the Monk's leave records Dan, Trev, Johnny and I were entitled to a full two weeks leave — somewhat in excess of our actual entitlement. The Monk, however, would be long gone before this was discovered so, thanks to the Monk, 16 of my last 30 days in FARELF would now be spent on leave in Singapore.

Later that week I was sent to BMH Singapore for my final examination by Captain Kelly, my treating dengue/meningitis specialist. After a thorough examination, Kelly declared himself well-pleased with my state of health, strongly advising me to have all the particulars of my illness recorded on my release documents. He also advised that I now had lifelong immunity from the particular strain of dengue I had contracted but, if I contracted another variant it could develop into the more severe dengue haemorrhagic fever and be life threatening — thanks a lot, Doc, the price of serving the nation!

On my return to Burma Camp, I underwent a further exhaustive pre-release medical examination by the Battalion MO. After noting my dengue fever and meningitis details on my medical record in case of any delayed after-effects, he declared me fit for release. Armed with my leave pay, received that day, I declared I was also fit

for Murph's farewell. We took over the small bar in the NAAFI, appointed a treasurer for the kitty, and settled in for some serious drinking. Songs were called for, so

Johnny and I led off with *We are from Roedean, good girls are we,* and the festivities never looked back.

Next morning, obliging to the end, Murph gave us a pre-dawn wake-up call before he left. I was both pleased and sorry to see him go. Pleased for him that he was on his way home early but sorry to see him leave because, since returning to Johore, he and I had become close friends and it would have been great to share the voyage home with him.

The day after Murph left was a holiday for the Battalion Sports Day – not that Dan, Trev and I took part. We spent the morning packing and handing in our bedding prior to departing on leave. Amidst all this, we had to change billets yet again to make way for the newly-formed Anti-Tank Platoon (now I knew what my Mobat drawing was needed for), who were taking over our billet. Including the move from Batu Pahat this was our fifth move in four months!

In order to complete our unexpected relocation and be ready to catch the recreation transport to Singapore we skipped *tiffin* in the cookhouse. Instead, we feasted on gash US Marine combat rations that Trev had scavenged from the supplies dumped in Borneo by the US Marines at the close of the exercise. Lucky the exercise had taken place in Borneo not Malaya — the dumped US rations would have fed a CT platoon for weeks.

During our stay in Singapore the weather was mostly overcast, not good for boosting my tan, but better for wandering around scouring the city for presents. This entailed several visits to Tang's Department Store on Orchard Road. These shopping trips were motivated not solely to purchase, and later collect newly engraved Selangor pewter, but also to ogle the Chinese floor supervisor, who filled her *cheongsam* like no other Chinese woman we'd ever seen.

'I'd crawl on my hands and knees over broken glass just to stick matches in her shit,' declared Johnny, ever ready with a lewd quip.

Later that night, we utterly lost our bearings and found ourselves in the notorious Bugis Street. Being strictly 'Out of Bounds' to Commonwealth service personnel and reputedly crawling with MPs, we had never previously ventured here to check out the 'ladyboys'. So, having found our way there by accident we settled in at a table and ordered beers. Watching the passing parade, we noticed Joe Belly disappearing into an alleyway with a tasty looking tart, so we waited to see how long his assignation would last. Well, it lasted quite a while because, by the time we had finished our beers, Joe had still not re-appeared and we'd had our fill of fending off 'girls' wanting payment to be photographed with them or their offers to partake in more carnal activities. It was time to up sticks before any MPs showed up — too close to demob to be busted or risk taking home some unwanted infection.

Encountering Joe in the UJ Club next morning the story of his night was revealed.

Waking up early the morning after with a mouth like the bottom of a parrot's cage, the first item he clapped eyes on was a pair of falsies hanging over a chairback. Further exploration of the flat-chested body lying beside him revealed appendages where he had not expected to find them. Chagrined, he was out of the bed, dressed, and hot-footing it back to the UJ Club with never a backward glance. It was only when he arrived back to the Club that he discovered his wallet was empty.

During our second week we splashed out for lunch at the Mont d'Or, a restaurant in the new Lido Cinema Complex. Here we experienced the best cuisine, served with great aplomb, in the most luxurious surroundings we had experienced since leaving Blighty. Such luxury made us feel quite prosperous, and we even looked the part when Trev produced a $50 note (the only one any of us had ever possessed) to pay the bill.

The weather on our last Saturday in Singapore had turned cool and wet and so after collecting our photographs from being developed, we headed to the Britannia Club for our last swim and, who should we find there but Sammy the Squeak. He was duly ducked several times in the pool and would have suffered a far worse fate had we known that, in our absence, he had been promoted to Lance-Corporal following Osbert's posting to Brigade. Later, we caught up with the Monk, shouting him a few beers for fudging our leave entitlements. It was at this time he confided that he was having second thoughts about entering the seminary and training for the ministry. He'd commenced his National Service as a tee-total divinity student but was knocking the beers back that night — indisputable proof that the Army drives a man to drink.

On return to Burma Camp my last full week in the Fed got off to a horror start: PT right after Reveille on Monday morning and the discovery that Sammy had been made up to Lance-Corporal. Evidently 'bubbling' and brown-nosing had its rewards. Thereafter, my last nine days in the Fed turned out to be among the most eventful of my time in Malaya.

The major scandal was that Sergeant Kaz's wife was seeking a divorce and custody of their children so she could become the second wife of their gardener in Singapore, a Malay Muslim with whom she had been sleeping. Apparently, Kaz was agreeable to the divorce but not to losing custody of the kids. The Army moved swiftly to put a stop to his wife's polygamous plans by finding her a berth on the *Empire Fowey*, the ship on which we were sailing home the following week.

The repatriation of the 5717 Intake, all 40 of us, including one on detachment in Singapore, was the largest single draft to be released since the Battalion's arrival in Malaya. The task of re-kitting us for a return to temperate climes, and ensuring we had completed and signed all the requisite forms, stretched the administrative capabilities of the Notts & Jocks to their limit. First, the QM found he had insufficient sea kitbags for everyone, and had to cajole the QM at 221 BVD to make up the shortfall. Second, there was only sufficient 37 Pattern webbing to equip half of us (although there was no shortage of blanco). The rest of us, including Trev and me, retained our 44 Pattern webbing, for which we were most thankful (no onboard blanco-ing for us, thank you very much!).

There may have been a webbing shortage but, strangely, there was an abundance of greatcoats which were re-issued to everyone — most essential since we were going

285

home to summer. Curiously, the greatcoats came with plastic GS buttons, in addition to which we were each issued with 15 brass Regimental buttons (if these had to be sewn on before we arrived back in Blighty I was in strife because I still had no cotton thread in my 'house-wife').

Tuesday morning brought an unwelcome shock. Believing that we had endured the last of RSM Twort's drill parades we found that we had to participate in the first of the newly introduced thrice weekly drill parades in preparation for imminent visits by the Commander-in-Chief, FARELF and the Colonel of the Regiment visiting from Britain. This was to be followed by a Trooping of the Colour Parade in November, all of which would happen long after Trev and I had left the Fed.

On the plus side, these parades kept us out of the office and being ordered around by the newly promoted Sammy the Squeak. With Osbert posted to Brigade, and Dan rarely present due to his footballing commitments, the workload was piling up, placing heavy demands on Sammy and compounding the matrimonial stress of Sergeant Kaz. Whenever Trev or I were given a job, we found some release formality that had to be attended to, and disappeared. The word from the rifle companies and other specialist platoons was that all their demobees had been released from work duties, but not so the Int Section.

This was when Trev and I learnt that Captain Pavior, totally exasperated with our endeavours to turn skiving into an art form, had written both of us excoriating release testimonials while we were on leave in Singapore, before going on leave himself. Even my *bete noir* Captain Sherry, now acting Company Commander, who had described me as 'arrogant, insolent, slovenly (and) idle' would not accept Pavior's references and replaced them, in my case, with the following glowing testimonial:

He has served as an Intelligence Section clerk since Jan 58. He is fairly intelligent but not very industrious. He is capable of doing a job accurately neatly and well, if supervised. Clean and well mannered. [87]

That week also saw the arrival of the first large draft to replace those of us about to be released. Having been flown out, these new recruits were whiter than white, which put our own tans into perspective. Compared with more deeply tanned lads, I was still a pale-skin, but alongside the new arrivals I looked genuinely bronzed. Thursday morning saw the draftees paraded in the shade of the veranda outside the Adjutant's office. This coincided with one of my rare spells in the adjoining Int Office. As the Adjutant was lecturing them about tropical conditions, especially heatstroke and sunburn, one of the new recruits crumpled to the ground.

'See what I mean?' observed the Toff, continuing his admonition regarding the risk of malaria, the importance of taking Paludrine, and the risk of venereal infections, etc, etc., without a pause.

---

[87] The good captain would no doubt have been astonished to learn that this 'fairly intelligent (but) not very industrious' soldier went on to obtain an honours degree from the University of Cambridge and even more astonished to learn that, later in life, he was awarded a Doctor of Philosophy.

Thursday morning saw me heading for the Armourer's Shop to stencil my sea kitbag, newly obtained from 221 BVD. The same night, Trev and Dan were rostered for guard duty. Trev was utterly incensed at copping guard duty so close to demob. He was even more incensed when Dan, whom CSM Morgan had managed to snare on one of his infrequent visits to camp, was made 'Waiting Man'. This was to enable him to depart early the following morning for yet another footballing commitment, thus sparing him the loss of a night's sleep.

Friday brought the surprise news that all the demobees had been granted a 48-hour leave pass that weekend because it was a Public Holiday. Having only just returned from leave Trev and I had little expectation of being granted a leave pass on our last weekend in the Fed. We concluded that the Adjutant and the RSM foresaw the havoc that 39 demobees, cashed up with a week's pay plus embarkation pay, could create if confined to camp over a long weekend.

Consequently, instead of slumming it in the NAAFI at Burma Camp, Friday night saw us embark on one last fling in Singapore. Before returning on the Sunday night, I met the Homans for a farewell dinner; excellent steaks, a few gins and tonic, and some lively conversation about Malaya/Singapore politics, before they drove me back to the Union Jack Club with messages to pass on to their two sons when I got home.

Back at camp we took advantage of the Monday Public Holiday having a good lie-in before breakfasting at the NAAFI. Here, to the background sound of Buddy Holly's *Every Day*, we were regaled with the story of the big camp drama over the weekend. Unknown to me while I'd been on leave in Singapore, Big Ned had returned to the Battalion having served his six months in detention for his Batu Pahat antics. His sidekick, Nog Norris, due for demob at the time of the fracas, had been returned to the UK but, since returning to camp, Ned had teamed up with another would-be hardman, 'Alf the Nutter'. After we'd left for Singapore on Friday night, the two of them had created mayhem in the 221 BVD NAAFI, beating the crap out of a couple of BVD squaddies who had made the mistake of taking them on. For this, they had been put in the Guard Room cell awaiting, in Ned's case, a possible second court-martial. On Saturday night, after serving them with their meal, one of the guards bolted the cell door but failed to replace the padlock. This omission did not go unnoticed by the prisoners. Ned was not only tall, but had abnormally long arms. Reaching down through the observation hatch, he was able to grasp the bolt, slide it back and open the cell door. He and Alf made their escape through the Guard Room, past the off-stag members of the Guard, who were either sleeping or playing dead. After their escape they rummaged through the rifle company lines for ponchos, rucksacks, *goloks* and other jungle kit, before raiding the cookhouse for food and disappearing into the *ulu*[88].

---

[88] I later heard from Chesh that Ned and Alf remained at large for over a week, evading the tracker dogs from the War Dog Wing by walking up stream beds. They were finally apprehended by the Guard, bollock-naked while taking a shower one night in the 'A' Company wash-house.

The holiday weekend culminated on Monday night when the stage was set for the 5717 Demob Party. In the main NAAFI, tables were pulled together to form a central stage, surrounded by chairs. With all demobees assembled, all dressed in T-shirts adorned with demob slogans, I was made 'Master of Ceremonies' and called up each of the lads in rotation by their home counties to do a turn. Pete Brumpton got proceedings off to a good start with his rendering of *I don't want to join the Army, I don't want to go to war* and, by the end of the night, everyone had been up on the impromptu stage to do something, even if only to show their rings if they failed to sing. Naturally, exposed rings were liberally doused in beer.

As the night wore on a few glasses were broken, leading to the intervention of the BOS who did his 'Have a good time by all means, but …' speech. He was drowned out by *Why was he born so beautiful* … At this stage the BOS might have let the party continue but, when a bottle, thrown by one of the more inebriated partygoers, crashed at his feet, the party came to an abrupt halt. A ripping time was had as we left the NAAFI with all the demobees having their T-shirts ripped off their backs.

Returning to our *basha*, Trev and I found our beds outside and doused in water (courtesy of Chesh and Dan, we later learnt). Having slept outside without mozzie nets, we were rudely awakened by the Orderly Sergeant soon after Reveille. Noticing our wet beds, he was all for charging us both for pissing the bed. Dan, one of the culprits saved the day, telling the Orderly Sergeant he'd seen some blokes emptying fire buckets over our beds as he was returning to the *basha* the previous night. His explanation managed to convince the Sergeant that the moisture was water and not filtered Anchor beer. Helpful to the end, Dan added that the culprits had taken off towards 'A' Company lines — which, in Chesh's case, was true.

This left us enough time to clean up the *basha* before getting bulled up for the 5717 Intake's final appearance on CO's Orders. True to form, Coco-Oscar, in his bumbling, incoherent way, spoke about *esprit de corps,* how proud we should be to have served in the Regiment; telling us how much he valued our service (even though he couldn't remember who I was when I was in hospital), how sorry he was to see us leave (really?), and what a jolly good job we had done. He went on to express the hope that, when we went back to civilian life, we would continue to take an interest in the Regiment and remember what the Army had taught us — self-discipline, smartness and comradeship. Finally, he exhorted us to always remember that:

'The Regiment has a reputation for maintaining standards, and we have only one standard — the best!'

As he spoke, snatches of one of our favourite songs floated through my mind,

> *We are the first Battalion, we are a fucking shower,*
>
> *Down to Bukit Timah, 90 miles an hour,*
>
> *Some silly bastard shouts 'Right Dress',*
>
> *You should have seen the fucking mess!*

291

> *We **were** the first Battalion we **were** a fucking shower.*

Whatever *esprit de corps* the 5717 Intake had developed, was owed solely to the raw recruits who had first met on a damp September morning in 1957, not to the Regiment. And especially not to the clowns in Coco-Oscar's circus who had subjected us to two years of bull, bullying, petty nit-picking, atrocious food, and overall military mindlessness.

Coco's address was followed by a lecture from the Adjutant on 'maintaining a high level of turn-out and discipline onboard the ship, and when we arrived back to the Depot'. Fat chance of that happening. Whatever time we might spend back at the Depot would be spent doing our utmost to demoralise the poor sods in basic training. The Toff also advised us that he did not mind us having a farewell party, but he did not want any rowdyism or brawling. He was a bit late for that admonition as we had pre-empted him by partying the previous night. Nevertheless, he was taking no chances. In addition to the regular Guard, a dozen sergeants and corporals were detailed to patrol the camp that night, ostensibly on the look-out for Big Ned and Alf the Nutter who were still at large. Little wonder the Battalion failed to even come face to face with any CTs when it could not even re-capture its own escaped prisoners.

With a pre-dawn start in the morning and the big demob party behind us, our last night in the Fed was a sedate affair. With Buddy Holly's *Everyday* playing in the background we quietly reminisced over our last few pints of Anchor and commiserated with the blokes we were leaving behind. The crowning denouement of the night was the hot gossip from the MI Room that Sergeant Kaz had caught a dose of the clap. Whether this was a farewell gift from his departing wife, or whether he had been playing away from home was not revealed.

'It's a getting closer', **one more night and an early breakfast in the Fed!**

CHAPTER 15
HOMEWARD BOUND!

Barely, it seemed, had our heads hit our pillows and Trev and I were being shaken awake by the guard. After a quick wash and shave, we stuffed the last few items into our kitbags and headed for the cookhouse for an early breakfast. True to form, even though it had been known for over a month that close to 40 of us were leaving early that morning, there was no early breakfast prepared. The one cook on duty managed to mackle together some scrambled eggs from powder which, together with stale white bread and a mug of tea, was it. A pedant might have described it as a breakfast because it broke our overnight fast, but a breakfast it was not. The Notts & Jocks' cooks had lived up to their reputation right up until our last meal.

First task after breakfast was to visit the REME *bashas* and let off a few firecrackers, in case they wanted an early wake-up to see us off. With Johnny being in Singapore, the Medics were spared but the RAPC and Orderly Room lines were not and we roused them with clanging dustbin lids. On returning to our *basha* Dan gave us a hand getting our baggage up the hill to the RV point on the square where we jumped aboard the waiting lorries.

'Goodbye, good riddance, and get fucked!' or words to
that effect, was our parting message to Burma Camp as
we drove out of the gate for the last time, cheering and
hollering and giving Piggy Gitt and the other RPs the
two-fingered salute for good measure.

At Victoria Dock, laden down with large packs, small
packs, sea kitbags and universal kitbags, but spared the
need to carry a rifle, we were marched by MPs to Godown[89] Number 3. True to the end our final departure
was another 'hurry up and wait' experience. For once the
Notts & Jocks had been over-efficient and delivered us
to the docks around an hour-and-a-half ahead of embarkation time. Lined up on the quayside, awaiting the arrival of other returnees we waited … and we waited …
and we waited, and the sun climbed higher in the sky,
and the mercury climbed higher up the thermometer, and
the sweat poured out of us until . . . finally, we commenced boarding.

Once on board the TT *Empire Fowey*, we cajoled the
Senior Deck Sergeant into allocating us to what, earlier
returnees had told us, was the best troop deck. Entering
the accommodation deck, I did a double-take because
standing across the room, partially hidden by the bunks,
was a familiar face. Carl Wright, the Troop Deck Sergeant, was a schoolboy rugby team mate who I'd last
seen when he, Gerry and I had toured Durham and Cum-
berland together with the Notts, Lincs & Derby Schools
in 1957. At rollcall I remained silent when he called my
name. He called it a second time and again I remained

---

[89] Godown – quayside warehouse,

silent. At his third, somewhat exasperated, call I responded;

'That the one from Henry Mellish, Sarge?' mentioning my school.

'Roger me dead with a ragman's trumpet!' he exclaimed. 'What the hell are you doing here, Bram?'

'Probably the same as you, Carl, going on demob.' That was it for the moment, but we caught up soon afterwards.

After depositing all our packs, other than our sea kitbags, into the hold we were issued bedding before changing our Straits Dollars into Sterling. It was later that morning when Carl and I caught up again and exchanged stories. The same age as me, he had been called up in early 1958 at a time when the Army was short of teachers. His school record saw him assigned to the Royal Army Education Corps and promoted to Sergeant before being posted to Hong Kong. While in Hong Kong he had applied for, and been offered, a place at university so had to apply for an early release in order to be back in England for the start of the academic year. Typically, the Army had blocked his request but, after enlisting the support of the local MP, his father had managed to secure Carl an early release.

By this time, it was lunch time — or was it *tiffin* since we were still docked in Singapore? Whatever it was, having not eaten since our token dawn breakfast, we were ravenous and tucked into our first shipboard meal — a marked improvement on Notts & Jocks tucker! After lunch we returned to our troop decks for an inspection and instructions on ship's procedures. Formalities completed, I returned to the upper deck to delight in the sight of the crew casting off, breaking my last link with FARELF. Surprisingly, it was a subdued departure as we quietly watched the quayside receding astern; no pipe band to pipe us off, as on our arrival, and no bald-headed old buffers waving gold-braided hats to bid us farewell, as there had been when we left Southampton 15 months earlier. Finally, the Notts & Jocks 5717 Intake was free of Coco-Oscar and his battalion of buffoons, slipping quietly away without fanfare having contributed diddly squat to bringing the Malayan Emergency to an end.

Three and a half weeks at sea, and it was 'Land ahoy!' as we entered the Solent, where we spent the day at anchor, awaiting a berth. During this frustrating delay, we drew our kit from the hold in readiness for disembarkation the following morning. Apart from the sight of England again, the other highlight of the day was being paid — a full two weeks' leave pay to take us up to 'Demob Day'. By mid-afternoon, the *Empire Fowey* was finally on the move, berthing in Southampton in the early evening alongside the *Queen Mary*. At 80,774 tons, or four times the size of our tiny troopship, the mighty *Queen* towered over us. Frustratingly, once docked, and with our wallets bulging with leave pay, we found ourselves marooned overnight aboard a 'dry' ship. The duty-free bar was closed because we were in port. True to form, the Army had reserved one last exquisite form of torment for our final night onboard — a bar with no beer.

Thursday, 28 August 1959, saw us disembarking after an early breakfast, our feet touching English soil for the first time in 15 months. Despite being burdened with my full kit and kaboodle, I jumped for joy. Once ashore, we were hustled to the railway station, and boarded a train under the direction of typically loud-mouthed, officious RMPs. Four and a half hours later we were back where it all began being met by the Depot RPs who, through our now veterans' eyes, looked nowhere near as intimidating as the ones who had greeted us off the train two years earlier. This time around, we would be seeing Civvy Street in two weeks, not two years. Arriving at the Depot, all we had to do was simply dump our kit into storage, collect our travel warrants which, amazingly, were made out and ready to collect, and we were free to head home.

Ten days demob leave and my National Service will be over.

EPILOGUE

Wearing my newly issued 37 Pattern battledress with mis-matched 44 Pattern belt and a back pack laden with presents, I boarded the train for home. Alighting at Attenborough station, the scene of my stilted farewell from my father two years earlier, I took the familiar route home, enjoying the balmy warmth of the late summer afternoon sun. Arriving at the gate I decided I was worthy of a front door entrance. After the initial surprise of my front door appearance I was greeted warmly; my mother overjoyed that I showed no apparent after-effects from my encounter with *aedes aegypti*, my father, seemingly over my whinging about the Army, equally pleased, and my brother, Ian, somewhat bemused by my moustache and perhaps a little overawed by my uniform, also happy to see me. Battledress quickly discarded, I wallowed in the luxury of a hot bath, soaking all the military grime out of my pores. At ease once again in some long-forgotten comfortable civvies, I rejoined the family and, over a few ales and the long-missed pleasure of a home-cooked meal, caught up on what had been happening on the home front during my absence.

Once back home it was as if a social programme had been planned for my first weekend. On Saturday it was the Rugby Club pre-season barbeque and, on Sunday, the annual cricket match between the Rugby Club and my local village Cricket Club. In the week that followed,

I re-acquainted myself with our two local pubs, catching up with village friends and all the local gossip. More especially, since Liz, my pre-departure love interest had moved on, I was keen to find out which of the local totty might be pleased to welcome home a randy soldier after fifteen months of involuntary celibacy. My initial lack of success in this pursuit suggested that my upper lip adornment was not helping my chances so this last vestige of my military persona was expunged before I returned to the Regimental Depot for final discharge formalities.

At the Depot, discharge procedures included another medical examination which revealed that, compared with my enlistment weight of 158 lbs, I now weighed 163 lbs. Those extra pounds could in no way be attributed to nourishment derived from Army food, but rather to money spent on beer. Had it not been for my encounter with dengue fever my weight gain would doubtless have been greater. Another part of the release process was being issued with our 'Certificate of National Service' (Army Book 111), mine containing the glowing 'Testimonial' describing me as 'fairly intelligent but not very industrious', and our Roneo-ed 'Certificate of Discharge' declaring we were now 'free to take up civil employment'. We were also given our Malaya campaign medals. The hand-over was such a non-event I cannot recall whether they were formally presented to us on parade or merely handed out with our discharge documents like baubels from a corn flakes packet. Probably the latter, since the medals came in utilitarian cardboard boxes with a crown printed on the lid and a label on the bottom stating, 'G.S.M.[90] WITH CLASP "MALAYA"', beneath which was typed my service number, rank, name and unit.

This cheapskate packaging was a stark contrast to the packaging of the *Pingat Jasa Malaysia (PJM)*, later awarded by the King of Malaysia in 2004 to all Malaysian and Commonwealth military personnel who served in the Malayan Emergency and in the Indonesia-Malaysia Confrontation. This medal came in a rich blue lined presentation box with the Malaysian coat of arms embossed in gold on the lid and an inscription inside. Not only that but the medal came with a miniature for formal dress occasions.

Typically, when the Malaysian Government had first approached the British Government regarding awarding the medal to eligible British citizens, permission was initially refused on the grounds that British Medals Policy prohibited the acceptance of medals from foreign nations. After intensive lobbying, the matter was referred to the Committee on the Grant of Honours, Decorations and Medals with a request to review its policy in respect of foreign awards and, specifically, the *Pingat Jasa Malaysia*.

Evidently not wishing to offend the King of Malaysia, the Committee's impeccably nuanced recommendation was that British citizens could accept the medal but recipients were not permitted to wear it. Deeply embarrassed that both Australian and New Zealand veterans of the Emergency were permitted to both receive and wear

---

[90] General Service Medal.

the *PJM*, this decision was eventually rescinded. The process took almost seven years, taking effect from Remembrance Day 2011.

Finally, on 10th September 1959, the nation's unwelcome intrusion into the young lives of those in the Notts & Jocks 5717 National Service Intake was over. Girded with our medals, discharge papers and demob pay, we headed out of the Depot gates for the last time, 729 long days after first clapping eyes on the 'Fortress Gothic' edifice that, thankfully, now no longer disfigures the local townscape.

Officially, we were to report to our allocated TA units that day to be enlisted on the Reserve for three-and-a-half years. In my case, I was supposed to report to the 8th Battalion (TA) HQ in Newark, between two and four o'clock that afternoon. At two I was still in the pub to which we had adjourned after leaving the barracks, and at four I was asleep on a bench on the bus station. I never did make it to Newark, and no Redcaps ever came knocking at my door during my period on the Reserve.

The pub in which the 5717ers gathered for their final farewells was well away from the barracks and close to the bus station. Being a mid-week lunch time, it was thinly populated; the regulars, as we were to discover later, made up largely of retired World War I veterans. As the beers flowed, the old soldiers became more and more disgusted at our antics, the final straw being when we pinned our medals onto our shirts and started dancing around the bar. At that point, the old timers had had enough and berated us over our behaviour and lack of respect for military tradition.

R A (BRAM) BRAMLEY

True, we had experienced nothing like what they had
suffered in the Great War but, like most people I had
spoken to since my return, these World War I veterans
had no idea that Britain was still actively engaged in a
guerrilla war in Malaya, from which we had only recently returned. Somewhat mollified by this enlighten-
ment the old veterans left us alone and went back to
chuntering into their beers. Unlike the well-reported Ko-
rean War, the first major post-WWII conflict in which
Britain was engaged, the conflict with the communists
in Malaya had never been declared a 'war', chiefly because of the insurance implications. It was only ever referred to as an 'Emergency' by the British and the Colo-
nial Governments of Malaya and Singapore — the
Emergency was not even a 'forgotten war', it was a truly
'unbeknown war'.

According to my Record of Service, 4th October 1959
was my last day of 'whole time National Service', meaning I was officially discharged from the Army. Coincidentally, that was my first day in college and, being a
Sunday, my first appointment was with the College
Dean, the Reverend J.S. Bezzant. During this induction
interview, I discovered that not only was the Dean a dis-
tinguished theologian but, during World War II, had
served as a Military Chaplain in the RNVR. Was there
to be no end to military incursions into my life? Seemingly not, because, when it came to my turn to recite the
Latin 'Grace' in the college hall before dinner, I chose
to assert my agnostic or, as the Army would have it 'agnotic', beliefs and advised the Steward of my intention
not to fulfil this obligation. The Dean was duly informed
and, in the words of the old sweat who stamped out my

dog tags, it was another case of: 'Reverend, man here doesn't like your God'. This time, instead of being issued with misspelt dog tags, I was summoned to the Dean's rooms to defend my 'agnotic' convictions to a former navy chaplain before being excused (Latin was never my strong suit, anyway).

If there was anything fortuitous about my National Service, it was being posted overseas. At that time, before 'gap years' became *de rigueur*, few teenagers had the opportunity to spend 15 months in a foreign land, so my posting to Malaya was an unexpected bonus. It exposed me to Malay, Chinese and Indian people and their cultures, and to unfamiliar landscapes and climatic conditions, as well as providing the opportunity to meet and mix with Australians and New Zealanders. Laidback and instinctively anti-authority, with a dry sense of humour they were my kind of people. They were also very direct — you always knew where you stood with Aussies and Kiwis, as my dunking at Batu Ferringhi Beach had demonstrated. Although by no means a decisive factor in my decision to migrate to Australia 15 years later, this initial contact gave me confidence that I would find Australia an amenable country in which to live.

Another advantage of a Far East posting was the voyage home. The 5717 Intake was fortunate insofar as the period we spent on operations was short-lived but not entirely without exposure to danger. The voyage home enabled us to unwind with our fellow conscripts, vent our spleens regarding the incompetence and injustices of Army life and to laugh at its absurdities, thus arriving home in a tranquil frame of mind to resume our civilian lives.

After meeting several conscripted Vietnam veterans in Australia, it seemed to me that they too would have benefited from a similar protracted journey back to 'normal' life. Other than those who returned aboard HMAS Sydney, usually with their units, to 'Welcome Home' parades, there was no welcome home for other returning National Servicemen who flew home directly from constant front line exposure. Winding down with their comrades, pre-discharge, either at sea and/or in a safe overseas location, may have helped their re-adjustment to civilian life and possibly reduced the incidence or severity of PTSD. Instead, due to the anti-war sentiment in the country, they were not welcome in RSLs and many chose not to reveal they had served in Vietnam. This was in stark contrast to the complete indifference that greeted the return of Malaya veterans to Britain.

One curious aspect of my National Service experience is that I made no lasting friends, even though I spent two years serving alongside most of the 50 men in my intake. My only enduring friendship from among my fellow National Servicemen is with David Cheshire, who I knew before we were called up. Notwithstanding the strong bond between Trev, Dan and myself, the 'Three Musketeers' of the Intelligence Section, these friendships did not endure beyond demob. What bound us together was our shared resistance to the arbitrary and often senseless nature of Army discipline, in the face of which we did our best to keep each other out of strife, and to support each other if we did fall foul of capricious Army discipline. Beyond that we had nothing much in common and soon lost touch. Of my other Army compeers, Murph was the one with whom I established the closest friendship and, the weekend after I was demobbed, I visited him in Liverpool but, even though we readily picked up the threads of our friendship, our lives soon grew apart.

When embarking on this memoir, I tried to trace some of my NS compeers through Forces Reunited. I could find none of my 5717 Intake on the website which said it all — so much for Coco-Oscar's exhortation to continue to take an interest in the Regiment. The only name I turned up was that of Osbert, the last person with whom I would have wanted to re-establish contact. Checking his Army record on Forces War Records, I discovered that, by the time he completed his six-year engagement, he had risen to the rank of Sergeant — truly astounding! More astounding still was the discovery that Coco-Oscar retired as a Brigadier.

Overall, my impressions of the Army's competence as a military entity were far from favourable. Given the British Army's history of success in a great many military conflicts, I can only conclude that the unit in which I served was atypical. It was poorly led and its leader, Coco-Oscar, was more concerned with appearances and impressing those above him than he was about the morale and wellbeing of his men for whom he showed little regard.

Later in life, on moving to Australia, I found public knowledge of Australia's involvement in the Malayan Emergency was no better than was Britain's

involvement in the UK. Media references about Australia's involvement in post-World War II military conflicts usually skip from Korea to Vietnam, and on to Iraq
and Afghanistan with seldom any mention of either the
Malayan Emergency or 'Konfrontasi'[91] in Borneo. Even
in the Australian War Memorial, one of most powerfully
evocative places I have visited, the Malayan Emergency
exhibit, through my eyes, at least, is totally underwhelm-
ing.

Given that 39 Australians[92] lost their lives during the 10
years that Australia was engaged in the Emergency it is
quite extraordinary that there is still no memorial in the
national capital to those who served and died in the undeclared wars in Malaya and Borneo as there is for those
who served and died in Korea and Vietnam. What is
even more extraordinary is that the Malaya and Borneo
campaigns are the only two post-World War II combat
operations in which Australia has participated that can
be deemed truly successful with both Malaya and Singapore achieving independence under democratic rule
even before the official 'Cessation of Hostilities on 31
July 1960. To echo the words of the late Brigadier Alf
Garland (former National President of the Returned &

---

[91] The undeclared war in Borneo from 1963 to 1966 arising
from Indonesia's opposition to the decision of Sabah and
Sarawak to join the Federation of Malaya to form the state
of Malaysia.
[92] Only two fewer than the 41 Australians lost in Afghanistan, a war that lasted twice as long.

Services League), who led the first overseas deployment of the Australian SAS to Borneo[93]:

No one knew we went up there, no one knew we fought there, now no one cares. It's a disgrace.

In conclusion, National Service had been an unwelcome intrusion into my teenage years and it was not an experience that I enjoyed. Even with the perspective of 66 years hindsight the dark tint in my spectacles has not become any rosier even though, thankfully, apart from my encounter with *Aedes aegypti,* I did not experience any other life-threatening situations. That said, and with the benefit of hindsight, I have to concede that I did derive some benefit from the experience. Being thrown together with fellow conscripts and career soldiers exposed me to an assemblage of men of widely varying intelligence, drawn from every social stratum. Whether they were in a position of authority or simply fellow squaddies, one had to learn to rub along with them: a valuable learning experience standing me in good stead for my subsequent working life.

As for what influence the Army had on me, there is no doubt that it reinforced my anti-authoritarian streak arising from being brought up by a domineering father. My strong distaste for regimentation came to light in my first job after graduating; a choice, I must concede, influenced by my father. I was employed by a large engineering company and my career there was short-lived. I was

---

[93] The Wild Men of Borneo - Australians in Battle 1950-2000 D.D. McNicoll, The Australian, Edition 1, Tue 25 Apr 2000, page 012

the company's first graduate trainee and they didn't quite know what to do with me and I didn't quite know what was expected of me. To this day, the vision of serried rows of clerks sitting at individual desks checking punched cards in a large open plan office with the supervisor seated at the back under the only clock in the room is imprinted on my mind. That business environment was far too regimented and reminiscent of the Army for my liking, so I quit.

For my father, who had lived through the Great Depression, my decision to leave a job without having another to go to was utterly unfathomable. It was time to leave home. After a summer sojourn working on a Cotswolds farm, I headed north for Scotland and embarked on a new career path in town planning: a path that would ultimately lead me to Australia.

ABBREVIATIONS

2i/c	Second in Command
ACC	Army Catering Corps
APTC	Army Physical Training Corps
BAOR	British Army of the Rhine
BHQ	Battalion headquarters
BMH	British Military Hospital
BOS	Battalion Orderly Sergeant
BVD	Base Vehicle Depot
Casevac	Casualty evacuation
CCF	Combined Cadet Force
CLF/GURDIV	Commander Land Forces/ Gurkha Division
CO	Commanding Officer
COS	Company Orderly Sergeant
CQMS	Company Quartermaster Sergeant
CSE	Combined Services Entertainment
CSM	Company Sergeant Major
CT	Communist Terrorist

FARELF	Far East Land Forces
Fed	Federation of Malaya (later Malaysia)
Ferret	Armoured fighting vehicle
FFI	Free from Infection
FTC	FARELF Training Centre
GCE	General Certificate of Education
GHQ	General Headquarters
GOC	General Officer Commanding
GPO	General Post Office
GSM	General Service Medal
HQ	Headquarters
IA	Immediate Action
IO	Intelligence Officer
IS	Internal Security
KDG	King's Dragoon Guards
KL	Kuala Lumpur
LZ	Landing Zone
MCP	Malayan Communist Party
Medevac	Evacuation home for medical reasons
MI Room	Medical Inspection Room
MMG	Medium Machine Gun

MNLA/MRLA	Malayan National Liberation Army/Malayan Races Liberation Army
MO	Medical Officer
MP	Military Policeman
MPAJA	Malayan People's Anti-Japanese Army
MRC(S)	Medical Reception Centre (Station)
MS	Motor Ship
MV	Motor Vessel
NAAFI	Navy, Army & Air Force Institute
NMBVAA	National Malaya & Borneo Veterans Association of Australia
NS	National Service
NZR	New Zealand Regiment
OC	Officer Commanding
OCS	Officer Cadet School
OGs	Olive Greens (light tropical dress)
OHMS	On Her Majesty's Service
OR	Other Ranks
ORBAT	Order of Battle
PAP	People's Action Party
POL	Petrol, oil and lubricants

PRC People' Republic of China

PRI President of the Regimental Institute

PTSD Post Traumatic Stress Disorder

PULHEEMS Physique, Upper limbs, Lower limbs, Hearing, Eyesight right, Eyesight Left, Mental Function, Stability (emotional), a system of grading physical and mental fitness used to determine the suitability of service people for posting into military zones.

QARANC Queen Alexandra's Royal Army Nursing Corps

QM Quartermaster

R&R Rest and Recuperation

RAAF Royal Australian Air Force

RAF Royal Air Force

RAMC Royal Army Medical Corps

RAR Royal Australian Regiment

RASC Royal Army Service Corps

RE Royal Engineers

REME Royal Electrical & Mechanical Engineers

RMP	Royal Military Police
RNZAF	Royal New Zealand Air Force
ROC	Republic of China
RP	Regimental Police
RSM	Regimental Sergeant Major
RSO	Regimental Signals Officer
SAF	Singapore Armed Forces
SAS(R)	Special Air Service (Regiment)
SDS	Signals Delivery Service
SEATO	South East Asia Treaty Organisation
SIB	Special Investigations Branch
SITREP	Situation Report
SLR	Self-loading Rifle
SMG	Sterling Machine Gun
SOE	Special Operations Executive
SSI	Staff-Sergeant Instructor
TA	Territorial Army
Tac HQ	Tactical Headquarters
TT	Troop Transport
UAR	United Arab Republic
USB	Unit Selection Board
VD	Venereal Disease

WD	War Department
WO2	Warrant Officer, 2nd Class
WOSB	War Office Selection Board
WRAC	Women's Royal Army Corps
WRAF	Women's Royal Air Force
WVS	Women's Volunteer Service
Z-Craft	Small tank landing craft

GLOSSARY

Banjo	- a sandwich or bread roll usually containing a fried egg
Basha	- a hut typically made of bamboo and palm materials
Boot walllah	- a servant who cleans boots
Bubble (to put the bubble in)	- to report someone (dob them in)
Char-wallah	- a servant who makes tea and snacks
Cheongsam	- a straight dress, usually of silk or cotton, with a stand-up collar and a thigh-high slit in one side of the skirt, worn by Chinese women
Creased	- tired, exhausted
Dhobi	- laundry

Flap — a panic/overreaction

Ferret — armoured scout car

Gash — surplus or waste material/equipment

Gibbered — drunk

Glasshouse — detention centre

Godolphin — corrugated iron hut

Golok — a bush knife like a machete

Gonk — to sleep

Grip, or to be gripped — to reprimanded or castigated

Gripe — to complain/whinge

Jalabaya — a traditional Egyptian garment native to the Nile Valley

Jambiya — an Arabian knife with a curved, double-edged blade.

Jankers — a colloquial name used by soldiers for 'Restrictions of Privileges', an official punishment for a minor breach of discipline entailing being confined to barracks and being required to do fatigues and attend extra parades wearing best uniform and full marching order.

Jig-jig	- sexual intercourse
Kampong	- a Malay village
Merdeka	- Malayan Independence
Nig	- raw recruit, newcomer or novice
Orang Asli	- a term used in Malaysia to describe Malays and indigenous peoples of Malaysia or, colloquially, 'sons of the soil'
Pokey Drill	- physical exercise using a rifle, designed to strengthen arm and shoulder muscles
Poncho	- a groundsheet
Rock-all	- to give someone a hard time
Sappers	- antiquated name for Royal Engineers
Scratcher	- bed
Skive	- to avoid work, to slack
Stag	- period of time on duty while on guard (usually 2 hours)

Stocius	- drunk
Tapes	- stripes or chevrons worn by NCOs
Tiffin	- lunch
Totty	- girls
Ulu	- jungle
Ulu-bashing	- slang for doing jungle patrols

SELECTED BIBLIOGRAPHY & REFERENCES

Barber, N. (2004). *The War of the Running Dogs: How Malaya defeated the Communist Guerrillas 1948-1960.* London. Cassell

Burgess, A. (2000). *The Malayan Trilogy.* London. Vintage

https://en.wikipedia.org/wiki/List_of_nicknames_of_British_Army_regiments#N

Kenneison, R. (2014). *Freddy Spencer Chapman: from John's to the jungle.* 'The Eagle', St John's College, Cambridge, Vol 96, 35- 42

Lees, F. (2009). *The Malayan Life of Ferdach O'Haney.* Singapore. Monsoon

Shindler, C. (2012). *National Service: From Aldershot to Aden: tales from the conscripts 1946-62.* London. Sphere

Spencer Chapman, F. (1949). *The Jungle is Neutral,* London. Chatto & Windus

Thambipillay, R (2011). *The Last Post: Story of the emergency &commemorative events (1948 – 1960),* Ipoh. Thambipillay

Thomas, L. (1967). *The Virgin Soldiers.* London. Pan Books

van Tonder, G. (2017), *Malayan Emergency: Triumph of the running dogs 1948-1960,* Barnsley. Pen & Sword Military

Vinen, R. (2014). *National Service: a generation in uniform, 1945-1963.* London. Penguin

ACKNOWLEDGEMENTS

In common with all authors setting off on their literary journey I had no idea of the number of people to whom I would be indebted by the time my story made it into print.

First and foremost, my thanks are due to my lifelong friend, David Cheshire, who shared this military experience with me and contributed the accounts of life in the jungle, which I escaped. Second, I am indebted to my soldier friend and military historian, the late Derek Napier, for his invaluable advice on the minutia of military matters (but acknowledging that any errors are mine alone).

Early in this writing journey it was thanks to Jackie Ryan that I found my way to the Queensland Writers Centre, which has proved to be an invaluable learning resource. The QWC was also the conduit through which I found other invaluable support: principally my editor Edwina Shaw, my hardest critic and most avid supporter; my publisher, Kylie Chan at Essential Self-Publishing; and website designer, Jemma Pollari.

My thanks are also due to Maggie Saldais for her early editorial advice and for her grammar tutorial; to Tammy Ortung, who edited the stand alone extract from the memoir that appeared in *As You Were: The Military*

Review Vol 18.; to Kevin Carter, editor of *Berita*, the now discontinued quarterly newsletter of the Queensland Branch of the National Malaya and Borneo Veterans Association Australia, who encouraged me to submit excerpts for publication; and to Anthony Fensom for his marketing assistance.

I would also like to acknowledge the assistance of Ian Anderson at Ipoh World for providing historical information about Ipoh and also Jennifer Brockman-Moore, Curator & Archivist at the Museum of the Mercian Regiment for her guidance regarding regimental history.

Finally, on a personal note, my heartfelt thanks go to my long-suffering wife Jenny who, having survived four years living with a PhD candidate, indulged me once again by tolerating my literary ambitions.

ABOUT THE AUTHOR

After completing his National Service in Malaya, the author re-armed himself with a degree from the University of Cambridge and headed north to Scotland to embark on a career in town planning. After working in Edinburgh and Glasgow and, later, in County Durham he emigrated to Canada in 1969. In Canada, he managed a regional planning commission in Nova Scotia for 18 months before relocating to Toronto where he worked on regional parks, recreation and leisure facility planning including a feasibility study for a domed stadium in Toronto. In 1974 he moved to Australia to work on the Whitlam government's growth centre programme. A year later, following the dismissal of the Whitlam government, he found himself in a career vacuum. This vacuum was filled by his appointment to lead the team that prepared the feasibility study and development plan for the Yulara Tourist Village (now Ayers Rock Resort) adjacent to the Uluru-Kata Tjuta National Park. Following this he joined an international consulting firm as a consultant to the tourism and leisure industries before establishing his own practice. Over this time, he has worked on a wide-ranging portfolio of projects throughout Australia and the Asia-Pacific region. In 1999 he was awarded a Commonwealth Product Development Grant to study heritage tourism initiatives overseas. On his return he took up a post-graduate scholarship examining why heritage tourism ventures fail and was awarded a PhD in 2003. Since that time, while aspiring to become a writer, he has travelled extensively for pleasure rather than for work. Bram lives in Brisbane with his wife where they share their backyard (and sometimes their house) with the resident wildlife.

www.ingramcontent.com/pod-product-compliance
Lightning Source LLC
Chambersburg PA
CBHW031042110426
42740CB00048B/786